THE
CASE
FOR
TELEVIS
VIOLENCE

THE CASE FOR TELEVISION VIOLENCE

JIB FOWLES

Sage Publications, Inc.
International Educational and Professional Publisher
Thousand Oaks   London   New Delhi

For information:

Sage Publications, Inc.
2455 Teller Road
Thousand Oaks, California 91320
E-mail: order@sagepub.com

Sage Publications Ltd.
6 Bonhill Street
London EC2A 4PU
United Kingdom

Sage Publications India Pvt. Ltd.
M-32 Market
Greater Kailash I
New Delhi 110 048 India

Printed in the United States of America

Library of Congress Cataloging-in-Publication Data

Fowles, Jib.
   The case for television violence / by Jib Fowles.
   p. cm.
   Includes bibliographical references (p.) and index.
   ISBN 0-7619-0789-0 (alk. paper)
   ISBN 0-7619-0790-4 (alk. paper)
   1. Violence on television. I. Title.
   PN1992.8.V55 F69 1999
   303.6—dc21
                                           99-6733

This book is printed on acid-free paper.

99   00   01   02   03   04   05   7   6   5   4   3   2   1

Acquisition Editor: Margaret H. Seawell
Editorial Assistant: Renée Piernot
Production Editor: Astrid Virding
Editorial Assistant: Patricia Zeman
Typesetter: Christina M. Hill
Cover Designer: Candice Harman

Violence is not a simple thing.

—Roland Barthes (1985, p. 307)

Far from being mindless, violence is usually the cutting edge of ideas and ideologies.

John Fraser (1974, p. 162)

Ultimately, however, the major limitations of mainstream research on television violence derive from its failure to address the meaning of violence, both on television and in everyday life.

—David Buckingham (1993, p. 12)

No one defends violence on television. And when Americans all line up on one side of an issue, you know something is terribly, terribly wrong.

—David Link (1994, p. 22)

Contents

Preface

In 1984, I was a witness at U.S. Senate hearings on the issue of television violence (Fowles, 1985). Paraphrasing my then recent book on television viewing (Fowles, 1982), I testified that children use television's often brutal fantasies for therapeutic purposes—as an antidote to the real world. I stated (Fowles, 1985), "The fantasy mayhem on the television screen—sometimes in the form of cartoons and sometimes not—helps the child to discharge tensions and animosities" (p. 66). According to Willard Rowland's (1997) review of these hearings, mine was a rare dissenting voice in what was otherwise a barrage against television violence (p. 116). I certainly felt like the odd man out; even the industry representatives on the panel, potential allies, eyed me quizzically. At that time, I recognized that sooner or later I would have to fully analyze the mistaken attack on television violence. The moment was not right, however: The anti-television violence edifice, seemingly respected by all, appeared to be impregnable, and not much scholarship had accumulated in any field that would lend itself to constructing a strong counterargument.

The passage of years has ameliorated this problem. Several capable overviews of the empirical literature on television violence have called the whole enterprise into question. From various academic fields has come corrective or at least probing work issued by American and more frequently British scholars. Now I believe a book-length argument favoring television violence, and explaining the errors of the anti-violence crusade, can be marshaled.

In the interim, I have been speaking publicly on the television violence controversy. While doing so, I learned early that I had the undesirable ability to make some people genuinely angry. Their voices climbed, they rose from their seats, and their forefingers were wagged my way like miniature blows. They were on the way to becoming almost violent. This hostile response, often from fellow professors, was initially startling and then puzzling. What I had believed I was doing—to the extent I had reflected on it at all—was little more than conducting an intellectual exercise, turning ideas around to determine if there was any merit to a point of view that contradicted conventional wisdom. Obviously, however, judging from the adverse reactions, something else was at stake. The more I mulled this over, the clearer it became to me that this response could not be fully explained within the framework of the television violence issue. It was not a simple matter of some people understanding things one way and me understanding them in another way. Grander contexts were being invoked—ones with powerful holds on people.

The issue of television violence is an ever-recurring one, alternately flaring and subsiding since the 1950s. Its very periodicity is telling of its essential nature. It has not been settled nor, as much as I might wish otherwise, is it likely to be soon. This suggests it cannot be resolved on its own terms. The controversy regarding television violence reflects festering wounds within American culture and, again, can be understood only with reference to larger contexts. Once studied this way, the controversy can offer a vantage point on certain struggles—cultural, social, and mental—buried in our way of life.

I praise the steadfastness and ingenuity of those who helped do the research for this book: Edwina Lewis, Natasha Calder, Sandy Shiver, Leslie Bellfore, Sue Moreau, Lori Keith, Cindy Schulz, Kelly Morris, Jennifer Wright, and Kristy Hill. Craig White, a true colleague, read and critiqued almost all the chapters; Cindy Schutz applied a fine editorial eye to three chapters; and my wife Joy and my daughter Celeste performed as thoughtful critics. Lori Keith and Susanne Gaddis also responded to individual chapters. The manuscript benefited from each reading; the lingering imperfections are of course my own doing.

Continuities in Violence

Beavis and Butt-head, the flagrantly imbecilic cartooned teenagers who appeared daily on the youth-oriented MTV channel, managed to create a large dent in American culture between their debut in 1992 and their cancellation in 1997. They were hugely popular with youngsters, having twice the ratings of any other MTV offering (Barrett, 1994, p. 88). To the delight of child and adolescent viewers, the two characters flunked all their courses, started fires, picked their noses, denigrated reading, indulged in the few prerogatives of youthful lust, and so on, all the while cackling moronically. The same strident idiocy that made them so attractive to youngsters also necessarily repulsed their elders; of all television shows, this was the most frequently banned by parents (Kolbert, 1995 p. H23).

Perhaps pervasive adult revulsion was part of the reason that in October 1993 many people were quick to accept wire service accounts of a house fire and death supposedly prompted by Beavis and Butt-head's pyromania. After a 5-year-old Moraine, Ohio, boy set his family's mobile home ablaze, killing his 2-year-old sister in the process, their mother claimed he was imitating the cartoon pair ("Mother Blames," 1993). This matter did not end just with the news stories and the usually mild admonitions. The outcry that followed was so pronounced that MTV took action, ordering the show's creator, Mike Judge, to remove any allusions to matches and fires in upcoming episodes. Even this concession, however, did not quiet the adverse reaction, and a week later MTV announced it would eliminate the early evening broadcast of the show (while lengthening the 11:00 p.m. show) ("MTV Moves," 1993). It seemed that the channel's executives had been quicker to censor the program than to alter its time slot; the first option had ethical but no financial consequences, whereas the second, resulting in smaller audience sizes, would certainly produce less advertising revenue. Mike Judge, dispirited by the turn of events, said wearily, "I've gotten so tired that I don't like fighting big battles" (Katz, 1994, p. 45).

The story of the Ohio fire appears to be a cautionary tale about the possible impact of televised misbehavior, a parable for the video age. A terrible tragedy had apparently resulted because a viewing child imitated a destructive act seen on the television screen. However, reporters' follow-up stories cast much doubt on the original version. The boy's family did not receive cable television and thus he could not have been a regular viewer of *Beavis and Butt-head* (Katz, 1994). He might have seen the program at nearby homes but for the fact that the entire trailer park was not wired for cable. According to neighbors, the little boy had been playing with matches for several years (Barrett, 1994, p. 87). The culpability of the fictional cretins dwindles to nought, however appealing it was in the search for scapegoats.

The spurious Beavis and Butt-head house-fire incident takes its place among a select group of similarly apocryphal stories—a folklore of false scares that, although small, is oddly persevering, recollected by many even after supposedly factual bases evanesce. A similar tale of a television-inspired transgression attempted to link the NBC broadcast of a made-for-television movie, *Born Innocent,* to a San Francisco rape that occurred 3 days after the broadcast. In the 1974 telecast, a 15-year-old girl was raped by four girls wielding a plumber's helper. Subsequently, in California a 9-year-old girl was sexually attacked with a beer bottle by four young girls and a boy. The mother of the Californian child filed an $11 million damage suit against NBC and its local affiliate, maintaining that the movie was to blame for the assault. The mother and daughter, Valeria and Olivia Niemi, retained attorney Marvin E. Lewis, who in another highly publicized case had won a $50,000 judgment for a woman claiming that a cable car accident caused her to become a nymphomaniac ("TV Wins," 1978). The fact emerged that the child most responsible for the rape of Olivia, Sharon Smith, had by her own account not watched the broadcast of *Born Innocent* (Schwartz, 1978). She never had a chance to testify about her lack of exposure to the program, however, because the trial judge dismissed the case when Lewis conceded he would be unable to prove NBC intended viewers to imitate the rape (Greenhouse, 1978). Subsequently, Sharon Smith (characterized by the defense as an emotionally disturbed child with a history of sexual deviance) was sentenced to 3 years in a federal facility (Liebert & Sprafkin, 1988, pp. 130-131). Any connection between the movie and the crime was unestablished; it could easily have been a matter of coincidence.

In another widely reported court case, the brutal detective series *Kojak* was accused of goading a young Costa Rican immigrant into an act of murder. Ronnie Zamora, who had killed his elderly neighbor during the commission of a burglary, was depicted in a 1978 trial as a devotee of violent television in general and *Kojak* in particular. The jury, however, was unimpressed by his lawyer's television-causes-murder defense and after a brief deliberation found Zamora guilty as charged (Irwin & Cassata, 1994). As opposed to the television-addled youth depicted in the news media, the jury viewed Zamora as a troubled boy brutalized by a stepfather, unwillingly transplanted first to New York City and then to Miami, destabilized by the drowning death of his closest friend, and possessed of a clear criminal bent. The jurors had listened to the testimony of a psychologist who had found Ronnie to be "emotionally disturbed, erratic, and unpredictable" as well as suicidal, "riding his bicycle into heavy traffic and standing under knives he had thrown into the air" (Liebert & Sprafkin, 1988, p. 127). They also had listened to the testimony of a psychiatrist who had asked Ronnie "Did television teach you to kill anybody?" and who reported the boy had answered "No" (Liebert & Sprafkin, 1988, p. 128). The novel defense implicating *Kojak* had been fabricated by Zamora's flamboyant lawyer, a man with a confessed penchant for seeking out press coverage (Rubin & Matera, 1989).

No one would want to argue that fantasies on television never have or never will inspire criminal behavior in real life. Even the number of incidents that are reported, however, with a press and reading public seemingly primed for such tales, is scant. Of this scant few, many of them cannot withstand investigation. The total number of antisocial acts directly attributable to television entertainment antics must be minuscule.

Exonerated, Beavis and Butt-head can take their places within a long lineage of similarly raucous entertainment acts, a fixture in the American comedic tradition. They join Laurel and Hardy, the Three Stooges, Abbott and Costello, Tom and Jerry, Wile E. Coyote and the Roadrunner, Cheech and Chong, Wayne and Garth—all of whom had their days of enthusiastic celebrity and simultaneously their detractors. Like Beavis and Butt-head, these acts have also been accused of undermining good taste and social order at the same time that they were regaling large numbers of delighted spectators. Repeatedly, audience members have been making one use of such performers while their critics have been making another.

Repeated Counts

Television has had no shortage of assaultive characters such as Beavis and Butt-head, rapists, and Kojak. Throughout the decades, various versions of Beavis and Butt-head's "frog baseball" (no description necessary) have popped up in the broadcast schedule, an expressive arena that has always resounded with thwacks, blasts, shots, pileups, punches, crunches, crashes, screams, and the occasional silent stabbing. Confronting this largess in what James Twitchell (1989) calls "concussive fictions," communication scientists early on began the apparently simple and straightforward task of tallying the number of violent acts on the medium. Continuities in violent content were to be met with continuities in research strategies.

At first, "violence counting" seemed to be an appropriate approach, one with dispassionate pretensions and the promise of robust findings. If done accurately—and in conception the research design did not seem intricate or formidable—such counts would have the ring of science to them and not be readily dismissible. It would only be later, on reflection, that violence counting became suspect.

The two earliest published violence counts (Head, 1954; Smythe, 1954) were conducted as the new medium of television came sweeping into America's households. Neither report defined exactly what was being tallied as violent content; perhaps both investigators considered depictions of violence as self-evident, or perhaps, on first attempting definitions, they found ambiguous instances so widespread that they shied away from the sort of definitional grappling that would entangle later researchers.

Reporting on three annual (1951-1953) studies done for the National Association of Educational Broadcasters, Dallas Smythe (1954) found an average of 6.2 violent acts or threats of violence per television hour (p. 150). He also discovered what each subsequent counter of video violence acts would generally confirm: "Children's drama had more than three times the frequency of violent acts and threats which was found in general audience drama (22.4 as against 6.0 per hour)" (p. 151). Stanley Head (1954), using a slightly different selection of content types, found an average of 3.72 "acts of aggression and moral transgression" per half-hour program, with more than twice as much (7.6) in children's shows (p. 184).

Other one-time counts of violence on television duly followed (Clark & Blankenburg, 1972; Dominick, 1973; Greenberg, 1980; Greenberg & Gordon, 1972; Harvey, Sprafkin, & Rubinstein, 1979; Potter & Ware, 1987; Slaby, Quarfoth, & McConnachie, 1976; Soley & Reid, 1985; Zusne, 1968). A more substantial, extended series of annual counts has been conducted since 1967 by George Gerbner, who is considered by many (Gunter, 1988, p. 28; Huston, 1992, p. 53; Liebert & Sprafkin, 1988, p. 87) to be the foremost authority on the quantity of television violence. Gerbner (1972) defines television violence as

> the overt expression of physical force against self or other, compelling action against one's will on pain of being hurt or killed, or actually hurting or killing. The expression of injurious or lethal force had to be credible and real in the symbolic terms of the drama. Humorous and even farcical violence can be credible and real, even if it has a presumable comic effect. (p. 31)

Although Gerbner has been faulted for the inclusion of comic violence (Blank, 1977, p. 275; Coffin & Tuchman, 1972, p. 16), the length of his time series, no matter what the definition of violence, is important in its own right because it should indicate what the general trend in violent content has been over several decades. According to Gerbner, the average hourly number of network prime-time violent scenes through the years is 5.3, with a peak of 6.9 occurring in 1984 and a low of 2.9 in 1993 (Gerbner, Morgan, & Signorielli, 1995, Table 1). By this measure, a decline in network violence is apparently under way. Gerbner's Violence Index, a composite of three submeasures, decreased from 181.1 in 1984 to 127.2 in 1993. Violence in Saturday morning network children's programming reached 32.0 violent scenes per hour in 1990 and then decreased to 17.9 in 1993; the average throughout the years has been 23.0 (Gerbner et al., 1995, Table 5). Gerbner and his associates (Signorielli, Gerbner, & Morgan, 1995), however, have suggested that violent content has been shifting to cable channels. Therefore, in their view the overall amount of violence available in the medium is in all likelihood constant.

In the mid-1990s, three well-funded and well-publicized studies renewed the research tradition of violence counting. In 1992 and 1994, the Center for Media and Public Affairs analyzed 18 hours of programming from 10 broadcast and cable channels in the Washington, D.C., area. Violence was defined as "a deliberate act of physical force that results in physical harm or destruction of property" and could appear in both news and entertainment shows. Funded by *TV Guide* and the Guggenheim Foundation, the study identified 1,846 violent acts in 1992 and 2,605 in 1994, a 41% increase in 2 years (Kolbert, 1994a). The four major networks (ABC, CBS, NBC, and Fox), widely criticized for their violent fare, apparently documented through a study they commissioned in 1995 and repeated in 1996 and 1997 that violence had decreased on their channels. Conducted by the UCLA Center for Communication Policy, this study used broader and perhaps more subjective criteria: Student researchers were asked to identify those acts of non-news violence that "raised concern" because they were "inappropriate" (Cole, 1996). In 1996, only 5 of 114 prime-time series "raised frequent concerns" about violent content compared to 9 the previous year. In 1997, the "frequent concerns" count decreased to 2 shows (Mifflin, 1998). The reports noted that cable channels "run much more explicit programming than is seen on the networks" (Cole, 1996, p. 122). Needing a count of its own, the cable industry retorted with a $1.5 million analysis of the 1994-1995 season that was not so forgiving of network broadcasting (*National Television Violence Study,* 1997). The National Cable Television Association study, led by a team of researchers from the University of California at Santa Barbara (UCSB), found that although on average 57% of all television shows contained violence (p. 139), the networks were close to that average with 44% (p. 88). The researchers had to concede, however, that pay cable channels far exceeded the average, with violence on 85% of their shows (p. 88). Follow-up studies over 2 years essentially confirmed the first findings.

The long-standing practice of television violence counts documents what is obvious to all: The amount of violence on the screen has been and continues to be voluminous and intractable. Although the violence on highly visible networks' series is surely on the decline, the violence on the less scrutinized cable channels is surely on the rise. This shift in content parallels, and may be related to, the shift in respective audience sizes as the networks' share of the prime-time viewership decreases toward the 50% level (from more than 90% as recently as the 1970s) while the cable channels' portion rises. Overall, the total amount of fantasy violence delivered by the medium is at least steady and may well be climbing. According to one cross-cultural survey, it is more prevalent on American television than in representative Asian (Japan) and European (Spain) countries (Takeuchi, Clausen, & Scott, 1995). Indisputably, scenes of violence predominate in the nation's favorite medium.

In addition to its repeated documentation of television's violence offerings, there are other continuities inherent in the violence count tradition—ones that are not so readily seen because they are subsurface and countervailing. From the 1950s to the present, this line of research, sturdy to all appearances, has been weakened by concealed defects serious enough for David Gauntlett (1995) to propose, "The view of many researchers that violence on television is something which can be simply counted up—an assumption shared by the popular press—has been of little help to the progress of meaningful research" (p. 15). There are four major flaws that obstruct "the progress of meaningful research."

First, the very accuracy of the counts is suspect—not solely because of minor definitional quarrels but also for unexpected reasons, with unexpected consequences. Even taken on their own terms, the summations of hostile depictions on television undoubtedly represent undercounts of the actualities and not inflated figures. Violence counters (Gerbner, for one) typically do not view sports programming as pertinent, do not develop coding schemes for such content, and therefore ignore an extensive area of televised combat. Interpersonal contesting and aggression are the essence of sports and the attraction for each broadcast's tens of millions of viewers. It is clear that football, boxing, and wrestling are violent sports but so are basketball and baseball in more stylized forms. Even a game such as tennis, ostensibly genteel, is premised on interpersonal aggression—on its displacement to a ball smashed repeatedly with an implement; the grunts from the participants tell reflective spectators of the retaliatory exertion being expended. The vocabulary for televised athletic events, so common as to go unnoticed, is replete with assaultive expressions: hit, strike, attack, bat, tackle, clip, slam, shoot, drive, dominate.

Another order of televised entertainment is also drenched in aggression but (with the exception of Gerbner) is almost never tallied. It is a particular cultural filter Americans possess that allows them not to perceive the hostility inherent in humor and in the highly developed television variety of it—the situation comedy. The most prevalent televised genre, with 46 of the 100 highest rated series of all time (Zillmann & Bryant, 1991, p. 262), situation comedies are everywhere construed as harmless and innocent, but on analysis they are revealed as thoroughly aggressive, with jokes and barbs (triggered by a "punch line," a revealing term) leveled at laughingstocks and scapegoats of all varieties. The elderly, the corpulent, the arrogant, the smitten, and the ditzy are all set up for the derisive laughter and surreptitious pleasure of audience members.

The next reservation about television violence counts, a more challenging consideration, regards their implication that television violence has a direct relationship to the outbreak of violence in the real world. Such a connection is not an element in this particular type of research because no data pertaining to this relationship have been gathered. In disregard of this limitation, the authors of the 1995 cable-funded UCSB violence count insisted that "exposure to televised violence contributes to a range of antisocial or harmful effects on many viewers" (*National Television Violence Study,* 1997, p. 6). Because they had not conducted any research of their own on this matter, this error is sufficient to erode credibility in the quantitative work that was actually done.

Television violence counts are frequently allowed to imply real-world violent effects because the word "violence" is used in both contexts and would seem to imply a semantic equivalency. Television violence and real-world violence, however, are not at all equivalent. Murder is a frequent crime on television but a rare crime in real life; slayer and victim are strangers on television but friends or family members in the real world. According to one study, (a) in the real world half of all murder victims are black, but on television only 7.3% are black, and (b) half of those arrested for serious crimes in the United States are black, but only 10% arrested on TV are black (Potter, Vaughan, & Warren, 1995, p. 513). John Fiske and John Hartley (1978) concluded, "It would appear that television violence is not the same as real violence" (p. 29). There is little chance they would be the same because the televised version is devoted to unworldly ends, in wholehearted service to dramatic conventions (Hodge & Tripp, 1986, p. 217). Television violence must occur after well-plotted intimations, it must be reasonably sanitary, and it must be thoroughly redressed and concluded at the close, with no lingering, unnerving aftereffects; in these particulars, it is far removed from common brutalities in everyday life.

The third reservation regarding violence counts expands on the second: There exists a fallacious underpinning to all violence counts that calls into question their relevancy in any way to the issue of televised violence and its effects. These studies' simplicity, which would seem to be their strength, may be their undoing. This literature can account for what is sent via television, but by its very nature it has nothing to contribute to an understanding of what is received by viewers and how it is processed. The condition of reception—about which violence counts research has nothing to say and can have nothing to say—is the central question in the television violence controversy and cannot lie concealed and unaddressed. In fact, there is ample evidence that the material sent is not at all the same as the material received—that each viewer ignores, selects, interprets, and misinterprets the content according to his or her needs and temperament at the moment. British scholar Barrie Gunter (1985) summarizes,

> In the effects research literature, it has become clear from behavioral, emotional, and perceptual measures of viewers' reactions to media content that the audience can be highly discriminating about violent portrayals and that unitary definitions of violence are relatively meaningless. (p. 11)

Even very young children are highly discrete and self-serving users of media violence (Buckingham, 1993; Noble, 1975). In short, reception is all, and violence counts reveal nothing about this.

Finally, the very act of counting violent incidents on television, an act that would seem to be unvarnished, is layered with unexpressed assumptions. People do not count things that are not of concern. Deciding to count these particular items is tantamount to labeling them problematic. Thus, even before an enumeration begins, its objects may be conceived of as rank, like cases of tuberculosis. There is an accusatory thrust to the acts of data collection and their public dissemination when there should not be ideally. Violence count researchers have managed in a clandestine fashion, and with the careless connivance of all involved, to have fashioned a "social problem," one whose existence or lack of existence demands much more deliberate thought.

This discussion of what should be the least convoluted treatment of television violence—the simple count of violent incidents—has unexpectedly brought us directly into the complexities of the matter. What exactly is being sent? More significantly, what exactly is being received and to what effect?

To proceed productively, at this point some specification of "television violence" is needed. For current purposes, television violence is limited to that appearing in entertainment in all forms; only news and documentaries are to be excluded. Within the realm of entertainment, violence can be defined broadly or narrowly; it will make little difference in terms of the investigation here. I find useful the broadest possible construction, which includes violence in cartoons, sports, and comedies, that on "reality" shows such as *Cops,* nature's assaults, and verbal and physical violence, but such breadth is not strictly required. No matter how it is described, this symbolic violence is clearly extensive; it permeates all channels. In form, it is highly reductive and stylized, having been formatted and performed by entertainment industry personnel so as to suit best the demands of the production and industry members' practiced intuitions about the users-to-be of that material (Saferstein, 1994). The violent content enters into very complicated relationships with audience members; to insist that the medium simply plasters this content on the minds of viewers is to profess ignorance loudly. Finally, television violence has been phrased as a social problem. Why it is conceived of in this way and what its actual cultural function proves to be are the subjects of this book.

Ups and Downs

Although the total volume of violent entertainment on television has to all appearances been consistently steady throughout the years, the critical response to the content has been consistently cyclic. Concern has flared and subsided, only to flare and subside again. As one measure of the nation's alternately increasing and decreasing apprehension, the number of citations to articles discussing television violence from 1950 to the present was determined in a magazine index

(*Reader's Guide to Periodical Literature*) and a newspaper index (*New York Times*) (Fowles, 1997). It was found that there have been six peaks of high numbers of articles regarding television violence (1964, 1969, 1972, 1977, 1981, and 1994) alternating with periods when very few were published. On average, 6 years passed between peaks. Assuming that magazine and newspaper editors have a well-developed sense of the interests of their readers or they would not occupy the positions they do for long, these peaks in article numbers can be taken as an indicator of peaks in public concern regarding television violence.

Representative of these peaks was the year 1972, for which the *Reader's Guide* listed 13 articles in general circulation magazines, and an additional 15 stories appeared in the pages of the *New York Times*. Most of the *New York Times* articles in 1972 pertained to the release of the Report to the Surgeon General on Television and Social Behavior. Titled *Television and Growing Up: The Impact of Televised Violence,* this report contained more than 40 technical papers stemming from 23 projects conducted by academic researchers (Surgeon General's Scientific Advisory Committee, 1972); it represents not only the largest investigation on television violence but also quite probably the largest concerted social science effort ever conducted. The story of its inception, submission, and reception epitomizes the regular episodes of anti-television violence fervor.

Although the origins of the Surgeon General's Report (as it came to be erroneously called) may well have lain in swelling public apprehension about television, the actual precipitating agent was a political one. In 1969, U.S. Senator John Pastore of Rhode Island called on the Secretary of Health, Education, and Welfare to investigate "whether there is a causal connection between televised crime and violence and antisocial behavior by individuals, especially children" (Cater & Strickland, 1975, p. 1). Three years and $1.8 million later, the six-volume document was delivered, only to be greeted with some confusion about what it actually concluded. Those with differing positions could extract from it different affirmations. From the summary, readers learned (Surgeon General's Scientific Advisory Committee, 1972),

> We have noted in the studies at hand a modest association between viewing of violence and aggression among at least some children, and we have noted some data which are consonant with the interpretation that viewing violence programs produces the aggression; this evidence is not conclusive, however, and some of the data are also consonant with other interpretations. (p. 7)

Not satisfied with scientific cautions, Senator Pastore quickly convened hearings in which under direct questioning he elicited the following clear statement from Surgeon General Jesse Steinfeld (as quoted in Liebert & Sprafkin, 1988):

> Certainly my interpretation is that there is a causative relationship between televised violence and subsequent antisocial behavior, and the evidence is strong

enough that it requires some action on the part of responsible authorities, the TV industry, the government, and citizens. (p. 114)

By orchestrating his witnesses and the news media's response to them, Pastore was able to recast the report as a clear indictment of television violence. In Robert Liebert's analysis of those events, "the weight of the evidence and the outcry of the news media did become sufficient to produce a belated recognition of the implications of the research" (Liebert & Sprafkin, 1988, p. 114).

All the parties in the recurrent television violence controversy had played their roles handsomely: the Polity, the Academy, the television industry, the news media, pressure groups, and the public. What was the final outcome? Television executives did appear to make concessions at Pastore's hearings and subsequently at industry conferences. Writing 2 years later, however, Douglass Cater and Stephen Strickland (1975) noted dryly that "there has been less than pervasive evidence that the commitments given to Pastore have been met with alacrity" (p. 3). They expressed hopes for the future—hopes that Liebert and Sprafkin said had not been realized as of 1988 (p. 115). In short, in the aftermath of the Report to the Surgeon General and Pastore's widely publicized hearings, it was soon business as usual for the television industry.

The pattern disclosed in the story of the 1972 report would seem to be the following: Public receptivity to the issue of television violence is sensed and acknowledged; from two venerable institutions—first the Polity and then the Academy—come declamations regarding it; the news media fan the flames; various reform groups rally; pressure is brought to bear on the television industry; the television industry acknowledges the concerns and then, owing to competitive motives, ignores them as soon as feasible; and matters return to their previous stasis. Willard Rowland (1983, p. 303) theorized that the struggle is a symbolic one from which all the contestants extract benefits: Communication science appears vigorous and needed; the government appears nurturant and moral; and the broadcast industry has the opportunity to make appropriately responsible gestures. Rowland's analysis hints at the possibility that the debate reflects the clash of broader social forces.

Another cyclical episode of anti-television violence virulence occurred between 1988 and 1995. As one measure of the issue's emergence, there were no *New York Times* articles on the topic in 1988 and 1990, but there were 22 in 1993 and 20 in 1995; similarly, there were no American magazine articles about television violence in 1990, whereas in 1993 there were 29 and in 1994 there were 22 (Fowles, 1997). Duly noted in the nation's press, five congressional hearings (two chaired by Illinois Senator Paul Simon) on the topic between 1988 and 1994 produced 88 expert witnesses; of those with academic or research appointments, Willard Rowland notes (1997, pp. 116-119), all had been selected for their known anti-television violence views. George

Gerbner (1993), perhaps the best known academic researcher on the subject, testified, "Our homes are drenched with carefully and expertly choreographed brutality such as the world has never seen and does not occur in any other industrial country" (p. 65). He stressed that "the consequences of being born into this, living and growing up with this, go far beyond imitative violence" (p. 66). Another well-reputed expert, Leonard Eron (1994), stated that a person's "observation of violence, as seen in standard everyday television entertainment, does affect the aggressive behavior of the viewer" (p. 97).

Congressmen seemed to be tumbling over each other to introduce new legislation regulating television content; at one point in 1993, there were nine bills on the docket designed to reduce video carnage (Gerbner, 1994). Chairman of the Federal Communications Commission, Reed Hundt, saying that the violence children view "affects their behavior negatively to some measurable and meaningful degree" (as quoted in Eggerton, 1994, p. 10), announced his agency's support for the pending restrictions. The First Amendment's stated protection of free expression restrained him no more than it did Attorney General Janet Reno, who maintained, "TV violence legislation will pass constitutional muster" (as quoted in McAvoy & Coe, 1993, p. 6). In addition, both presidential candidates entered the fray: In 1995, Bob Dole's campaign speeches attacked the entertainment media, insisting they were "bombarding our children with a destructive message of casual violence" (as quoted in Balz, 1995, p. A4), whereas in his 1996 State of the Union message, President Bill Clinton proposed that V- ("violence") chips be installed in all new television sets so that parents could block objectionable content, and he piously urged the media to create "television shows you'd want your own children and grandchildren to enjoy" (as quoted in Mitchell, 1996, p. A12). Because of their high positions in the nation's government, all these individual's pronouncements were repeated numerous times in the press. Lower echelons of government were happy to chip in: Although they themselves had done no research on the topic, three doctors from the U.S. Public Health Service wrote the following in the *Journal of the American Medical Association* (Rosenberg, O'Carroll, & Powell, 1992): "Exposure, especially of impressionable children and youths, to the creatively captivating scenes of aggression and violence depicted in the media fosters our acceptance and expectation of violence in America and probably contributes to the frequency of aggressive acts themselves" (p. 3071).

The attack on television violence also issued from other august institutions. The American Medical Association (AMA, 1996) reiterated its long-standing opposition to video havoc and solemnly informed its members,

An extensive body of research amply documents a strong correlation between children's exposure to media violence and a number of behavioral and psychological problems, primarily increased aggressive behavior. The evidence further shows that these problems are caused by the exposure itself.

Although the topic, being semiotic and behavioral, was outside the association's area of expertise in physical medicine, it was apparently too tempting a target to resist attacking. The AMA vocally supported the anti-TV violence bills, with its president warning, "Children's exposure to violence in the mass media can have lifelong consequences" (Jones, 1995, p. 6). The association's journal had previously published an article in which the author, Brandon Centerwall, had examined correlations between the diffusion of television and crime rates and made the remarkable assertion that "television is a causal factor behind approximately one half of the homicides committed in the United States" (Centerwall, 1992, p. 3061). Because it appeared in this respected publication, the claim was taken seriously, and Centerwall became something of a minor celebrity, featured at conferences and in interviews everywhere.

Other prestigious associations joined in the clamor. The American Academy of Pediatrics took up the cause, urging the networks to cut down on violent offerings and broadcast more educational programs. Speaking for the academy, Dr. Victor Strasburger affirmed, "We are basically saying the controversy is over. There is clearly a relationship between media violence and violence in society" (as quoted in "Doctors Push," 1995, p. A16). The American Academy of Child and Adolescent Psychiatry issued a similar position statement, as did the American Public Health Association and the National Association of Attorneys General. The organization with the most sensible claim to expertise on the topic, the American Psychological Association, also weighed in by stating, "In addition to increasing violent behaviors toward others, viewing violence on television changes attitudes and behaviors toward violence in significant ways" (American Psychological Association, 1993, p. 33). All these position statements received mention in the news, further credentializing the movement against television violence. In 1993, the Harry Frank Guggenheim Foundation, which supports research on the causes and consequences of violence, generously distributed to press outlets copies of a speech given by Leonard Eron at the Harvard School of Public Health. Eron had begun his remarks about television violence, "The scientific debate is over" (Eron, 1993, p. 14), and was now widely and appreciatively requoted.

Taking heart from governmental and professional authorities, many reform groups joined in the onslaught. The National Foundation to Improve Television (NFIT, 1996), headquartered in Boston, declared in their recruitment brochure,

> Three different Surgeons General, the U.S. Attorney General's Task Force of Family Violence, the American Medical Association, the American Academy of Pediatrics, the American Psychological Association, and many others have spoken out about the dangers of television violence. It is time to add your voice.

One of the foundation's announced plans was to initiate lawsuits "with the goal of forcing our regulators to restrict the broadcast of excessively violent programming" (NFIT, 1996). The president of the National Family Association, Barbara Hattemer, insisted television teaches "that violence is an everyday occurrence and an acceptable way of solving problems" (1994, p. 360). The leader of another group told a 1996 television talk-show audience (Lieberman, 1996),

> Today we are addressing what few recognize as the number one health problem in America: media violence. As a psychiatrist and the chairperson of the National Coalition on Television Violence, I can tell you that more lives are damaged or destroyed by the effects of on-screen violence than by any other medical problem.

Her claim was left undocumented.

Many of the vocal reform groups were rooted in religious interests. Morality in Media, a large interfaith organization based in New York City, found television violence to be among its foremost concerns: "violence in the media may be understood as a presentation designed to appeal to base human instincts of actions contrary to the dignity of the person" (p. 7). The group was determined to challenge the television industry: "We believe we can change 'them' by putting up a red light on that TV freeway to decadence" (Morality in Media, n.d., p. 25). The American Family Association (headed by perhaps the best known of the anti-television crusaders, the Reverend Donald Wildmon) renewed its campaign in the 1990s by instituting consumer boycotts against the sponsors of what they thought to be the most violent programming. Burger King was the object of the protesters' wrath in 1990 and 1991: "Some of the programs which Burger King helped sponsor included *Ruthless People, Octopussy, Platoon, Child in the Night, Beverly Hills Cop II, Throw Momma From the Train, Hardball,* and *The Nasty Boys*" (American Family Association, 1990). Some of the religious rhetoric took on an ominous tone: Evangelists Phil Phillips and Joan Hake Robie (1988) instructed their followers that "the media is [sic] not going to self-impose restrictions on its own use of violence. We must act now. God has given us a commission like no other" (p. 244).

The bashing of television violence seeped into the public consciousness, and in the absence of any contrary arguments it took hold. The same people who might view a televised slugfest in the evening hours voiced reservations about "television violence" when quizzed by poll-takers in the daylight. Survey after survey (their sheer volume is indicative of the fervor regarding the issue) in the 1990s depicted a public uneasy about video mayhem, at least when asked about it specifically. The percentage of Americans who linked television violence to real-world violence varied according to the polling firm and its client, the year conducted, and the precise wording of the question, but the percentage was never below 55. At the top end, 88% of the respondents in a 1993 Gallup poll, when asked about the influence of television on crime, said it was either "important" or "critical" (U.S. Department of Justice, 1994, p. 221). The *Los Angeles Times* conducted its own national poll in 1993 and determined that 79% of those polled thought there was a connection between violence in televi-

sion entertainment and viciousness in real life ("Most Believe," 1993). In a
Times Mirror poll in the same year, 78% agreed that media violence was a
cause of the breakdown of law and order (U.S. Department of Justice, 1995,
p. 238). In a 1995 Gallup poll, 75% of Americans believed "there is a relationship between violence on television and the crime rate in the United States"
(U.S. Department of Justice, 1995, p. 223). According to a 1994 Harris poll,
61% of Americans agree that television contributes "a lot" to violence in the
nation (U.S. Department of Justice, 1994, p. 238). Also, at the low end, 56% in
a *New York Times* national poll in 1995 believed that violence in the media contributes to teenage violence (Kolbert, 1995, p. H23).

During the 1990s' panic regarding television violence, only one person
dared to counterattack publicly—the actor Michael Moriarty. His is a cautionary tale. A graduate of Dartmouth College and a Fulbright Scholar at London's
Academy of Music and Performing Arts, Moriarty has achieved artistic success as a published poet, an accomplished composer and performer for both
jazz and classical music, and a much-experienced Broadway and film actor.
His widest exposure came with the role of District Attorney Ben Stone on the
NBC crime series *Law and Order.* In November 1993, Moriarty and the show's
producer, along with other television industry figures, were invited to meet
with Attorney General Janet Reno, who was promoting the curtailment of television violence. When Reno harangued her visitors and refused to engage in a
dialogue, Moriarty took offense. His rejoinder by letter stated, "The next time
you invite me to a meeting where only one side gets to ask questions, send a
subpoena" (Preiss, 1997). At a press conference and in subsequent interviews,
Moriarty spoke out strongly in defense of television violence. He told one in-
terviewer (Kalbacker, 1994),

> Dramatic violence is the most effective tool for telling the invisible tale of good
> and evil. Violent drama has been the hallmark of every major civilization since the
> Greeks. It is not a disease. It is an immunization against the disease. (p. 139)

To another he said, "We look at violence in drama like we look at a car accident.
It's a way of coming to terms with our mortality, and with potential disaster"
(Proffitt, 1994, p. M3). In addition, Moriarty was troubled by the Attorney General's casual dismissal of the notion that censoring television violence con-
flicted with the First Amendment: "To threaten us with unconstitutional legislation—It's an outrage!" (as quoted in Proffitt, 1994, p. M3). The government's
attack on television violence, Moriarty believed, was an attempt to deflect attention from its inability to control violence in the real world (Proffitt, 1994).

So strong was the campaign against television violence at that time that
Moriarty's principled stance was not without personal consequences. Pressure
from the U.S. Department of Justice, and even stronger pressure from those
within the television industry who did not want to further fan the controversy,
led to his release from his starring role in *Law and Order.* As he tells it, "I was

forced to resign under what is known as constructive termination. In other words, they made the terms so demeaning, I was forced to resign in protest" (Johnneysee, 1995). Work in films and television dried up, although he did secure a role as Professor Higgins in a Broadway revival of *My Fair Lady*. His wife and son grew uncomfortable under the pressure (Kalbacker, 1994, p. 140), and in the end Moriarty believed the best course for his family was to move to Canada. He told a *New York Times* reporter, "I'm being forced to move to Canada to recover my artistic freedom" ("A Question," 1996, p. 13). Moriarty was a true casualty in the war against television violence.

The existence of this repeated cycle of ferocious concern and then apathy is telling in its own right. The matter has never been laid to rest, nor is it ever likely to be. Each convulsion of public debate predicts the exhausted lull that will follow and sets the stage for the next round, several years later, of rhetorical frenzy. One reason the debate cannot be settled may be the vocabulary by which it is conducted. The words used to describe television are often polarizing terms that defeat clear thought. Television is a "vast wasteland," the "boob tube" that delivers "eye candy," content of "the lowest common denominator," to "couch potatoes." Striking preemptively, this arsenal of derogatory terms can obliterate the phenomenon than needs to be understood and remove it from any possibility of understanding. This vocabulary, useful for combative purposes but useless for intelligent comprehension, suggests a grander reason that the issue of television violence can never be settled for good. To all appearances, no one truly wants to conclude the debate. Cynthia Cooper (1996) refers to "years of repetitive inquiry with very few results" (p. 135). The matter must have a certain utility, one waiting to be detailed, that sustains its survival.

The recurrence of the social issue of television violence is analogous to the recurrence of the individual's daily viewing of some version of video violence. Just as, in the large, social forces on a regular basis like to have a go at television violence, so too in the small does each viewer take in a frequent dose of television violence, whether that symbolic aggression comes in a blatant form (an action-adventure movie or an MTV video) or in a cleverly disguised one (such as a situation comedy or a golf match). The need for society to launch periodic attacks on television violence mimics the need for individuals to aggress within the permissible domain of television violence.

In the Long Run

The history of the television violence controversy can be extended no further than the diffusion of the medium in the 1950s, but at that point the debate grafts neatly onto a long tradition of loudly voiced concerns about popular entertainment content—a tradition stretching back several centuries if not millennia. One observation frequently and correctly made is that the critique of popular diversions with their highly emotive content is always most pointedly directed at the newest entertainment medium, whose initiation into social life occurs as it bears the brunt of antagonistic criticism (Cumberbatch & Howitt, 1989, p. 37; Pearson, 1983, p. 208; Twitchell, 1989, p. 222; Wartelia & Reeves, 1985, p. 119). In a clear formulation of this idea, Steven Starker (1989) notes,

> Each technological innovation, or new media application, promptly has been declared a serious threat to the character and mental abilities of children, the behavior of teenagers, the morality and intelligence of adults, and the sanctity of the American way of life. Newspapers, comics, paperback books, magazines, romance and detective novels, movies, radio, television, video games, and recently computers have all engendered critical books and articles by alarmed experts. (p. 5)

In the twentieth century, before social scientists began to concentrate on television, radio and movies captured their attention (Luke, 1990, Chapter 2). In their analysis of the scientific study of these three electronic media, Ellen Wartella and Byron Reeves (1985) remark that "we are impressed by the overwhelming similarity in the research studies from epoch to epoch, with a new technology substituted as the object of concern" (p. 127). As movies, broadcast radio, and television were introduced in turn, each was soon followed by a cluster of research efforts aimed at determining the extent of its supposed toxicity. Although very few social scientists studied more than one medium, Wartella and Reeves (1985) hypothesize that the famous Payne Fund research program (Charters, 1933), studying the effects of movies on the young, set the pattern for the empirical study of the three media. The Payne Fund scholars, many of whom were trained at the University of Chicago within a tradition of social issue research, conceived of the film medium as a potential problem—one capable of causing negative effects—and approached their subject from this alignment. In one of the Payne Fund studies, unpublished at the time but recently recovered (Jowett, Jarvie, & Fuller, 1996), the authors declared the following about movie crime's effects:

> From a sympathetic interpretation of the plot and emotional stress of the criminal in the photoplay, it is quite possible for one of normal or even superior intelligence under the stress of circumstances to succumb, at least temporarily, to some of the suggestions toward crime included in the photoplay. (p. 210)

These pre-television era studies by social scientists were not conducted in a vacuum but were carried out within a generally apprehensive climate regarding new media, one in which public uneasiness led to a search for decisively stated judgments from authorities of all sorts. Movies were the recipients of much vitriol from cultural leaders. Dr. A. T. Poffenberger, professor of psychology at Columbia University, affirmed in a widely quoted 1921 article, "Motion Pictures and Crime," that movies "might easily become a training school for anti-Americanism, immorality, and disregard for law" (as quoted in Jowett,

1976, p. 144). Typifying this position, a 1932 author declared (as quoted in Pearson, 1983, p. 32), "Hollywood's worst in the movie line has recruited hundreds of [slum boys] for the gangs of race-course roughs, motor bandits, and smash-and-grab thieves." Lee de Forest, a developer of early radio technology, was widely and appreciatively requoted when he lamented in a fantasized speech to broadcasters (de Forest, 1950),

> What have you gentlemen done with my child? He was conceived as a potent instrumentality for culture, fine music, the uplifting of America's mass intelligence. You have debased this child, you have sent him out in the streets in rags of ragtime, tatters of jive and boogie woogie, to collect money from all and sundry, for hubba bubba and audio jitterbug. . . . Murder mysteries rule the waves by night and children are rendered psychopathic by your bedtime stories. (p. 443)

The various print media, as they too had developed and come to entrance large numbers of people, were similarly reviled by culture critics. Between the attack on radio and the one on television, there occurred a 1950s campaign, silly in contemporary eyes but deadly serious at the time, against comic books. Frederic Wertham, a psychiatrist, reported in his extremely popular *Seduction of the Innocent* (1954),

> The average parent has no idea that every imaginable crime is described in detail in comic books. . . . If one were to set out to show children how to steal, rob, lie, cheat, assault, and break into homes, no better method could be devised. (p. 157)

The good doctor asserted, "Our researches have proved that there is a significant correlation between crime-comics reading and the more serious forms of juvenile delinquency" (p. 164)—research that he neglected to include. In language foreshadowing the caveats of television researchers decades later, Wertham wrote, "Crime comics are certainly not the only factor, nor in many cases are they even the most important one, but there can be no doubt that they are the most unnecessary and least excusable one" (p. 166). Encouraged by Wertham's success, Senator Estes Kefauver, in 1954 Juvenile Delinquency Subcommittee hearings, felt justified in haranguing the president of a comic book publishing company regarding one of its garish covers (as quoted in Starker, 1989): "This seems to be a man with a bloody ax holding a woman's head up which has been severed from her body. Do you think that is in good taste?" (p. 83). In his thorough analysis of the 1950s' clamor regarding juvenile delinquency and the media, James Gilbert (1986) concludes that the episode simply "indicates the reappearance of an old worry" (p. 4).

A century earlier, the appearance of "penny dreadfuls" (serial sections of novels) in England in the 1840s and of dime novels later in the United States prompted a torrent of learned and wordy reproach. Commenting on "the desire of the mass audience for a literature of violence," David Brion Davis (1986,

p. 41) notes that violence, especially homicide, has been a staple in American novels and stories since 1800. In 1856, the poet Samuel Taylor Coleridge (as quoted in Starker, 1989) lashed out at the popular pastime of novel reading:

> It conveys no trustworthy information as to facts; it produces no improvement of the intellect, but fills the mind with a mawkish and morbid sensibility, which is directly hostile to the cultivation, invigoration, and enlargement of the nobler faculties of understanding. (p. 8)

The origins of the modern campaign against the excesses of popular culture lie in eighteenth-century England. Author Henry Fielding railed in 1751 against "too frequent and expensive Diversions among the lower kind of People" (as quoted in Pearson, 1984, p. 97). Increasingly during that period, violent British pastimes—bear baiting, bull baiting, cock fighting, and so on—were coming under censure. In his description of this development, Robert Malcolmson (1982) observed that "many of the attacks on traditional recreations betrayed a pronounced class bias. The reformers' energies were mobilized largely against popular amusements; few were so indelicate as to storm the citadels of genteel pleasure" (p. 35); that is, the blood sports of the populace were proscribed, but the blood sports of the aristocracy, such as fox hunting, were not. An increasing wage-earning population, enjoying increased leisure, was turning to lurid newspapers, magazines, novels, and storypapers, which irritated the more proper segments of British society. Like Malcolmson, Herbert Gans (1974) interprets this critical invective as stemming from class antagonisms: The new literate, urban strata with their recreational pursuits were believed to be threatening to the traditional gentry, resulting in a shower of cultural criticism from on high (pp. 52-56).

The Continuous Spectator

Although the historical continuities in violent entertainment offerings are important, as are the continuities in censorious criticism, most important are the continuities in spectating. People have liked, and continue to like, observing violent spectacles. James Twitchell (1989) factually notes, "We have craved violent spectacle whether it was carved on cave walls, engraved on Persian tablets, enacted in Roman coliseums, or imaged in pixels on illuminated screens" (p. 235). In this regard, television would seem to be providing updated and streamlined content for an age-old human proclivity. This service may account in part for the medium's popularity: Americans on average spend 80% of their total media time with television (Cutler, 1990, p. 38).

Several provisional statements regarding the viewing of television violence are offered here. First, watching this content is an entirely voluntary behavior. Virtually no one is compelled to observe this order of content; even toddlers, chancing on material too explosive, will exercise discretion by leaving the room or trying to change the channel. (As Chapter 2 explores, this essential stipulation of voluntariness is violated in every laboratory study on the topic.) Second, the voluntary viewer knows that the content is symbolic and is not live. If the spectator does not perceive the content as symbols at a distance, it will soon produce a contrary and unwanted effect, and the spectator is likely to defect, which neither the broadcaster nor the spectator desires. Third, the voluntary spectator views the violent entertainment in a relaxed, nondidactic frame of mind (Csikszentmihalyl & Kubey, 1981). The spectator is actively seeking release and not instruction. Television viewing is mainly the occasion for discharge, not absorption. Every viewer knows this, but every social critic, spine stiffened, forgets this fact. Voluntary, symbol seeking, and relaxing are features of television violence spectating that will recur in the following chapters. They are set as a challenge to the frequent misconstruction of television viewing as an inflicted, passive, and possibly overstimulating activity.

2

Violence Viewing and Science

It is widely believed that empirical research has absolutely demonstrated the perils of viewing televised entertainment mayhem. There is good reason for this belief: It is affirmed everywhere, creating a tight discursive skein of conventional wisdom. After Leonard Eron (1993) proclaimed in his testimony at Senate hearings that "the scientific debate is over" (p. 95), Senator Paul Simon was moved to say, "We are past questions on the research" (as quoted in Bruning, 1993, p. 7). Dr. Victor Strasburger, speaking on behalf of the American Academy of Pediatrics, asserted, "We are basically saying the controversy is over. There is clearly a relationship between media violence and violence in society" ("Kids' Doctors," 1995, p. 6). Newton Minow, the former Federal Communications Commission (FCC) chairman famous for labeling television a "vast wasteland," reiterated regarding studies of television that "all of them consistently show that television violence contributes to real violence" (Minow & LaMay, 1995, p. 28).

Despite such assertions, we are now going to explore this particular and substantial literature, the body of scientific studies on the effects of viewing televised violence, to determine if it indeed affirms what it is often represented to affirm. Is there concurrence within the "violence effects literature" regarding negative consequences? If possible, we want to determine if this literature is sturdy and possesses an obvious integrity; we want to test its mettle.

The violence effects literature comprises one of the larger bodies of studies in the social sciences, but what cannot be learned, once inside this discourse, is why indeed it is so voluminous. Richard Sparks (1992) observes that although television violence is "one of the most extensively researched and best-funded areas in the whole of social science, this entire body of work is virtually devoid of any comment on why this should be so" (p. 19). I return to this item following our excursion.

The exact size of the television violence literature remains in dispute. Disagreements about the size of the literature hinge on such matters as subject-area definition (does cartoon violence count? violence in commercials? verbal aggression?), on whether a particular paper reports on a full-fledged study or on a portion of one or is merely a rephrasing of another paper, and on the size and substance of a particular piece of research. Hearold (1986) identified 168 studies, whereas Freedman (1984) maintained, "The actual literature on the relation between violence and aggression consists of fewer than 100 independent studies, and the majority of these are laboratory studies" (p. 229). Comstock and Strasburger (1990), however, allude to "over 1,000 articles, including reviews" (p. 32). A literature review by Haejung Paik and George Comstock (1994) set the number at 217 studies published between 1957 and 1990 (p. 522). Not more than 25 original studies were added in the 1990s. Of this total number, the majority of studies by far were conducted in the United States (Comstock & Palk, 1991, p. xii); the empirical approach to the issue of media violence is for the most part an American preoccupation.

A few general observations about the content of this literature can be made at the outset. Invariably, the subjects are the young, from nursery school children to college students; they are to be scrutinized by adult experts. Thus, several conditions immediately obtain: Violence viewers are conceived of as immature and malleable and are to be monitored by unimpeachable scientists. Furthermore, any approach to this topic other than an empirical one has been shunted aside. Thus, the compass points by which the research is to be steered are the child vis-à-vis the adult and the scientific and quantitative as opposed to the nonscientific and humanistic. Moreover, there is no other possible relationship between the young viewer and the violent content than a particular prespecified effect or the lack of this effect. In the words of Carmen Luke (1990), "The viewer, conceptualized on the basis of a cause-effect rationality, could only be seen as a passive, cognitively and experientially blank target upon which media messages would inscribe effects" (p. 3).

By description, this body of research is often segmented into three groups according to the research methodology employed. Such a triage does do a disservice to a few major and revealing studies that fall out of this classificatory scheme, but they will be resuscitated here in due course. Meanwhile, the standard three-part division is a useful convenience.

First are the large number of experiments conducted in a laboratory setting. Typically informed by social learning theory, these experiments attempted to link a controlled stimulus to a learned response. Social learning theory, derived from behaviorism and much in vogue among psychological researchers in the 1950s and 1960s, holds that behaviors are not instinctive but are learned in the process of socialization (Grixti, 1985, p. 67). A tendency toward aggression, for example, would be produced by whatever reinforcements occur in a child's surroundings, including the available media. In the most famous of these laboratory experiments, psychologists Albert Bandura, Dorothea Ross, and Shelia Ross (1963) worked with four groups of nursery school children. The first experimental group saw a live man or woman strike an inflated plastic Bobo doll (which obligingly rolls upright when knocked down) while gleefully shouting, "Sock him in the nose," "Kick him," and "Pow." The second experimental group was exposed to similar antics from the same male or female, except exposure came via a film. The stimulus for the third group was a cartooned cat pummeling the Bobo doll. As a control, the fourth group saw nothing. Children in all four groups were mildly frustrated (by being shown toys that they were not allowed to play with) before they were taken into another room with more toys and an actual Bobo doll.

Bandura et al.'s (1963) control group children displayed the least amount of aggression toward the inflated figure, whereas the children exposed to the film and the cartoon aggressed the most. Bandura et al. concluded, "The results of the present study provide strong evidence that exposure to filmed aggression heightens aggressive reactions in children" (p. 9).

The number of laboratory studies done on the topic began to taper off as questions were raised about the artificiality of the laboratory setting; attention then turned to field experiments that might be closer to actual viewing conditions. The best of the field studies featured large numbers of subjects who were exposed to violent or nonviolent television content and then observed in natural settings. For example, Milgram and Shotland (1973) executed a series of such studies, employing hundreds of subjects. They had arranged to have two contrasting episodes of the program *Medical Center* produced—one in which a central character is driven to smash open charity collection boxes and another in which he does not. Through a ruse, subjects were individually frustrated in a situation where a similar collection box stood unattended: Would they steal the money as the fictional character had? Subjects who had viewed the destruction of the collection boxes were no more likely to imitate that behavior in real life than were subjects who had not seen that scene. Milgram and Shotland repeated their field experiment eight times, with successively greater methodological refinements but with no change in findings. They noted, "We did our best to find imitative results, but all told, our research yielded negative results" (p. 65). Although this study and others found no cause-and-effect relationship, some studies did—enough so that one review of the field experiments concludes that on balance they do indict television violence (Wood, Wong, & Chachere, 1991).

In the third type of violence effects research, know as correlational studies, researchers do not manipulate variables in the attempt to isolate effects. These more naturalistic studies amass large collections of data pertinent to, on the one hand, violence viewing, and on the other hand, behavioral measures. Correlations between the two variables are then calculated; correlations could range from 1.00 (daytime correlates with subsequent nighttime at 1.00) to −1.00. The great vexation about correlations is that they cannot in and of themselves specify causes; causal statements can only be ventured and rationalized as best as possible by the analyst, to be accepted or not by others. There is a high correlation between my advancing age and the proliferating number of television channels, but no one would presume the first factor is the cause of the second.

What is probably the most cited research within the violence effects literature is a correlational study in design. Leonard Eron, Rowell Huesmann, and their collaborators conducted longitudinal research on hundreds of individuals from an upstate New York county, collecting data on viewing preferences and aggressive behavior. Information on the subjects was first gathered in 1960 when they were in the third grade and then gathered again when they were 19 years old and 30 years old. For males, a preference for television violence at age 9 apparently correlated with antisocial behavior at ages 19 and 30, leading Eron (1987) to identify television violence as a prime cause of subsequent aggression (p. 440).

On the essential question of whether televised violence instigates real-world aggression, the violence effects literature—whether laboratory experiment, field experiment, or correlational study—has been summarized at several points in its evolution. Some of these overviews conclude that the case against television violence is a strong one. For example, Andison (1977) reviewed 67 studies appearing between 1956 and 1976, reporting on 73 separate investigations into the effects of television violence. By his count, there had been 31 laboratory experiments, 22 field experiments, and 20 survey studies, with a total of more than 30,000 subjects. Andison's conclusion, that television violence "probably does stimulate a higher amount of aggression in individuals within society" (p. 323), was more fully supported by the laboratory experiments than by the field experiments or the surveys. Andison said that this discrepancy might have resulted from nonlaboratory methods that "were not rigorous enough and therefore underestimate the relationship" (p. 322), although he admitted such an explanation was not found elsewhere in the literature. The fact remained that the degree of effect varied according to the methodology used.

Another systematic overview of the television effects literature was conducted by Susan Hearold (1986), who identified 230 studies of television's effects, both antisocial and prosocial. Data from more than 100,000 subjects yielded 931 measurable effects and 112 correlations (p. 85). According to Hearold, exposures to antisocial content (679 of them in this literature) did produce antisocial results, typically 30% greater than neutral treatments (p. 108). She noted, "The implication of that is if subjects watched the antisocial treatment, usually violent programs or episodes, they would be elevated from the 50th to the 62nd percentile in antisocial behavior, typically physical aggression" (p. 108).

In 1994, Haejung Paik and George Comstock published a meta-analysis that accumulated the results of 217 violence studies. They concluded, "We find a positive and significant correlation between television violence and aggressive behavior" (p. 516). According to their statistical analysis, and in keeping with Andison's (1977) findings, the correlations were twice as high for laboratory experiments than for surveys. Again, different methodologies produced different results.

If these overviews by Andison, Hearold, and Paik and Comstock regarding the influence of television violence on aggressive behavior were the sole ones, and the conclusions in them were the only conclusions drawn, then televised violence would seem to be guilty as charged.

Some researchers have not been shy about drawing inferences from what they believe exists in the scientific literature to hazard guesses about the contribution of television to hostility in the real world. In 1990, George Comstock said that television was the cause of between 5% and 15% of aggressive behavior (Comstock & Strasburger, 1990, p. 40), although 1 year later he decreased the range to between 4% and 10% (Comstock & Paik, 1991, p. 267). Leonard Eron believed that television was responsible for 10% of violence in young people, whereas George Gerbner stated that "no more than 5 percent" of real-life aggression can be traced to the medium (as quoted in Storm, 1994, p. A10). In the view of Brandon Centerwall (1993), the summary evidence is so decisive that if only televised violence could be eliminated, "there would be 10,000 fewer homicides each year in the United States" (p. 63).

Indictments of television violence do not end with so-called imitative effects. Not only does video viciousness stand accused of prompting hostile behavior but also it is charged, somewhat contrarily, with making viewers fearful or of numbing them altogether to concerns regarding interpersonal malice. In a cunning labeling of this array of possible impacts, Ronald Slaby (1994) posited an "aggressor effect" (the standard, whereby the viewer expresses more hostility toward others), a "victim effect" (in which viewers of television become more timid or paranoid), and a "bystander effect" (that, often referred to as "desensitization," entails the hardening of attitudes upon witnessing wrongful incidents).

The victim effect is most closely associated with the extensive work of George Gerbner and his associates and followers. In addition to his annual violence count, Gerbner also releases from time to time updates of his cultivation analysis, which describes the audience effects said to be "cultivated" by exposure to television. Gerbner and his colleagues derive statistical correlations between the amount of self-reported television viewing time and various professed attitudes. According to their analysis, the greater the amount of viewing, the more likely the viewer is to overestimate the actual level of threat in the world. Gerbner and Gross (1976b) relate, "The prevailing message of television is to generate fear" (p. 42) as they leap fearlessly from numerical correlations to cause-and-effect statements.

The bystander effect, or desensitization, is promoted in a much smaller literature, originating with four laboratory studies by a team of two researchers, Ronald Drabman and Margaret Hanratty Thomas (Drabman & Thomas, 1974a, 1974b, 1976; Thomas & Drabman, 1975). The four published studies were variations of a single experimental procedure: Small numbers of third- and fourth-grade students were individually asked to watch younger children over a television monitor while the adult experimenter stepped out of the room. What the 8- to 10-year-olds were actually seeing was a staged videotape in which kindergarten actors became progressively more abusive toward each other. The experimenters wanted to determine if subjects previously exposed to violent footage would take longer to notify an adult than subjects exposed to nonviolent footage or no film at all. Invariably, the hypothesis was confirmed: The children who had seen the violent content were slower to report misbehavior. Although this could have been interpreted as evidence for a cathartic or discharging effect, in that the violence-exposed children were perhaps more relaxed and tolerant, the experimenters represented their findings as evidence of desensitization.

In the view of Ronald Slaby (1994), the aggressor effect, the victim effect, and the bystander effect "have been conclusively demonstrated" (p. B2). He asserts dramatically, "Although not all of these effects occur in all viewers and some viewers are more susceptible than others, it appears that no viewer is immune" (p. B2). Despite affirmations such as this, close scrutiny of this body of research raises many doubts.

Examining the Research

For the moment, it is prudent not to question the forces that gave rise to the violence effects literature and have sustained it for five decades nor to tease out the unarticulated assumptions enmeshed in it. Let us begin by taking this extensive literature entirely on its own terms. What will become clear is that although the majority of the published studies on the topic do report antisocial findings, the average extent of the findings is slight—often so much so that the findings are open to several interpretations. The less artificial and more naturalistic a study is, the tinier the findings are likely to be (Andison, 1977, p. 322; Paik & Comstock, 1994, pp. 526-527). Jonathan Freedman, a skeptical reviewer of this body of studies, has observed, "The further people are from the data, the more excited they are by it" (as quoted in Storm, 1994, p. A10); conversely, the closer one draws to this literature, the less compelling it may appear.

Those who pore over the violence effects literature agree that the case against televised fantasy viciousness is most broadly and clearly made in the large number of laboratory studies, such as those done by Bandura. Overall, these studies offer support for the imitative hypothesis—that younger viewers will exhibit a tendency to act out the aggression seen on the screen. In this group of studies, many find the issue reduced to a pristine clarity, parsed of all needless complexity and obscurity, and answered with sufficient experimental evidence. What is found in this literature can be rightfully generalized to the real world, some believe, to spark a host of inferences and even policies. However, the laboratory is not the real world, and may be so unreal as to discredit the results.

The unnaturalness of laboratory studies is frequently commented on by those who have reservations regarding this research (Buckingham, 1993, p. 11; Gunter & McAteer, 1990, p. 13; Noble, 1975, p. 125), but the extent of the artificiality is rarely defined, leaving those who are unfamiliar with these settings or the nature of these experiments with little sense of what is meant by "unnatural." This feature deserves elaboration. Most behavioral laboratories are located within or adjoin a university campus, itself a location somewhat displaced from conventional locations and certainly removed from the everyday experiences of the children who were frequently the subjects of these laboratory experiments. Selected as a subject, the child would have to be brought by a parent or teacher to a strange universe, with buildings of a size, number, and configuration usually foreign to the child—a setting populated exclusively by adults and lacking other children, pets, houses, stores, or other items familiar to the child.

From the child's perspective, the behavioral laboratory may be stranger still. The setting is institutional, with hard surfaces and angles. There are none of the textures of a home nor the school's familiar displays of handwork. Other youngsters are also arriving, few of whom the child is likely to know, but all of whom are to comprise a novel social group to which the child must be aware and attuned. Around and above the children are adult strangers with clipboards who are in charge.

Now in a room with other unmet children, the child may be unexpectedly frustrated or angered by the experimenters—shown toys but not allowed to touch them, perhaps, or spoken to brusquely. The child is then instructed to look at a video monitor. It would be highly unlikely for the young subject to sense that this experience in any way resembled television viewing as done at home. At home, everything is known; here, everything is unknown, demanding attentiveness. At home, the lights are low, the child may be prone and comfortable, and viewing is nonchalant; here, the room is overlighted, the child is seated upright, and the viewing is concentrated. Most signally, at home television viewing is an entirely voluntary activity: The child is in front of the set because the child has elected to do so and in most instances has elected the content, and he or she will elect other content if the current material does not satisfy. In the behavioral laboratory, the child is compelled to watch and, worse, compelled to watch material not of the child's choosing and probably not of the child's liking. The essential element of the domestic television-viewing experience, that of pleasure, has been methodically stripped away.

Furthermore, what the child views in a typical laboratory experiment will bear little resemblance to what the child views at home. The footage will comprise only a segment of a program and will feature only aggressive actions. The intermittent relief of commercials or changed channels is missing, as are television stories' routine endings bringing dramatic closure in which everything is set right, with the correct values ascendant.

The child then may be led to another room that resembles the one in the video segment and encouraged to play while being observed. This is the room that, in Bandura et al.'s (1963) famous experiment, contained the Bobo doll identical to the one shown on the screen. Is it any wonder that uneasy children, jockeying for notice and position in a newly convened peer group, having seen a videotaped adult strike the doll without repercussions, and being tacitly encouraged by hovering experimenters who do not seem to disapprove of such action, would also hit the doll? As Noble (1975) wryly asked, "What else can one do to a self-righting bozo doll except hit it?" (p. 133). There are typically only a limited number of options, all behavioral, for the young subjects. Certainly, no researcher is asking them about the meanings they may have taken from the screened violence.

In summary, laboratory experiments on violence viewing are concocted schemes that violate all the essential stipulations of actual viewing in the real world (Cook, Kendzierski, & Thomas, 1983, p. 180) and in doing so have nothing to teach about the television experience (although they may say much about the experimenters). Viewing in the laboratory setting is involuntary, public, choiceless, intense, uncomfortable, and single-minded, whereas actual viewing is voluntary, private, selective, nonchalant, comfortable, and in the context of competing activities. Laboratory research has taken the viewing experience and turned it inside out so that the viewer is no longer in charge. In this manner, experimenters have made a mockery out of the everyday act of television viewing. Distorted to this extent, laboratory viewing can be said to simulate household viewing only if one is determined to believe so.

Beyond the particular charade of the viewing experience that the clinical setting establishes, laboratory experiments on any topic are susceptible to two possible contaminants. The first is "experimenter expectancy bias" as labeled by Robert Rosenthal (Rosnow & Rosenthal, 1997, p. 43), a leading investigator of the phenomenon. More than 450 experiments, conducted by Rosenthal and many others, have demonstrated that premonitions of experimenters are highly likely to be realized in the results of their work (p. 46). In a typical study, student experimenters were engaged to elicit from subjects guesses about the worldly success or failure of people by looking at their photographs (Rosenthal & Fode, 1961). Half the student experimenters had been primed to expect high success ratings, whereas the other half, using the same photographs, had been led to believe that failure judgments were expected. Indeed, the "success" experimenters all found higher success scores than any of the "failure" experimenters. There is good reason to believe that experimenter expectancy bias may have tainted the results of many laboratory studies on media-inspired aggression because many academic researchers harbor suspicions about the excesses of popular entertainment. Regarding this prejudice, Robert Thompson observed (as quoted in Storm, 1994), "Television has been a threat to the academy for so long, one would suspect any purportedly legitimate analysis of something the academy so seriously doesn't like. It is like dogs making the cat policy of a city" (p. A10).

Second, all laboratory experiments are hounded by the "good subject effect" because scrutinized subjects often desire to perform suitably in the eyes of the observer (Rosnow & Rosenthal, 1997, p. 64). That is, subjects will adjust their behavior or attitudes in the light of what they perceive to be the "demand characteristics of the experimental situation" (p. 64). For example, Borden (1975) demonstrated that subjects' aggressiveness (calibrated by the level of electrical shock the subject would administer to a bogus competitive opponent) could be influenced by whether the experimental observer was male or female or whether the experimental observer was identified as a member of a karate club or of a pacifist group.

Borden notes, "In sum, the results indicated that the subjects' aggressive behavior was apparently a function of their expectations of approval for such behavior, based on the inferred or explicit values of the observer" (p. 567). The children in Bandura et al.'s (1963) experiment, or in any number of similar studies, may have behaved in ways in which they intuited were what the experimenters desired.

So wayward is the laboratory experimental situation that many anomalous findings regarding aggression have been derived. In one experiment, erotic content produced more aggressive responses (measured by the apparent application of electrical shocks to insulting experimenters) than did aggressive content (Zillmann, 1971). In another experiment, subjects who were treated nicely and then shown violent footage acted afterward in a more generous manner than subjects similarly treated and shown a neutral film or no film (Mueller, Donnerstein, & Hallam, 1983). A humorous film, in contrast to a neutral film, produced more aggressive responses (Tannenbaum, 1972, p. 330). Even viewing *Sesame Street* or *Mister Roger's Neighborhood* induced a threefold increase in aggression among preschoolers who initially measured low in aggressiveness (Coates, Pusser, & Goodman, 1976). Gauntlett (1995) reflects,

> This assortment of findings suggests that the arousal produced by watching television [in laboratory experiments] may be a more salient "effect" than any of the more specific "effects" which are "found" by tests which, by their design, are incapable of revealing any potential effect other than the one they seek to measure. (p. 20)

That general levels of arousal are elevated in subjects through the unnaturalness the laboratory experiment process would explain why aggression and other findings would occur (Cumberbatch & Howitt, 1989, p. 37; Singer & Singer, 1988; Tannenbaum, 1972). The arousal that occurs in the laboratory experiments, and that may be its main effect, is the opposite of what occurs domestically, in which drowsiness is a more likely outcome (Kubey & Csikszentmihalyi, 1990, p. 81).

The inadequacies of laboratory research on television violence effects are apparent in the small body of research on the matter of desensitization or, as Slaby (1994) called it, "the bystander effect." The few attempts to replicate the finding of the four Drabman and Thomas experiments (Drabman & Thomas, 1974a, 1974b, 1976; Thomas & Drabman, 1975)—that children exposed to violent footage would take longer to call for the intercession of an adult supervisor—have produced inconsistent results. Horton and Santogrossi (1978) failed to replicate in that the scores for the control group did not differ from the scores for the experimental groups. In addition, Woodfield (1988) did not find statistically significant differences between children exposed to violent content and children exposed to nonviolent content. Her explanation for this lack of replicated findings was that throughout the years children have been exposed to so much television violence and are so thoroughly desensitized that no experimental treatment is going to differentiate. Woodfield admitted, however, that no longitudinal data existed to corroborate this conjecture.

A third attempt to replicate by Molitor and Hirsch (1994) did duplicate the original findings, apparently showing that children are more likely to tolerate aggression in others if they are first shown violent footage. An examination of their results, however, does give rise to questions about the rigor of the research. This experiment was set up with the active collaboration of the original researchers and may be less of an attempt to replicate (or not) than an attempt to vindicate. Forty-two Catholic school fourth- and fifth-grade children were assigned to two treatment groups (there was no control group). As for all laboratory experiments, the viewing conditions were so thoroughly alien that results may have been induced by subtle clues from the adult laboratory personnel, especially for obedient children from a parochial school setting. Children shown violent content (a segment from *Karate Kid*) waited longer on average before requesting adult intervention than did children shown nonviolent content (footage from the 1984 Olympic games). Again, this finding could be interpreted as evidence of catharsis: The violent content might have lowered levels of arousal and induced a momentary lassitude. The findings could also have resulted from a sense of ennui: Postexperiment interviews revealed that all the children shown *Karate Kid* had seen the movie before, some as many as 10 times (p. 201). By comparison, the Olympic contests might have seemed more exciting and stimulated swifter reactions to the videotaped misbehavior. The first author was one of the laboratory experimenters; therefore, the specter of expectancy bias cannot be dismissed.

Even if desensitization were to exist as a replicable laboratory finding, the pressing question is whether or not the effect generalizes to the real world. Are there any data in support of the notion that exposure to television violence makes people callous to hostility in everyday life? The evidence on this is scant and in the negative. Studying many British youngsters, Belson (1978) could find no correlation between levels of television violence viewing and callousness to real violence or inconsiderateness to others (pp. 471-475, 511-516).

Research by Hagell and Newburn (1994) can answer the question of whether some youngsters who view heightened hours of television become "desensitized" to violence and embark on criminal lives; unexpectedly, teenage criminals view on average less television, and less violent content, than their law-abiding peers.

Reviewers of the small desensitization literature conclude there is no empirical evidence that anything like the bystander effect actually exists in real life (Gauntlett, 1995, p. 39; Van der Voort, 1986, p. 327; Zillmann, 1991, p. 124). Even George Comstock (1989), normally sympathetic to the violence effects literature, concedes about desensitization studies that "what the research does not demonstrate is any likelihood that media portrayals would affect the response to injury, suffering, or violent death experienced firsthand" (p. 275).

I now turn from the contrivances of laboratory research to the more promising methodology of field experiments, in which typically children in circumstances familiar to them are rated on aggressiveness through the observation of their behavior, exposed to either violent or nonviolent footage, and then unobtrusively rated again. Although this literature holds out the hope of conclusive findings in natural settings, the actual results display a disquietingly wide range of outcomes. Some of the data gathered indicate, instead of an elevation in aggressive behaviors, a diminishment in aggressive behaviors following several weeks of high-violence viewing. Feshbach and Singer (1971) were able to control the viewing diets of approximately 400 boys in three private boarding schools and four homes for wayward boys. For 6 weeks, half the boys were randomly assigned to a viewing menu high in violent content, whereas the other half made their selections from nonaggressive shows. Aggression levels were determined by trained observers in the weeks before and after the controlled viewing period. No behavioral differences were reported for the adolescents in the private schools, but among the poorer, semidelinquent youths, those who had been watching the more violent shows were calmer than their peers on the blander viewing diet. The authors concluded that "exposure to aggressive content on television seems to reduce or control the expression of aggression in aggressive boys from relatively low socioeconomic backgrounds" (p. 145).

Although Wood et al. (1991) report that the eight field experiments they reviewed did, overall, demonstrate an imitative effect from watching televised violence, other reviewers of this literature do not concur (Cumberbatch & Howitt, 1989, p. 41; Freedman, 1988, p. 151). McGuire (1986) comments dismissively on "effects that range from the statistically trivial to practically insubstantial" (p. 213). Most decisively, Gadow and Sprafkin (1989), themselves contributors to the field experiment research, concluded their thorough review of the 20 studies they located by stating that "the findings from the field experiments offer little support for the media aggression hypothesis" (p. 404).

In the aftermath of the thoroughgoing artificiality of the laboratory studies, and the equivocation of the field experiment results, the burden of proof must fall on the third methodology, that of correlational studies. In the search for statistical correlations (or not) between violence viewing and aggressive or criminal behavior, this literature contains several studies impressive for their naturalness and their size. Not all these studies uncover a parallel between, on the one hand, increased levels of violence viewing and, on the other hand, increased rates of misbehavior, by whatever measure. For example, for a sample of 2,000 11- to 16-year-olds, Lynn, Hampson, and Agahi (1989) found no correlation between levels of violence viewing and levels of aggression. Nevertheless, many studies do report a positive correlation. It should be noted that the magnitude of this co-occurrence is usually quite small, typically producing a low correlation coefficient of .10 to .20 (Freedman, 1988, p. 153). Using these correlations (small as they are), the question becomes one of the direction(s) of possible causality. Does violence viewing lead to subsequent aggression as is commonly assumed? Could more aggressive children prefer violent content, perhaps as a vicarious outlet for their hostility? (In fact, it was demonstrated in one study that aggressiveness precedes a preference for violent programs; see Atkin, Greenburg, Korzenny, & McDermott, 1979.) Could any of a host of other factors give rise to both elevated variables?

Following his substantial correlational study of 1,500 London adolescents, Belson (1978) highlighted one of his findings—that boys with high levels of exposure to television violence commit 49% more acts of serious violence than do those who view less—and on this basis issued a call for a reduction in video carnage (p. 526). Closer examination of his data (pp. 380-382), however, reveals that the relationship between the two variables is far more irregular than he suggests in his text. Low viewers of television violence are more aggressive than moderate viewers, whereas very high violence viewers are less aggressive than those in the moderate to high range. Moreover, "acts of serious violence" constituted only one of Belson's four measures of real-life aggression; the other three were "total number of acts of violence," "total number of acts of violence weighted by degree of severity of the act," and "total number of violent acts excluding minor ones." Findings for these three variables cannot be said to substantiate Belson's conclusion. That is, for these measures, the linking of violence viewing to subsequent aggression was negated by reverse correlations—that aggressive youngsters sought out violent content (pp. 389-392). Three of his measures refuted his argument, but Belson chose to emphasize a fourth, itself a demonstrably inconsistent measure.

Correlational studies can never escape the fact that correlations are not causes. Buckingham (1993) noted, "One may well discover that children who are violent watch a lot of violent television, but this does not prove that violent television causes real-life violence" (p. 11). Even Leonard Eron, whose attempt to determine causality with his longitudinal data comprises the most frequently cited correlational study (analyzed in detail in the following section), concedes that his research cannot definitively settle the issue of causal direction. He said (as quoted in Storm, 1994), "It's in the laboratory where you can actually show cause and effect" (p. A10), turning the matter back to the manipulations of experimenters.

For the total television effects literature, whatever the methodology, the reviews mentioned earlier by Andison (1977), Hearold (1986), and Paik and Comstock (1994) are not the only ones that have been compiled. Other overviews reach very different summary judgments about this body of studies in its entirety. A review published contemporaneously with that of Andison considered the same research projects and derived a different conclusion (Kaplan & Singer, 1976). Kaplan and Singer examined whether the extant literature could support an activation view (that watching televised fantasy violence leads to aggression), a catharsis view (that such viewing leads to a decrease in aggression), or a null view, and they determined that the null position was the most judicious. They wrote, "Our review of the literature strongly suggests that the activating effects of television fantasy violence are marginal at best. The scientific data do not consistently link violent television fantasy programming to violent behavior" (p. 62).

In the same volume in which Susan Hearold's (1986) meta-analysis of violence studies appeared, there was also published a literature review by William McGuire (1986). In contrast to Hearold, it was McGuire's judgment that the evidence of untoward effects from violence viewing was not compelling. Throughout the 1980s, an assured critique of the violence effects literature issued from Jonathan Freedman (1984, 1986, 1988). Freedman cautiously examined the major studies within each of the methodological categories. After discussing the possibilities of experimenter-induced results in laboratory studies, Freedman stated that laboratory experiments "have little relevance to the question before us" (1988, p. 149). With regard to field experiments, Freedman concluded, "I think it is fair to say that most psychologists would not consider this mixture of results convincing evidence of a phenomenon" (1988, p. 151). Regarding correlational studies, he noted that "not one study produced strong consistent results, and most produced a substantial number of negative findings" (1988, p. 158). Freedman's general conclusion is that "considering all of the research—laboratory, field experiments, and correlational studies—the evidence does not support the idea that viewing television violence causes aggression" (1988, p. 158).

Freedman's dismissal of the violence effects literature is echoed in other literature reviews from British scholars, who may enjoy an objective distance on this largely American research agenda. Cumberbatch and Howitt (1989) discussed the shortcomings of most of the major studies and stated that the research data "are insufficiently robust to allow a firm conclusion about television violence as studied" (p. 51). David Gauntlett (1995), noting that "the time has come for firm conclusions to be drawn from this unprecedentedly voluminous body of work" (p. 1), analyzed at length most of the consequential studies. He believes that "the work of effects researchers is done" (p. 1) but not for the same reasons that some American scholars believe this to be true. In Gauntlett's view, "The search for direct 'effects' of television on behavior is over: Every effort has been made, and they simply cannot be found" (p. 120). Ian Vine (1997) concurs: "Turning now to the systemic evidence from hundreds of published studies of the relationship between viewing violence and subsequent problematic behaviors, the most certain conclusion is that there is *no* genuine consensus of findings" (p. 138).

Although the violence effects literature is flimsy at best, it is often represented as sturdy and unreflectingly accepted as such. New studies that assert that their results build on a tradition of firmly substantiated research findings are rarely called to task for this bandwagon claim. An example is one of the more widely cited research efforts into the effects of viewing on aggression conducted by Tannis MacBeth Williams (1986) and colleagues. They began their report on the introduction of television into a Canadian town previously unable to receive transmissions ("Notel") by stating, "The most important question was whether the aggressive behavior of Notel children would change following the reception of television in their community. Our prediction, *based on the findings obtained in most previous research* (italics added), was that it would increase" (Joy, Kimball, & Zabrack, 1986, p. 313). Building on this putative research base, the investigators observed the free play of Notel's first and second graders just before television arrived and then returned 2 years later for a second observation of the same children. Using a checklist, the observers kept track of incidents of physical and verbal aggression. They concluded that "the finding that Notel children displayed more aggression 2 years after the introduction of television into their town further strengthened the evidence for a relationship between television and aggression *demonstrated previously in laboratory, field, and naturalistic studies* (italics added)" (Joy et al., 1986, p. 339).

A close reading of the Notel study, however, reveals that it was no stronger than the research tradition it invoked and, indeed, perhaps in several ways even weaker. The independent variable was not violent content alone but all the programming of the newly introduced channel. Even if a child had wanted for some reason to view much violent content, it would have proven impossible: The government-run CBC station carried only two crime or detective shows each broadcast week (Joy et al., 1986, p. 335). The remarkably small size of the study (16 Notel children) makes it dangerous if not foolhardy to proffer sweeping generalizations about the large-scale effects of television. Coding of aggressive behavior was not done blindly but rather by researchers with full knowledge of the pre- and postconditions and with a large stake in the outcome; there was no special effort to correct for the possibilities of experimenter expectancy bias.

The findings of the Notel study are nowhere near as decisive as the authors represent, and they contain several truly perplexing anomalies. In addition to

Notel, researchers had also collected data from a comparably sized town with one channel ("Unitel") and another with four channels ("Multitel"). One might reasonably predict, if television causes aggression as claimed, that aggression levels in Notel would be considerably below those of Unitel and Multitel before the medium arrived and then increase to approximate the levels of the two television-suffused communities. This is not at all what the data describe (Joy et al., 1986, p. 320). At the start, the measures of physical aggressiveness were the same for the three communities. Why was this the case? If television causes aggression, why weren't the levels in Notel initially lower and the levels in Unitel and Multitel higher? After television arrived, the reported levels of aggressiveness rose much higher in Notel than in Multitel or Unitel. Why should Notel's children after 2 years be more aggressive than the children who had had television all their lives? Shouldn't it be the other way around? The researchers acknowledged this inconsistency and offered lamely that perhaps "the social constraints which operate in children's play groups" had broken down in Notel (p. 323), although why these restraints had not broken down long before in Unitel and Multitel is not discussed. The data from the 16 Notel children are so inconsistent that they cannot be reasonably said to support any conclusion. This study simply perpetuates the weaknesses of the violence effects literature.

No matter how suspect this literature is, support for its thin findings still abounds. In particular, the work of George Gerbner and that of Leonard Eron are tenaciously believed to have proven the menace of television violence. When the *New York Times* in a 1994 front-page article reexamined the issue of television violence, the two authorities quoted at the start of the article were Eron and Gerbner (Kolbert, 1994b). On the Internet, for the American Psychological Association home page of March 1996, the document "Children and Television Violence" began with reference to George Gerbner and Leonard Eron. Time and again, when material on television violence is offered to a general readership, it is Eron and Gerbner who are cited as pillars of the research effort.

Although the bystander effect can be set aside because of the weakness of the research, the extensive, decades-long research of Leonard Eron into an aggressor effect and that of George Gerbner into the victim effect resist dismissal for their bulk if nothing else—not only of their own extensive publications but also of the concurring commentary from others. The research by Eron and Gerbner requires additional, separate analyses.

Leonard Eron and the Tail That Wags the Dog

According to psychologist Leonard Eron, he did not set out to indict television violence but simply to identify through naturalistic research the particular causes of aggression in youngsters. Eron told a reporter (as quoted in Storm, 1994), "Actually, television is just an incidental finding. But it turns out to be the tail that wags the dog, because we got a lot of financial support through that" (p. A10).

Seemingly, the more Eron and associates were able to place the onus for aggression on televised carnage, the more financial support they were able to obtain; theirs was a research agenda that was handsomely sustained for three decades and was able to extend internationally into six countries. As results accumulated from this longest-ever longitudinal study of viewing and aggression, so did the recognition showered on Eron; he was invited to testify at numerous congressional hearings, was a featured speaker at countless conferences, and in 1980 was the recipient of a lifetime award, the Distinguished Professional Contribution to Knowledge Award, from the American Psychological Association. Throughout his long career, Eron (1993) consistently maintained that "the observation of violence, as seen in standard everyday television entertainment, does affect the aggressive behavior of the viewer." His findings are commonly taken as proof positive of the aggressor effect resulting from heavy violence viewing.

The study that launched Eron's longitudinal research program was conducted in 1960 in a semirural, upstate New York county (Eron, 1963). The subjects were 875 third graders who were 8 or 9 years old. It was found that boys who favored violent television programs (as identified by their parents) were more likely to be aggressive at school (as nominated by their peers). Eron conceded, however, that causality could not be demonstrated through this correlation (p. 196): Did viewing violence lead to aggression, did aggressive children like violence programs, or were other variables involved? Eron nonetheless ventured that television violence did produce aggression, basing his claim on Bandura et al.'s (1963) experiments. Also reported were two irregular findings: For girls, no relationship between violence viewing and aggressiveness could be discerned, and for all children there was a negative correlation between total television viewing time and aggressiveness, raising the possibility of a cathartic or reductive effect.

For a follow-up study done 10 years later, Eron, colleague L. Rowell Huesmann, and their research team were able to locate and interview 427 of the original subjects who were at that time 18 or 19 years old (Eron, Huesmann, Lefkowitz, & Walder, 1972). Again, preferences for violent programs were positively correlated with peer-nominated aggressiveness. With longitudinal data in hand, Eron believed himself to be in a position to address the matter of causality. Through the use of cross-lagged correlations (in which a variable at Time 1, such as violence viewing in 1960, is correlated to a variable at Time 2, such as aggressiveness in 1970), the researchers thought they could suggest which variables were antecedents and possible causes. They conceded at one point, "Of course, one cannot demonstrate that a particular hypothesis is true" (p. 257) through the use of correlations, but they ventured forth undaunted. They found a correlation of .31 between males' preference for violent content at age 9 and peer judgments of aggressiveness at age 19, a correlation higher than that (.21) between violence viewing and aggression at third grade and in their view suggestive of a causal flow. They concluded by stating that "it was demonstrated that there is a probably causative influence of watching violent television programs in early formative years on later aggression" (p. 263).

Several concerns about this study need to be laid out for inspection. From a methodological perspective, for cross-lagged correlations to be above reproach, and apples not be compared to oranges, the measuring sticks at the two points in time must be identical. This was not the case here. First, the means of identifying violence preferences varied. Although 9-year-olds are quite capable of specifying their favorite shows, the researchers chose to have their mothers name three most-watched programs; ten years later, the subjects named four. This discrepancy in measurements may partly explain the curious datum that the preference for violent content at age 9 does not exhibit a significant correlation (.05) with a preference for violent content at age 19 (Eron et al., 1972, p. 256). There is virtually no demonstrated continuity in viewing habits. Second, the measures of aggressiveness differed (p. 254). To the peer ratings of 1960 were added in 1970 the subjects' self-ratings of antisocial behavior and a psychological test of predisposition to delinquency. When the peer ratings were done in 1960, the subjects picked the most aggressive students in their classroom, but when the ratings were conducted in 1970 the most aggressive could be selected from throughout the high school class, a far larger group. Because the subjects were no longer in school in 1970, they had to recall who had been the more aggressive a year or two earlier.

Although the authors highlight the peer rating of aggression for boys in 1970 that did correlate with earlier violence viewing, they chose not to discuss two other proposed aggression measures that did not correlate significantly: self-ratings of antisocial behavior and psychological test results on predisposition to delinquency (Eron et al., 1972, p. 256). That is, of the three measures of aggression they had selected for boys, only one correlated with previous viewing. Another research team, with another hypothesis, might have decided that on balance the evidence could not support causal inferences for boys, but Eron and his colleagues simply chose to emphasize the one in three that did.

Although for boys one of the three possible indicators of aggression did correlate with earlier violence viewing, for girls not a single one correlated. Although measured levels of aggression may indeed be lower for girls, if there is merit to Eron et al.'s (1972) thesis there should still be correlations between girls' earlier violence viewing and later aggression; there are none. Why the statistical relationship should be found for one gender but not for another is a conundrum, suggesting the tentativeness of the entire effort (Sohn, 1981).

To summarize the review of Eron et al.'s famous 1970 longitudinal study, the research format contained the possibility that there might be six cross-lagged correlations (three for boys and three for girls) between earlier violence viewing and later aggression. Had these six correlations materialized, then there would have been clear evidence (but still not proof because the study is only a correlational one) in support of Eron et al.'s causal hypothesis. All six did not materialize, however. Five were simply not in the data; only one was in the data, and it was only moderate (.31). It is difficult to believe that a study with such a weak single finding has been taken so seriously by so many thoughtful people.

Eron's well-funded research continued. In 1981, he and his associates returned a third time to the upstate New York site, where remarkably they were able to reinterview almost all the individuals (409 subjects in total) with whom they had talked in 1970 (Huesmann, Eron, Lefkowitz, & Walder, 1984). The chief findings reported from this second follow-up study are that aggressiveness persists across generations (from the parents of the subjects to the subjects' children) and through the subjects' own lifetime, although the correlations demonstrating this persistence are not as high as might be expected (.50 for boys and .35 for girls). Although this study is often represented as the culmination of a 22-year research effort into the relationship of television and antisocial behavior (Mortimer, 1994), the medium as a cause of aggression recedes almost entirely in the published report. In fact, the word "television" does not appear in the text. Instead of highlighting the "learning" of aggression from television, the authors pointed to other instigators of aggression—familial, neurological, and genetic—and in doing so undermined their previously exclusive focus on television violence. A person can only wonder about this odd turn. In the view of one skeptic (Sohn, 1982), there is one plausible reason for the missing television data: A long-term correlation between violence viewing and aggression had not been confirmed (p. 1293).

In the early 1980s, an international research effort began to command the attention of Eron and Huesmann. In 1986, they reported on results of 3-year-long studies on grade-school children from five countries (the United States, Finland, Poland, Australia, and Israel). A sixth study done in the Netherlands was published separately (Wiegman, Kuttschreuter, & Baarda, 1992). In their summation of the research, Eron and Huesmann state "that the correlation between exposure to media violence and aggression is a consequence first of exposure promoting aggressive acts and second of aggressive acts stimulating exposure" (p. 243). The actual results, however, are so uneven and so varying from study to study that it is difficult to be sure the correlation they point to truly exists or, if it does exist, that the relationship is causal or, if causal, that it is of the nature and order that they indicate.

For example, in the American study (which was conducted by Huesmann and Eron), positive correlations were found between violence viewing and peer-nominated aggressiveness for both boys and girls, in partial contradiction to their earlier studies (Eron, 1963; Eron et al., 1972) that found correlations only for boys. Moreover, this time the correlations were higher for girls than for boys, confounding much of the researchers' earlier rationalizing about the lack of female findings. Although Eron (1963) had previously found correlations for violence viewing and aggressiveness but not for total viewing time, in the later study (Huesmann & Eron, 1986), girls' regularity of total television viewing better correlated with aggressiveness than did their violence viewing (p. 55). The study does not venture reasons for these unexpected developments.

In contrast, in the Finnish study the correlations between violence viewing and aggressiveness were positive for boys (.21) but for girls were statistically insignificant (p. 97). In the Polish study, although average violence viewing increased during the 3-year research period, aggression decreased (p. 139), defeating the main hypothesis. For the Australian children studied, the result was null: "Present data did not indicate that a relation exists in Australia between children's early violence viewing and the level of their aggression 3 years later" (p. 192). Positive correlations were found for city children in Israel but not for rural children (p. 223). Finally, the Dutch researchers, like the Australian researchers, could discern no correlation: "These results give no support for the hypothesis that television violence viewing will, in the long term, contribute to a higher level of aggression in children" (Wiegman et al., 1992, p. 155).

Summarizing the findings of Eron and Huesmann's (1986) multinational research, there were 14 opportunities to find positive correlations between violence viewing and aggressiveness (for both genders, five national studies plus two in Israel). Of these 14 opportunities, positive correlations were found in only 5 (both boys and girls in the United States, Finnish boys, and Israeli urban children). What of the 9 unfulfilled opportunities? Even from internal evidence there is little reason to accept Eron and Huesmann's causal assertion.

This examination of Eron's work from the 1960s to the present must conclude that his television research is insubstantial—that its conclusions are not satisfactorily supported by the evidence presented. The widely varying findings cannot be considered steady, replicated support for Eron's hypothesis. In comparing Eron's research to that of others, Cumberbatch and Howitt (1989) find that it is "inferior in every respect and yet has been widely cited as definitive research linking television violence with aggression" (p. 45). Eron (1995) seems unmoved by such criticism and continues to proclaim, "There can no longer be any doubt that heavy exposure to televised violence is one of the causes of aggressive behavior, crime, and violence in society" (p. 1).

George Gerbner's Mean World

In contrast to Leonard Eron, George Gerbner believes he has discerned different results from televised mayhem. According to Gerbner, whatever television folds into the actual maliciousness of the real world is trifling. "Whereas, the contribution of television to the *perception* (italics added) of violence is much higher. People are almost paralyzed with fear," he informed a *New York Times* reporter (Kolbert, 1994, p. A13).

The main tenet of Gerbner's cultivational analysis is that those who view the most television are subject to a "cultivation" effect, whereby their outlooks measurably draw closer to the distorted world of television content. Although Gerbner insists that "the term *cultivation* for television's contribution to conceptions of social reality is not simply a fancier word for effects" (Gerbner, Gross, Morgan, & Signorielli, 1986, p. 23), in actuality it is. Although Gerbner and associates have examined several cultivational themes, such as the "mainstreaming" of beliefs (Gerbner, Gross, Morgan, & Signorielli, 1982) and estimates about the aged (Gerbner, Gross, Jackson-Beeck, Jeffries-Fox, & Signorielli, 1980), the research most relevant to the violence debate concerns heavy viewers' perceptions of crime rates (Gerbner, Gross, Eleey, Jackson-Beeck, & Signorielli, 1977) and of their chances of being the victims of crime (Gerbner & Gross, 1976a). Gerbner's hypothesis is that heavy viewers, due to the lessons of the medium, will overestimate the amount of crime in national life and reveal a "cultivated" fearfulness about being a crime victim.

The core of Gerbner's work consists in statistical computations of data originally collected by the National Opinion Research Center (NORC) for its annual General Social Survey. From a national sample of adults the General Social Survey gathers information on opinions and behaviors of interest to social scientists, including estimated television viewing hours. It is worth noting that Gerbner is concerned not with the viewing of violence per se (for this he has no data) but rather with the viewing of any and all television content. Gerbner computed correlations between respondents' viewing times and matters such as estimates of the likelihood of being the victim of a crime and the extent of one's fearfulness about being a crime victim. The resulting data allowed Gerbner to confirm his hypothesis: The greater a person's viewing time, the more likely the person is to overestimate the chances of being a crime victim and to express heightened fears of crime (Gerbner, Gross, Jackson-Beeck, Jeffries-Fox, & Signorielli, 1978, p. 206). Gerbner's heavy viewer perceives a mean world.

Nancy Signorielli (1990), Gerbner's long-time research associate, summarized "the mean world syndrome" as follows: "In most subgroups those who watch more television tend to express a heightened sense of living in a mean world of danger and mistrust and alienation and gloom" (p. 102). From her perspective, this is not the end of the matter because fearful people are more readily controlled,

more susceptible to deceptively simple, strong, tough measures and hard-line postures—both political and religious. They may accept and even welcome repression if it promises to relieve their insecurities and other anxieties. That is the deeper problem of violence-laden television. (p. 102)

Tyranny supposedly looms.

The correlations generally found in cultivation analyses, as Potter (1994) notes, are low, typically between .15 and .30. Potter stated, "This means that the exposure variable usually predicts less than 3% of the variance in the cultivation indicators" (p. 16); the remaining 97% must be explained by other factors. No matter whether the correlations are large or small, however, the fact remains that they are only correlations reporting on the extent that two factors are likely to co-occur in time.

Many people have heard of George Gerbner and his research, but far fewer know that his work has been roundly criticized by other social scientists. The surprising number of studies questioning Gerbner's cultivation analysis can be categorized into two groups. The first group says in essence that, if a correlation does exist between heavy viewing and distorted outlooks on crime, the co-occurrence of the two factors is best explained by a third variable. The second camp doubts whether the correlation exists at all.

As an example of studies that have uncovered missing variables, Jackson-Beeck and Sobal (1980) examined the original NORC data to determine if "heavy viewers' life circumstances" could explain both their extended viewing and their pessimism and anomie. They found that heavy viewers tended to be uneducated, poor, unemployed, and asocial; these factors could produce Gerbner's two variables. Doob and Macdonald (1979) questioned whether Gerbner's results could not be caused by the actual crime rates in respondents' areas of residence. The following was their commonsensical hypothesis: "People who watch a lot of television may have a greater fear of being victims of violent crimes because, in fact, they live in more violent neighborhoods" (p. 171). In two high-crime neighborhoods and two low-crime neighborhoods, 300 interviews were conducted. Adult respondents were asked, among other questions, about the extent of their weekly television viewing and about their estimated likelihood of being a victim of crime. The researchers easily replicated Gerbner's finding in that people who watch much television are more likely to indicate fear of their environment. This relationship statistically disappeared, however, when the researchers controlled for the actual incidence of crime in the neighborhood. Real crime, not television, was the cause of fearfulness. Corroborating this conclusion, research reported by Tyler and Cook (1984) documented that people's fear of being victimized is dependent not on media exposure but on their personal experience with crime.

Skogan and Maxfield (1981) showed that advancing age was a missing variable that could account for both increased viewing and increased fear: "There is no evidence here of any relation between media attentiveness and fear of crime" (p. 179). Among children, Roberts (1981) demonstrated that fearfulness was a correlate of age and gender (younger children and females were more afraid) rather than of viewing spans.

Other studies have identified Gerbner's missing third variable as being of a psychological nature rather than a sociological one. People who are constitutionally fearful may stay indoors and watch more television (Kubey &

Csikszentmihalyi, 1990, p. 168; Zillmann & Wakshlag, 1985, p. 154). Wober and Gunter (1982) identified a third variable that they termed "locus of control"—the extent that individuals believe they are in control of their own fates or not. Those respondents who were least likely to believe they were masters of their own situations were most likely to both watch much television and evince fear of being victimized. In an experiment by Wakshlag, Vial, and Tamborini (1983), it was demonstrated that people who are apprehensive about crime will seek out media content that features the restitution of justice—exactly what violent television programs standardly offer. Boyanowsky (1977) also determined that threatened people will select violent media content to deal with their anxieties. According to Dolf Zillmann (1980),

> It appears that the findings reported by Gerbner and Gross are equally (if not more) consistent with the alternative causal possibility. Anxiety may foster heavy viewing of programs that feature suspenseful drama. Unlike the Gerbner-Gross proposal, such an expectation is not based on the consideration of fear-inducing stimuli alone, but on the suspense-resolution unity instead. (p. 159)

From the second critical camp emerge doubts about the very existence of any correlation between heavy viewing and fear of victimization. Rubin, Perse, and Taylor (1988) administered questionnaires to a sample of 392 adults regarding their viewing and their social outlooks. They wanted to correct for a possible "response bias" in Gerbner's cultivation analyses because preliminary evidence suggested that NORC's negatively phrased questions elicited overly negative responses; Rubin et al. posed mostly positive questions. The result was that, "contrary to cultivation assumptions, ritualistic, heavy television exposure was not linked to negative effects" (p. 126). In fact, higher viewing levels correlated with a sense of being safe and not of being fearful (p. 125).

Two independent and sophisticated reanalyses of Gerbner's data also suggest that the original correlation might not have existed. Michael Hughes (1980) pointed out that the Gerbner team had not controlled their analysis for many variables that might have introduced a false correlation. For example, it is known that African Americans on average watch more television than others and are more apprehensive about their neighborhoods, but more than likely it is the life situation of many African Americans that leads directly to fearfulness—more so than media exposure. A reasonable analysis would control for the variable of race, but Gerbner did not and therefore perhaps inflated the correlations he found between heavy viewing and fear of victimization. Numerous other variables could also have been controlled to isolate the one factor of television-viewing time, but they were not. Hughes recomputed Gerbner's NORC data while simultaneously controlling for sex, race, educational level, age, hours worked per week, income, number of memberships, church attendance, and size of community—all pertinent to the amount of viewing time or degree of fearfulness and possibly inducing a spurious correlation. The results of Hughes's calculations caused Gerbner's findings to virtually evaporate. In fact, one reversed direction, suggesting "that those who watch television heavily are *less* likely to be afraid of walking alone at night in their neighborhoods" (p. 295). Hughes concluded that the impact of television on national life is much more complex than Gerbner's scheme could possibly encompass: "Trying to uncover the effect of television by comparing heavy and light watchers is bound to result in inconsistent and largely uninterpretable findings" (p. 301).

The second reanalysis of Gerbner's original data that reached similar conclusions was conducted by Paul Hirsch (1980, 1981). Hirsch had noticed that Gerbner had segmented the questionnaire respondents into viewing groups ("Heavy," "Medium," and "Light") in arbitrary and sometimes inconsistent ways. In his reanalysis of the NORC sample, Hirsch formulated two new categories: nonviewers and extreme (more than 8 hours daily) viewers. Contrary to Gerbner's theory predicting that fearfulness increases with viewing time, Hirsch learned that nonviewers were the most fearful. A second anomaly was that extreme viewers appeared to be less cultivated by television than heavy viewers. Like Hughes, Hirsch introduced multiple controls on the NORC data to try to isolate the single variable of television viewing. Once this was done, Hirsch found that the relationship between viewing time and supposedly television-induced effects was generally a patternless, nonlinear one. This led him to conclude that "acceptance of the cultivation hypothesis as anything more than an interesting but unsupported speculation is premature and unwarranted at this time" (pp. 404-405).

Without stating it explicitly, Hughes (1980) and Hirsch (1980, 1981) raised the possibility that the Gerbner team had, whether consciously or not, manipulated the data to produce the correlations they reported between the amount of viewing and the amount of fearfulness. Although respondents' hours of daily viewing in the NORC tabulations is a continuous variable from zero to 24, Gerbner elected to segment this range into three particular categories: light (0-2 hours), medium (3 hours), and heavy (4 or more hours). According to Hirsch (1980, p. 412), with other data sets Gerbner used at least five other different hourly definitions of these three viewing categories. In one study (Gerbner et al., 1979), for example, 3 hours of viewing was defined as light for one sample and as heavy for another. Potter (1991) states that these shifting definitions can have a profound effect on the correlations produced; in fact, by moving the definitional lines, virtually any result can be produced (p. 581).

Second, questions have been raised about the particular items that Gerbner selects—or does not select—as measures of apprehension. Hughes (1980) pointed out that Gerbner had ignored certain NORC questionnaire items that were logically related to Gerbner's interest in violence but that if used would not confirm the findings Gerbner reported. The items pertained to the application of violence in the real world, and when Hughes correlated them to levels of television viewing it was found that those people who watch television more were less likely to approve of real-world violence (p. 297).

Just as Hughes and Hirsch found little support for Gerbner's cultivation hypothesis among Americans, other researchers working in other countries also failed to find evidence of it. In England, Piepe, Crouch, and Emerson (1977) conducted 842 interviews, asking about levels of television viewing and apprehensions; they found no correlation. Also in England, Wober (1978) obtained viewing data and victimization estimates from more than 1,000 adults: Heavy viewers did not feel more insecure than light viewers. Hedinsson and Windahl (1984) found scant evidence of any cultivation effects among Swedish schoolchildren, and Bouwman (1984) reported a null result for a Dutch sample. As Richard Sparks (1992) stated, cultivation effects do not travel well (p. 92).

Even if Gerbner's cultivation correlation does exist in the United States, it is only a statistical correlation. Gerbner's imputation of a causal flow—that high levels of viewing produce as an effect the exaggerated perception of the world as a mean and fearful place—is contestable. Disputing Gerbner, Zillmann (1991) argues that the causal flow is in the opposite direction and that fearfulness leads to television viewing, especially of violent content, to reduce the initial level of apprehension: "It would thus appear likely that repeated exposure to dramatic portrayals of violent crime reduces rather than increases affective reactions, especially fear reactions" (p. 123).

Horace Newcomb (1978) challenged the basis of cultivation research by pointing out that Gerbner assumes precisely the matters that he should be testing (p. 273). For example, Gerbner assumes that television is ruled by violence, whereas another observer might insist that television is ruled by the triumph of justice and order in the face of violence. Gerbner assumes that viewers are "unsuspecting," "defenseless," and cannot perceive programming as largely fictional; the purposive and selective viewer has no place in Gerbner's scheme. According to Gerbner, viewers all receive similar messages, and they receive one kind of message rather than another. These are all testable items, but they go unexamined by Gerbner. By limiting the range of meanings that the content might offer, and limiting the range of interpretations that viewers might make, Gerbner constricts the broadness of the television experience.

For a quarter century, doubts have been raised about the merits of Gerbner's cultivation analysis—doubts serious enough that, in any other branch of social science, the matter would have been set aside. Gerbner, however, seems impervious to this ongoing criticism and indeed is unwilling to make any methodological adjustments in light of it (Potter, 1994, p. 23). The efforts of Gerbner's skeptics languish largely unnoticed while Gerbner's reputation soars. Why is this the case?

Science, or "Politics by Other Means"

Do the assertions of Eron and Gerbner, as well as those of tens of others who claim to have found negative effects of violence viewing, thrive to an unwarranted extent because their presentation is couched as "scientific" or "objective"? If so, then a few words about the conduct of science may be in order.

Stephen Jay Gould states near the beginning of his masterful *The Mismeasure of Man* (1981) that "Science, since people must do it, is a socially embedded activity" (p. 21). Pure and dispassionate in conception, the actual conducting of science must necessarily be sullied by its human agency, even under the best of conditions. This is even more true in the social sciences than in the natural sciences because when human activity is the object of study, it invites the subtle, unavoidable application of the prejudices and predispositions that govern the categorizing of the social world by all humans, including scientists. Negative and positive judgments find their way through facades of objectivity.

The opportunity for prejudicial contamination occurs throughout the process of carrying out social science. Even to initiate a scientific study, which by its nature must be finite, a near-infinite number of assumptions—a few examined but most unrecognized—must be made. Philosopher of science Helen Longino (1990) points out that "the relation between hypothesis and evidence is mediated by background assumptions that themselves may not be subject to empirical confirmation or disconfirmation, and may be infused with metaphysical or normative considerations" (p. 75). Even if data are then scrupulously collected, it is the case that the ones that are collected have been deemed relevant, perhaps incorrectly, and all other possible data have been excluded, perhaps incorrectly; as Steve Woolgar (1988) suggests: "Facts are the upshot of knowledge practices, rather than their antecedents" (p. 83). The interpretation then given to the data obtained can only be highly subjective: It is hoped that it is informed, of course, but we must ask, informed by what? John Ziman (1984) comments, "Scientific knowledge is essentially *underdetermined:* In principle, there are any number of possible interpretations of a finite set of observations" (p. 104).

The opportunity for the introduction of bias at every step of the way means that it is likely that social science will always be served up with impurities, greater or lesser. These flaws very often are expressive of the power relations in the social world and disclose an unreflecting seeping through of the scientist's personal notions of preferred social arrangements. To the extent that the scientists are white males over 30 years old—this describes most of the authors of the violence effects literature, including Eron and Gerbner, and most social scientists in general—then one has every right to expect that studies may be tainted by perspectives favoring this group at the expense of others. As Sandra Harding (1991) rephrases Karl von Clausewitz's dictum on war, "Science is politics by other means" (p. 10). Even the very act of selecting a subject for scientific study can be fraught with political implications because it institutes a relationship of the superior and the inferior, the knowledgeable and the unknowing. Science can all too readily lord it over its subjects.

Gould (1981) presents two sterling examples of social science gone awry, both of which contrived to find "that oppressed and disadvantaged groups—

races, classes, or sexes—are innately inferior and deserve their status" (p. 24). Craniologists in the nineteenth century calculated brain sizes of various groups to make inferences about mental superiority. Samuel George Morton (1799-1851), a Philadelphia surgeon, poured lead shot into his large collection of skulls and determined that whites on average had the largest cranial cavities, Indians ranked next, and blacks had the smallest cavities. Morton's data have survived, and Gould was able to recalculate the means. He learned that, contrarily, there were no significant differences in average skull sizes among the races: "In short, and to put it bluntly, Morton's summaries are a patchwork of fudging and finagling in the clear interest of a priori convictions" (p. 54).

Subsequently in France, Paul Broca (1824-1880), a professor of clinical surgery, calculated the brain weights of all the corpses he autopsied and reported that those of males averaged 1,325 grams, whereas those of females averaged 181 grams less (1,144 grams). The difference, Broca believed, confirmed the inferiority of women. Broca had also noted the heights and ages of his cadavers, and with this information Gould (1981) was able to conduct a reappraisal. Brain weight increases with height and decreases with age; controlling for these variables greatly narrowed the gender difference. Gould also proposed controls for the degenerative diseases that the older female population would have suffered, and he conjectured that the difference would then disappear: "In short, Broca's data do not permit any confident claim that men have bigger brains than women" (p. 107). Craniologists, in attempting to make the case for superiority based on brain sizes, were only elaborating their own prejudices.

Gould's (1981) second example of tendentious social science is the twentieth-century practice of IQ (intelligence quotient) testing. Gould understands the development and implementation of "scientific" IQ tests as a stratagem designed to rationalize the containment of impoverished social groups. The use of IQ tests to indicate the intrinsic merit of various groups, in Gould's analysis, is crippled by two inherent flaws. First, the tests do not measure innate intelligence but rather reflect environmental factors such as access to education. Second, "the assumption that test scores represent a single, scalable thing in the head called general intelligence" (p. 155) is fallacious. There are many facets to intelligence—more than can be captured by a paper-and-pencil test. Developed with Army recruits during World War I, IQ tests were taken to prove the superiority of certain groups and led directly to the Immigration Restriction Act of 1924, which aimed at excluding all except northern Europeans. Gould noted, "The eugenicists battled and won one of the greatest victories of scientific racism in American history" (p. 232).

In a similar manner, prejudices of several sorts could have contaminated the violence effects literature that, as with Gould's two examples, is largely a white male enterprise. As such, the question of the effects of television violence is cast as a power issue and is infused with the ideology of power. Pure and powerful scientists are poised to save powerless children, who are being assaulted by the bully television and its vicious content. In this scheme, scientists become saviors, and society becomes beholden to them, but only if the evil can first be documented.

I do not believe that Eron or Gerbner, or to the best of my knowledge any of the scientific contributors to the violence effects literature, falsified their data to reap the social rewards. There is nothing about Gerbner's or Eron's data that smells the least bit fraudulent. Just the opposite is true: Most of Gerbner's cultivation data are generated not by himself but by the NORC, whereas Eron's data are so wracked with pervasive inconsistencies that connivance seems highly unlikely. Gerbner is guilty of, I am convinced, a convenient and biased manipulation of the NORC data once they are in his possession, eschewing some analyses in favor of others that support a predetermined position. Eron is guilty of, as best as I can tell, not questionable data manipulation but rather questionable interpretations once the procedures are complete. Both scientists may well have begun with personal and condemnatory assumptions about television, both armed themselves with licit data, and both managed to arrive at the positions at which they started. If this is so, their work is not science so much as legerdemain.

What might their motives be? Funding is a never-ending problem in the social sciences, but this particular line of research, especially when positive findings occur, has been generously supported, allowing both scholars to enjoy prolonged and productive careers. Research support for this topic is not only "the tail that wags the dog," as Eron reported, but also virtually the entirety of the dog, both defining the research question and outlining the answer. Publications are the coin of the academic world, bartered quickly for salaries and collegial reputation, and this line of research with its positive findings has translated into hundreds of publications during four decades for Gerbner and for Eron. Their high standing is certified in the large number of personal awards they have garnered. Executing their research agendas, they have become men of position and power. Also, they have done it in agreeable ways—by siding with elite culture against the crassness of popular culture and by defending the supposedly defenseless.

Eron and Gerbner have been fortunate that their contributions have been to the ordnance of choice in the wider war on television violence. That is, in the campaign against television violence, it is the "scientific" violence effects literature that campaigners choose to wield. Politicians pick up this cudgel and so do advocacy groups. Why science, when other rhetorical tactics might serve? Science is draped in a convenient myth—the myth of complete objectivity. Helen Longino (1990) states, "The myth of scientific value neutrality that is a consequence of the more general view that scientific inquiry is independent of its social context is, thus, a functional myth" (p. 924). Its function is to let science proceed unimpeded, to pass sentries without its biases being questioned. "Scientific objectivity" is a stealthy weapon.

In the end, one must wonder if social science truly has much besides incidental information to contribute toward an understanding of television violence or the cultural war against television violence. Its "objectivity" can mask motives that need to be made more visible. It is premised on a cause-and-effect model when this may be incapable of describing the relationship of the forces at work. The rigor of the scientific method allows it to take only minute pinches of reality—a disadvantage in measuring the glacial changes wrought by the medium of television. In this instance, science has largely been concerned with behavioral outcomes when the real outcome may well be interior and semiotic. To study the circulation of meanings, which is the essence of the production and consumption of symbolic violence, traditional social science has few tools to employ and few active lines of research to pursue. Other, more global approaches would seem to promise greater success.

James Carey (1989) posits two overarching and contrasting conceptualizations of public communication: the metaphor of transmission "whereby messages are transmitted and distributed in space for the control of distance and people" (p. 15) and the contrasted concept of communication as ritual, "the representation of shared beliefs" (p. 18). Carey finds the transmission view, which has guided communication science for decades and is the model for the violence effects literature, to be threadbare. Instead, he urges that social communication be conceived in more complex, communal, and ritualistic ways, a to-and-fro of cultural creation. In this manner, Carey believes, communication studies can be reinvigorated and the essence of public communication recognized (p. 35).

Turned Against Itself

Presume, for argument's sake, that the dismantling of the violence effects literature, and of its scientific matrix, is not convincing so far. We have been working from the inside out, first raising general questions about the innards of the discourse and then unraveling specifically the work of its two figureheads, Leonard Eron and George Gerbner, before taking on in a wholesale fashion the scientific approach to this topic. One may still harbor, however, a sense that the literature, with its overall slight findings of television-inspired aggression, has validity. In this case, I have no other choice but to turn the literature against itself, to select substantial studies done outside laboratories and with large numbers of respondents that could find no evidence of a relationship between television violence and real-world aggression or, even more interesting, that found evidence of a reductive or cathartic effect whereby exposure on a large scale to violent content was linked to reduced aggressiveness and criminality.

Hennigan et al. (1982) developed a study of the relationship between television viewing and violent crime that was most impressive in that it was national in scope and used unobtrusive measures. Their research, employing historical data, exploited the fact that between 1949 and 1952 the FCC had enforced a freeze on new television station licenses. Although some cities already had licensed stations, others were not to get their first until afterward. The researchers identified 34 cities that had received no television broadcasts during the freeze and then picked a comparable sample of 34 cities with broadcasting. If television influences real-world violence, for 1951 the nontelevision cities should have had lower violent crime rates than the television cities; the crime rates should have continued to lag through the freeze. By 1955, after the freeze had been over for 3 years and television stations were operational everywhere, the rates for the two groups of cities should have been similar. None of this appeared in their data analysis, however. The authors determined that "there was no consistent evidence of an increase in violent crime due to the introduction of television in the years tested" (p. 473).

In an equally broad-based and most remarkable study, Messner (1986) concentrated not on the totality of broadcast content but on violent programs alone. His hypothesis was that, for large populations, "there will be a significant, positive relationship between levels of exposure to television violence and rates of violence crime" (p. 220). For the 1980 fall television season, Messner accepted the National Coalition on Television Violence's (an antiviolence advocacy group) identification of the five most violent programs aired, shows such as *The Dukes of Hazzard* and *The Incredible Hulk*. He then determined how popular these particular programs were in the nation's Standard Metropolitan Statistical Areas (SMSAs) by checking the local Nielsen ratings for November. Next, he correlated the SMSAs' television violence viewing with their 1981 rates of violent crime as reported in the FBI's "Uniform Crime Report." As Messner stated, "The results are quite surprising" (p. 223). The SMSAs in which large audiences were attracted to violent television programming tended to exhibit lower rates of violent crime (the correlation was $-.25$). Among other analyses, Messner also studied the population of males aged 18 to 34 to determine if the negative correlation also held for them too, and it did (p. 227). Viewing television violence was not related to an increase in violent crime but rather to a decrease. Messner noted, "The data consistently indicate that high levels of exposure to violent television content are accompanied by relatively low rates of violent crime" (p. 228).

There are no comparably recent and comparably large-scale studies from Great Britain, but there is a sizable one that hints at what might be found. Data collected from 2,039 adolescents included information on violence viewing and on aggressiveness (Lynn et al., 1989). Television violence ratings were established by asking the children to rate on a 5-point scale the violence in 43 popular programs; these data were then averaged to establish a violence rating for each show. Each child was asked to record using a 4-point scale the extent to which each of the 43 programs was viewed. Frequencies of viewing multiplied by violence ratings produced a child's total measure of violence viewing.

The children were also administered a standardized questionnaire that calibrated aggression, psychoticism, and neuroticism. The correlation between psychoticism and aggression was high (.43) and that between neuroticism and aggression was much lower (.10), whereas for violence viewing and aggression the correlation was nonexistent (–.03) (p. 153). Lynn et al. (1989) noted that "the amount of viewing of TV violence evidently has no effect on aggression" (p. 154). The authors tested the hypothesis that the correlation of aggressiveness would increase with age and the cumulative effect of violence viewing, as the television-violence-causes-real-life-aggression theory would suggest. As age increased, however, aggression decreased (p. 154).

The findings of these substantial studies complement many other studies that could not find a positive relationship between violence viewing and aggression (Feshbach & Singer, 1971; Greenberg & Wotring, 1974; Hagell & Newburn, 1994; Harris, 1992; Hartnagel, Teevan, & McIntyre, 1975; Heath, Kruttschnitt, & Ward, 1986; Holz, 1971; Milavsky, Kessler, Stipp, & Rubens, 1982; Milgram & Shotland, 1973). Thelma McCormack (1993) comments about anti-television violence advocates: "In theory they base their policies on scientific evidence of harm but, in practice, choose the evidence selectively" (p. 20). Because these contrary studies are not touted by reformers and have few partisans, they go largely unnoticed. They will not go away, however.

Discourse Within Discourse

Opened up for inspection, the sizable violence effects literature turns out to be an uneven discourse—inconsistent, flawed, pocked. This literature proves nothing conclusively, or equivalently, this literature proves everything in that support for any position can be drawn from its corpus. The upshot is that, no matter what some reformers affirm, the campaign against television violence is bereft of any strong, consensual scientific core. Flaws extend through to the very premises of the literature—flaws so total that they may crowd out alternative viewpoints and produce in some a mind-numbed acquiescence. Specifically, the literature's two main subjects—television and the viewer—are assumed to be what they are not.

Viewers are conceived of as feckless and vacuous, like jellyfish in video tides. Viewers have no intentions, no discretion, and no powers of interpretation. Into their minds can be stuffed all matter of content. Most often, the viewer postulated in the effects literature is young, epitomizing immaturity and malleability. This literature, wrote Carmen Luke (1990), "had constructed a set of scientifically validated truths about the child viewer as a behavioral response mechanism, as passive and devoid of cognitive abilities. The possibility that viewers bring anything other than demographic variables to the screen was conceptually excluded" (p. 281). Although there is ample evidence that the young are highly active, selective, and discriminating viewers (Buckingham, 1993; Clifford, Gunter, & McAleer, 1995; Durkin, 1985; Gunter &

McAteer, 1990; Hawkins & Pingree, 1986; Hodge & Tripp, 1986; Noble, 1975), this is never the version in the violence effects literature.

Television, on the other hand, is seen as powerful, coercive, and sinister. The medium is not a servant but a tyrant. It rules rather than pleases. It is omnipotent; it cannot be regulated, switched, modulated, interpreted, belittled, welcomed, or ignored. All the things that television is in the real world it is not within the violence effects literature.

The relationship between television content and viewers, as implied in this research, is one way only, as television pounds its insidious message into a hapless audience; there is no conception of a return flow of information by which viewers via ratings indicate preferences for certain content rather than other content. The only result allowable from the viewing experience is that of direct and noxious effects. Other possibilities—of pleasures, relaxation, reinterpretations, therapy, and so on—are not to be considered. The television viewing experience, twisted beyond recognition, is conceived of in pathological terms; in fact, a large amount of the research throughout the past decades has been funded by national mental health budgets.

All these preconceptions apply before a bit of research is actually conducted. The surprising result is not that there have been worrisome findings reported but that, given these presuppositions, the negative findings were not much grander still.

A question raised at the outset regarded the volume of this body of studies can now be rephrased: Given the shortcomings of the literature, and its lack of consensus and of productive lines of research, why has it become so extensive? An answer to this question is that this literature continues to be nurtured by a second and encompassing discourse—the one that represents and misrepresents the smaller effects literature. Unlike what it encases, the larger discourse is univocal, unanimous in its opposition to television violence (although it does include a variety of intensities). From the larger public discourse, the violence effects literature draws its nourishment. Sustenance comes in the forms of funds, endorsements, the provision of communication outlets, and receptivity to studies producing the "right" answers. Participants in the larger discourse generously sustain the smaller "scientific" one because in the campaign against television violence science is an ideal weapon—a clean bomb of sorts.

The war on television violence, the larger discourse, has united many allies with otherwise weak ties—prominent authorities and grassroots organizations, liberals and conservatives, and the religious and the secular. We must ask why they put aside their differences, lift their voices together, and join in this particular cause. This implausible alliance constitutes a force field that waxes and wanes throughout the decades, losing strength at one point and gaining it at another; it would seem to have a rhythm all its own. What can account for the regular reoccurrence of this public discourse denouncing television violence?

3

The Whipping Boy

If there were a broad and causal connection between the viewing of symbolic, two-dimensional televised scrapes and the menacing aggression lurking in the three-dimensional world, then this relationship would surely be reflected in national crime trends. Crime is, after all, a definitive, quantifiable indicator of the amount of asocial viciousness in a population. One could expect that, should television violence proliferate, rates of violent crime would also increase. And, it does appear that television violence has been slowly growing in volume and intensity since 1950. Although the networks have recently been televising fewer bloodbaths, because of the expanding number of cable channels there is overall somewhat more violence available in the medium (*National Television Violence Study,* 1998, p. 117). Moreover, each annual contribution to the mountain of violent offerings may well have had a cumulative effect, further boosting crime measures. We should logically expect a steady increase in national violent crime data during the television era. Conversely, a drop in violent crime rates would cast doubt on any linkage between television violence and antisocial behavior.

Striking testimony to a television violence/crime wave connection has come from Brandon Centerwall (1989). Examining the increasing incidence of homicide in the United States during the 1960s and early 1970s, Centerwall notes that the statistical trend paralleled the diffusion of television sets approximately 15 years earlier. He argues that the earlier development caused the latter, with the time lag allowing for the indoctrination of the young into the ways of video slaughter and then the years for them to mature into killers. Centerwall (1992) writes, "The introduction of television in the 1950s caused a subsequent doubling of the homicide rate, i.e., is a causal factor behind approximately one half of the homicides committed in the United States" (p. 3061). In support of his thesis, Centerwall (1989) cites similarly accelerating trends for television-ridden Canada and the lack of such high crime rates in South Africa, which had no television until 1975.

Centerwall's (1989) data that attempt to link the spread of television to the rise in United States' homicides, intriguing as they may seem, are more readily explained in terms of a factor he chooses to slight (p. 8): the grandest demographic event in post-World War II America—the unanticipated surge in births between 1947 and 1964 (peaking in 1957) known as the baby boom. Murders are disproportionately the handiwork of young males, and throngs of this type were maturing in the 1970s, producing irregularly high homicide rates (McGuire, 1986, p. 191; Skogan, 1989, p. 239). It was shrewd of Centerwall to select Canada as his other test case because Canada and the United States were among the very few countries to experience the postwar bulge in birth rates (Jones, 1980, p. 21). South Africa, with its low pre-1975 murder rates, did lack television, but more significantly it lacked a baby boom.

When America's violent crime statistics are extended beyond Centerwall's cutoff date of 1975 and beyond the dates of his publications, to the present, then the weakness of his causal argument becomes clear. Violent crime in the 1980s remained high, but as the baby boom cohort members aged past their 30th birthdays in the 1990s, crime began to decline. From 1991 to 1997, the commission rates of violent crimes (which the Federal Bureau of Investigation [FBI] specifies as the number of murders, forcible rapes, robberies, and aggravated assaults per 100,000 Americans) decreased each successive year ("FBI Reports," 1997). Confirmation of this decline comes from a second set of government statistics, the National Crime Victimization Survey, a poll of 94,000 people conducted annually by the Census Bureau for the Department of Justice. This large sample's experience with violent crime has been declining since 1992, and in 1996 it reached its lowest point since the surveys began in 1973 (Butterfield, 1997). Moreover, in a longer but less noticed trend, rates for property crimes (burglary, auto theft, and larceny and theft) have been decreasing in the United States since 1980 (U.S. Department of Justice, 1997, p. 306).

The reasoning here seeks to underscore the fact that as more entertainment violence has become available on television, crime rates in the United States have been decreasing, thus erasing positive correlations and causal imputations. Critics of this argument might point to criminological trends other than commission rates—to evidence that arrests and incarcerations are reaching new historical highs with each passing year. In 1997, there were 1.6 million Americans behind bars or 615 inmates per 100,000 citizens; the rate had almost doubled since 1985, when it stood at 313 (U.S. Department of Justice, 1997, p. 510). The United States has the highest rate of incarceration in the world save Russia, which has 690 convicts per 100,000 people ("Prison Population," 1997).

Thus, an anomaly exists in that crime rates are decreasing in the United States at the same time that imprisonment rates are increasing. Much of the explanation for this puzzling turn of events lies with the so-called War on Drugs;

arrest rates for either buying or selling drugs (not counted in the FBI's "Uniform Crime Reports" as either violent crimes or property crimes) virtually doubled between 1980 and 1994 from 256.0 per 100,000 Americans to 510.5 (U.S. Bureau of the Census, 1996, p. 210). In the thoughtful analysis of Yale Law School professors Steven Duke and Albert Gross (1993), the government's decision to ferociously pursue drug infractions has produced widening circles of criminality beyond the increasing arrests for narcotic use and supplying: the robberies and burglaries necessary to obtain the means for purchasing drugs whose prices have been elevated because of interdiction pressures; the internecine struggles and murderous wars among drug organizations; the proliferation of handguns; the corruption and subversion of the justice system; and so on. The authors observe that "what most of us think of as manifestation of the drug problem are usefully thought of as by-products of criminalization" (p. 9). The public's unquestioning support for the War on Drugs suggests a prevailing apprehension and consequent repressiveness; these create conditions conducive to more imprisonments across the board and for longer periods of time. Therefore, incarcerations can increase as crime rates continue to decrease.

Television is not a schoolhouse for criminal behavior because, as a rule, televised amusement is not successful for any didactic purpose. Viewers turn to this light entertainment for relief, not for instruction. Video action exists, and is resorted to, to get material out of minds rather than to put things into them. The following is an example of the uninstructive nature of the medium: Although gender stereotypes predominate in programming, Durkin's (1985) thorough review of the pertinent studies uncovered no consistent relationship between subjects' amount of viewing time and their stereotypes of sex roles. Also, in a subsequent demonstration of television's inability to teach, the amount of viewing time by boys and girls did not correlate with gendered behaviors such as washing dishes and taking out the garbage (Morgan, 1987). Closer to the current topic, there was no demonstrable statistical relationship between a viewer's favorite aggressive television hero, the one with whom the viewer is most likely to identify, and any imitated attitudes or behaviors (Howitt & Cumberbatch, 1974, p. 219). Todd Gitlin (1994) states, "Violence on the screens, however loathsome, does not make a significant contribution to violence on the streets. Images don't spill blood" (p. B5). Because images do not cause spilled blood, there are scant outwardly behavioral implications to watching television violence—there are only interior, psychic implications.

It is curious that, although crime is on the decline in the United States, Americans continue to believe it is on the rise (U.S. Department of Justice, 1997, p. 134). Only 25% in a 1996 national poll thought crime was decreasing (U.S. Department of Justice, 1997, p. 134). Although the murder rate is decreasing steadily, coverage of murders has skyrocketed (Kurtz, 1997), further inflaming the mistaken impressions of citizens. News editors and producers are not generating this coverage due to some ideological agenda of their own;

they are doing it because, in their drive to augment audience sizes, they must act on their strong intuitions that the public demands such reportage. Because there is little resistance and no backlash from viewers and readers regarding crime stories, it appears likely that the editors are correct. A conclusion is that the public, entering into a strongly fearful and repressive period, wants stories that articulate its anxieties.

Into this curdling ethos the matter of television violence wanders. Although symbolic violence demonstrably has no relationship to hostile behavior and should be discarded as a possible cause, its sinister reputation lives on. It lives on because the issue is in a clandestine fashion serving other purposes and other contentions. Richard Sparks (1995) explains, "Both crime and television function as metaphors for contemporary troubles" (p. 58). What exactly are these other troubles?

The Whipping Boy

In this chapter, I argue that the issue of "television violence" is much like an empty sack and that into it is periodically and surreptitiously stuffed all matter of other issues and struggles. This deceit is not a conspiracy executed by a few but something that people everywhere do to themselves as they thoughtlessly seek outlets for contentious sentiments. Many of these other contentions are suppressed in public discourse because of the threat that their debate may pose to social order; the citizenry hears all too little about the contests between races, genders, and generations, although these frequently unacknowledged struggles roil national life. When University of Texas law instructor Lino Graglia uttered arguably racist statements against affirmative action in 1997, he was operating well within his First Amendment rights and within the privileges of his position as a tenured professor, but the resulting clamor was enough to quiet him momentarily (Mangan, 1997); to all appearances, the lid is not to be lifted off such issues, at least not in public. Denied full expression, these rankling conflicts slip stealthily into the sack of television violence, a subject that for various reasons is allowed articulation. Once in the public arena, even if in disguised form, such matters can be gratifyingly thwacked by the dominant and the righteous.

Just as in European history a child from the highest classes might have had a whipping boy to take the punishment that the privileged child deserved, so is television violence a whipping boy, a stand-in replacement for transgressions and clashes transpiring elsewhere. David Buckingham (1997) concurs: "The debate about children and media violence is really a debate about other things, many of which have very little to do with the media" (p. 45).

There are several reasons why television violence is such an exemplary— one might even say perfect—whipping boy. First, it is a large target present in one form or another in every household every evening and every weekend. It is not elusive. Second, if one puts on blinders, there might seem to be some correspondence between the mayhem on the television screen and aggression in the palpable, living mode. Both televised entertainment and the real world deal in hostilities.

Third and most signally, television violence performs ideally as a whipping boy because the issue attracts no supporters. Virtually no one speaks out in defense of television violence—the very idea seems silly to most. David Link's (1994) is a lonely voice when he protests, "No one defends violence on television. And when Americans all line up on one side of an issue, you know something is terribly, terribly wrong" (p. 22). Even television industry representatives, whose companies' well-being absolutely depends on the delivery of animosities in symbolic form, rarely get beyond conciliatory statements when compelled to address the matter; in a poll of entertainment industry executives, 78% expressed concern about the content of action dramas on television (Guttman, 1994). In 1993, Ted Turner, perhaps the most conspicuous and enduring industry leader, said in congressional testimony that television was "the single most important factor causing violence in America" (Turner, 1994, p. 105). Lacking the support of its own purveyors, television violence offers zero resistance to the campaign against it. For violence bashers, there is no worry that conditions might worsen as a result of the critical onslaught, no sense of possible retaliation, and thus their campaign can proceed without caution. The object of derision simply stands still and takes all the abuse that can be heaped on it. As a whipping boy, television violence could hardly be improved.

Television violence survives not as an ever-present whipping boy but as an occasional one. When cultural pressures build for several years and they cannot find a direct outlet, then television violence surfaces to absorb obligingly some of the flak. Once the displaced aggression has been vented at television violence, the issue resubmerges, continuing on its decade-long cycle. The bursts of the anti-television violence campaign amount to a regularly recurring melee for the otherwise restrained forces for containment and propriety in American culture; when the issue does resurface, these forces can have at it with license and with glee. The issue is never settled, nor is it likely to be, because to do so would mean eliminating this sector's truly perfected whipping boy.

What exactly are the real conflicts that are displaced to the contrived whipping boy of television violence? They are several in number and of two kinds. Most struggles entail the mightier overwhelming the frailer, but in some conflicts the weaker retaliate through moral exertion.

High and Low

The idea that the attack on television violence is in actuality an attack by the upper classes and their partisans (especially from the Academy) on the culture of the majority, and that class conflict lies at the very heart of the antiviolence critique, is not a novel one (Fowles, 1992, Chapter 7; Gans, 1974; Pearson, 1983,

p. 208; Petley, 1997). In this interpretation, the most current television reform movement is simply the latest manifestation of the ceaseless struggle between the higher and the lower, the patrician and the plebeian, the bourgeoisie versus the proletariat, the gentry over commoners, the dominant against the dominated.

There appears to be potential merit to an approach that seeks to explain the anti-television violence campaigns in terms of concealed class antagonisms—of high culture against popular culture. Before this analysis can proceed, however, it must first negotiate with a contrary position, one arguing that the United States is now a virtually classless society. If in fact the nation were largely destratified, the implication would have to be that class conflicts were at most a minor contributor to the violence debate. And, according to a 1996 *New York Times/CBS News* national poll, only 3% of Americans situate themselves in the upper class and only 8% in the lower class, whereas a vast majority (approximately 87%) believe they belong in the middle. Judith Blau's (1989) research regarding the social distribution of artistic preferences led her to conclude,

> My empirical results suggest that owing to rising levels of education and urbanization, a universal culture has been spawned, and the process of modernization has eradicated the consequences of class differences since the various institutional arts are now rooted in more or less the same social-economic matrix. (p. 4)

This homogeneity of classes and culture, if it exists, is caused by television, theorized W. Russell Neuman (1982). He asked a sample of adults from different educational backgrounds to view certain broadcast programs, interviewed them afterward regarding their responses, and found there was little variation according to years of schooling. He noted, "We take the lack of differential response in this case as possible evidence of a cultural leveling phenomenon" (p. 486).

Everyday experience, however, suggests that social classes have not expired. Americans constantly make class judgments about one another. They unreflectingly note outward appearances and speech patterns and then proceed to classify tentatively. When it is necessary to go further, one person learns about the other's occupation and education, the place of residence and the automobile driven, vacations and pets, and locates that person socially. Especially when matters of courtship and marriage occur, notions of class rank crop up. The term *classy,* much in vogue to indicate selfless benevolence and implacability, suggests the positive premium still placed on ideals of upper-class life. Characters in films and television programs radiate class information about themselves to audience members who know precisely how to gauge such clues. Social stratification may not be as rigid as it was in the past, and in America it is undoubtedly less formidable than it is in most other industrial countries, but it remains a viable gradient of the social landscape. As Michael

Argyle (1994) comments, "Class systems appear to be an inevitable feature of human society" (p. 63).

Embarking on a social class analysis of the anti-television violence crusade, we encounter the work of Pierre Bourdieu. The preeminent living theorist and researcher into matters of class and culture, Bourdieu (1984) is perhaps best known for his work on the segmentation of society according to preferences in aesthetic taste (for instance, going or not going to art museums). Bourdieu's fascinations with class and culture may be partially explained by the facts that he is a trained sociologist and therefore is likely to see social class and its concomitants everywhere he looks, and that he is French and lives in a society in which social class considerations are much more prevalent than they are in the United States. Bourdieu is not without his detractors (Fowler, 1997; Lamont, 1992, pp. 181-188; MacLeod, 1987), but their critiques are not pertinent to the use to which his work will be put here. Because of his background and training, the social classes and their imperatives that may be obscured to Americans are clear to him. He can point the way toward understanding the little acknowledged pressure that class structure can bring to bear in such human affairs as the anti-television violence crusade.

The concept of *habitus* lies at the center of Bourdieu's work. Although the theorist's intellectual intensity and opaque writing style sometimes seem to render the term elusive, its meaning is simple and not remarkably different from that of the English word "habit." Habitus is the system of predispositions ingrained in a particular group or social class. It manifests itself in similar thoughts, behaviors, expressions, leisure pursuits. The shared habitus unites and defines the social entity. Habitus, however, does not shackle individuals; in Bourdieu's scheme, there is ample room for idiosyncratic action.

Another concept special to Bourdieu is *capital*—a term broader and at the same time more specific than was "capital" as used by Karl Marx. Capital is approximately equivalent to social power. In addition to conventional economic wealth, there are several other kinds of capital in Bourdieu's system. Cultural capital (expressive preferences gained primarily through education), symbolic capital (prestige and honors), and social capital (whom one knows) work together with financial capital to define a person's location in the social structure. Social action then becomes a function of class habitus and personal capitals. A final term from Bourdieu's work is *reproduction,* which is the manner by which social classes reproduce themselves and, in doing so, preserve status differences. The reproduction of habitus is the key work of a social class.

Although Bourdieu does not discuss television in his magisterial *Distinctions* (1984), it does not take much imagination to extend his analysis into the domain that is of interest here. Bourdieu does offer leads: People are classified according to a system of oppositions (e.g., "she is this, but not that") that "has its ultimate source in the opposition between the 'elite' of the dominant and the 'mass' of the dominated, a contingent, disorganized multiplicity, interchangeable and innumerable, existing only statistically" (p. 468). There is great tension between Bourdieu's dominant elite and dominated masses—a tension manifested in the dominants' "apocalyptic denunciations of all forms of 'leveling,' 'trivialization,' or 'massification,' which . . . betray an obsessive fear of number, of undifferentiated hordes indifferent to difference and constantly threatening to submerge the private spaces of bourgeois exclusiveness" (p. 469). He conveys clearly in his opening pages (pp. 1-2) that taste (cultural capital) functions as a marker of social class; therefore, different preferences in expressive diversion (such as watching television violence or not) can be used to situate a person hierarchically. Extending these thoughts can lead one to see that an attack on the most popular medium, on television and especially its violent content, would be in reality an attack by the dominant, with their "excessive fear of number" and their wish to maintain exclusivity, on the habitus of the dominated. To reconfirm social distinctions, members of the dominant need only profess an opposition to television violence; this affirmation becomes a badge of membership in the higher class.

By exploiting Bourdieu's (1984) analytical scheme, we come to see television violence as an issue in the largest social struggle—that of the privileged (those with baccalaureates, the dominant) against the rest (the dominated). Television violence is the rhetorical issue of choice in the dominants' efforts to demean and control the dominated.

In the derisive vocabulary of the dominant, violent content is delivered via the "mass media." This term is used so much that it seems unremarkable, even natural, but repetition has concealed its derogatory nature. Programming is not received by a mass, an undifferentiated horde; it is received by individuals. In fact, there is no mass, there are no masses. The first modern expression of this deflating rejoinder is the following often-quoted text from Raymond Williams (1958):

> I do not think of my relatives, friends, neighbors, colleagues, acquaintances, as masses: We none of us can or do. The masses are always the others, whom we don't know, and can't know. . . . Masses are other people. There are in fact no masses; there are only ways of seeing people as masses (p. 299)

Echoing Bourdieu's (1984) statement that masses exist "only statistically" (p. 468), John Carey (1990) wrote,

> The mass is a metaphor for the unknowable, the invisible. . . . The metaphor of the mass has the advantage, from the viewpoint of individual self-assertion, of turning other people into a conglomerate. It denies them the individuality which we ascribe to ourselves, and to people we know. (p. 44)

When dominant Americans chastise the nonexistent phenomena of the "masses" and their "mass medium" of television, with its evil content of television violence, what they are really endeavoring is to disparage and suppress the culture of the dominated. These figments refer to no social reality; their invocations are comments on the motives and social loci of those who give voice to them.

That the anti-television violence crusade is an attempt by the patrician to deride the plebeian is indicated by the composition of the body of witnesses at the five congressional hearings on television violence held between 1988 and 1995. Considering the 36 nonindustry witnesses who testified reprovingly against television violence, would they conform to the senior, white, male epitome of the dominant in American life? Indeed they did. Only 7 of the 36 (20%) were women. None were black or Hispanic. The 29 white males were identified as presidents, professors, directors, representatives, senators, senior scientists, and other distinguished titles that suggested they were well advanced in their careers. It is this patrician sector of society that for reasons of its own leads the attack on rowdy television violence.

The means by which one enters into society's dominant segment, and in doing so learns to effect reproachful views on television violence, is higher education or the Academy. Henry Giroux (1988) offered, "The university, with relative autonomy, functions largely to provide and legitimate the knowledge, skills, and social relations that characterize the dominant power relations in society" (p. 156). The general veneration that greets the Academy is a sign of its near-sacred station and of the importance of its role in, as Bourdieu would view it, the reproduction of the dominant and the dominant's habitus. Through the Academy's portals enter callow youths selected as the most promising for cultivation, who will metamorphose within the institution and exit as a new corps of society's officers—as upright members of the dominant. While within the Academy, the novices will experience a reverse-prestige system: The more conjectural and useless a course of study is (e.g., the liberal arts), the more it is esteemed. The fact that the practical is less valued and the impractical is valued more suggests that the nominal purpose of the Academy (applicable knowledge) is not the true purpose, which is class indoctrination.

The passage into the dominant sector that the Academy affords is, like all ritualistic passages, an arduous one—it occupies one fourth of the young person's school years, and it entails an enormous financial outlay for that person's sponsors. That applicants scramble to attend the best colleges suggests the importance of the collegiate process; the fact that they cannot buy their way in reveals that it is not financial capital but cultural capital that is at stake. The young person and the sponsors are willing, even anxious, to invest the requisite time and money because the investment ensures ultimate acceptance and sinecure in the favored status of the dominant. To have a bachelor's degree is to have the credential of the dominant; not to have a college degree is to remain forever among the dominated.

As keepers of the Academy and as those who make actual its mission, professors are highly valued, almost revered, members of society. They are coddled, given fewer duties than most employed people, and granted time off for one third of the year. Their autonomy (they are little accountable) replicates the autonomy of the Academy; their privileged position replicates the lofty status of the institution. Although their rewards in terms of Bourdieu's financial capital are middling, the cultural capital they accrue cannot be surpassed. It follows that, as they go about their duties in preparing a new cadre to enter the dominant sector, they are unlikely to undermine the culture of the established. Clearly, their role is to reproduce the dominant habitus.

Regarding television, the supposed addiction and marker of the deprecated dominated, professors strive to regard it with condescension or an affected indifference. Ellen Seiter (1996) observed, "A studied, conspicuous ignorance about television is a mark of distinction (like all distinctions, it is valued because it is so difficult to maintain)" (p. 141). Professors' general attitude toward television becomes more pointed when the topic of television violence is discussed; as the staff of the Academy, professors are quick to assert piously that television is dangerously violent. Among college communication teachers, two thirds of a sample of 486 agreed that television "increased aggressive behavior" (Comstock & Paik, 1991, pp. 287-288). Also, from another canvass, of 68 scholars who had published papers or reports specifically on television's effects, 80% concurred that television violence produced aggressiveness (Comstock & Paik, 1991, p. 287).

Professors researching television's effects, therefore, seem to occupy a doubly honored position in the hallowed halls of the Academy. Not only are they, like their colleagues, performing the crucial service of reprovisioning the dominant classes but also they are breathing life into a key issue in the struggle between the dominant and the dominated. They may devote their entire careers to demonstrating the dangers of television violence and are bound to receive approbation from the dominant class as a result. No wonder the position of television-effects researcher has proven so attractive.

As a caveat to what has been said about professors and their service to the dominant strata, it must be noted (if it has not occurred to the reader already) that professors sometimes work contrarily, apparently taking issue with the dominant habitus and siding with the dominated. This occasional ploy should not be misread, however. Because such a professor's stance is rhetorical only, and without true immersion in dominated life, it poses little danger of contaminating students. No student is going to defect because of it. Awareness of the disenfranchised on the part of college students simply puts another arrow in the quiver of the dominant habitus and prepares collegians to better occupy their ruling positions when they graduate. The occasional Marxist professor is a form of inoculation against the possible ravages of the underclass's habitus.

In conclusion, the television violence debate, devoid of any true content, has been stuffed within intimations of the everlasting class war. In the struggle between the patrician and the plebeian, television violence is the challenge that can be spoken aloud—the disguised expression of the dominants' diminishment of the dominated. As such, the issue has signifying properties, tagging the privileged. It is because this topic does define social boundaries, and because few other topics are publicly useful for this, that people invest so much energy in the antiviolence campaign. The elite crusader against television violence is saying, "I belong here, and not there. I am this, and not that."

Once the social class skirmish has again exhausted itself and a quiet sets in, members of the dominant class revert to their unselfconscious viewing of televised mayhem. What was previously rejected as base now returns as unremarkable. Even college professors view, and among them even communication teachers do so. During one lull, a study (Bybee, Robinson, & Turow, 1982) found that media professors did not restrict their childrens' viewing anymore than did the rest of the population.

The Saved Versus the Damned

Recalling from Chapter 1 that many of the groups organized in opposition to television violence have religious ties, we now turn to a second societal dimension—and when reduced to essences, a second polarity—that figures into this moral crusade. In this instance, the contestants and their motives are not as camouflaged as are those in other struggles. The partisans on the attacking side are maximally explicit and vociferous; they stand for religiosity, conservative beliefs, "family values," and are against licentiousness, media excesses, symbolic violence, and so on. Those under attack—the entertainment industries and, by extension, all sorts of permissive people—respond first with incomprehension and then with annoyance, wishing the conservative and fundamentalist contingent would disappear. It would be easy for the political Left to ignore the religious Right if the latter did not comprise a well-defined and adamant voting bloc.

The cultural axis in operation could hardly be more different from the vertical one that would describe social classes stacked from bottom to top. Here, the axis and its poles can be understood as horizontal, stretching from the most conservative to the most free-thinking. Those gathered at the conservative and evangelical pole come from a range of social strata (Romanowski, 1996, p. 35), although they are frequently depicted by their opponents as occupying lower-status positions exclusively. Seeking certainty in the literal word of the Bible, believing in creationism and patriarchal traditions, and adhering to long-standing customs and attitudes, those clustered at this pole are often moved to take issue with the novelties of social transitions and the uncertainties of modern life.

As conservatives react negatively to social changes of greater and lesser profundity, they may be performing services for American civilization more important than they would recognize. The passage of time witnesses American culture venturing into areas rarely if ever visited before and never on such a large scale (for example, in matters of widespread individuality or of social inclusivity); some sort of conservative movement may prove useful, much like a sea anchor during turbulence, for steadying the vessel of culture.

Fundamentalists rail against the expanding, heaving tableau of television violence, and in organized fashion they strike out against it. The American Family Association (AFA), headed by the Rev. Donald Wildmon, has objected strenuously to video carnage; in 1993, Randall Murphree, editor of the association's *AFA Journal,* wrote, "Violence on the small screen continues to invade America's homes as television offers more graphic murders, bloodier assaults, and general mayhem. And all the while, the dramatic effects on society grow more and more alarming" (p. 5). In 1997, the AFA announced that, by their count, violence incidents in prime-time network programs had increased 31% from the previous year (AFA, 1997)—an increase far in excess of those noted by other monitors. As an example of the AFA's activities, in August 1997 its "Action Alert" roused its members to contact CBS and "express your concerns about their dangerous agenda of expanding the limits of violence on television through *Brooklyn South" (Smith, 1997).*

The issue of television violence affords groups such as the AFA the sanctioned opportunity to carry out a cultural attack—to have at their opponents, to condemn immoral depictions and the entertainment industry that produces and distributes them, and to remonstrate against whatever it is in spectators that leads them to relish such productions. Doing so, fundamentalism affirms its presence to others through an issue that is allowed to capture media attention and affirms its role to itself as a guardian of traditional mores. Television violence allows conservative forces the opportunity to carry their standard forward.

The Dark Other

Analysis based only on dominant-dominated or conservative-liberal axes cannot do justice to the many struggles inherent in a massive and highly variegated society. Other contentions find their outlet roundabout in the spurious assault on the nation's whipping boy. For example, the attack on "the Other" in society, an attack that new patterns of decorum have disallowed voicing in public, continues deceptively, hidden in the rhetorical sack of television violence.

Perhaps the most elaborated and certainly the most cited treatment of the concept of the Other occurs in Edward Said's (1978) *Orientalism.* The Orient, remarked Said, was one of Europe's "deepest and most recurring images of the Other" (p. 1). He wrote, "The Orient was almost a European invention, and had been since antiquity a place of romance, exotic being, haunting memories and landscapes, remarkable experiences" (p. 1). Orientalism had its purpose as "a Western style for dominating, restructuring, and having authority over the Orient" (p. 3). Although superiority over the Other was one motive for this ideological phenomenon, another was self-referential in nature: "The Orient has helped to define Europe (or the West) as its contrasting image, idea, personality, experience" (p. 1). From Said, we derive that the Other, the "not-us," is a fabrication of its definers used both to regulate those classified as the Other and to distinguish the culture of the definers. The Other is a mechanism for emphasizing differences and disregarding similarities in order to maintain group solidarity among the "us." The Other differs conceptually from the mass in that the mass can be a part of the us, even if a discredited part, whereas the Other never is a part of us.

In the United States, the Other is a Dark Other—blacks and, to a lesser extent, Hispanics. The Dark Other is the recipient of an undeniable racial assault, continuing and perhaps even strengthening in the post-civil rights era. One striking form of the assault on the Dark Other is the so-called War on Drugs mentioned previously. Baum (1996) states, "The War on Drugs is about many things, but only rarely is it really about drugs" (p. xi). The War on Drugs had its inception in the 1968 campaign speeches of Richard Nixon, following the assassinations of Martin Luther King Jr. in April and Bobby Kennedy in June and in anticipation of the impending defeat in a real war in Vietnam. On Nixon's election, the War on Drugs began in earnest and continues to this day.

The War on Drugs promoted definitions of legal and illegal drugs that favored whites at the expense of the Dark Other; whites' alcohol and prescription tranquilizers (both of whose records of extensive abuse and human damage are well documented) enjoy legal protection, whereas blacks' marijuana and cocaine (the health effects of which, on examination of the data, appear to be negligible) were proscribed (Duke & Gross, 1993, pp. 76-79). Of course, there is nothing inherent in these drugs that allocates them to the legal or illegal categories; these allocations are socially determined—that is, they are determined by "people like us" in denigration of the Other. With these definitions in place, ably masking the real agenda, the war against the Dark Other could proceed.

Recall that between 1980 and 1994 the drug arrest rate doubled in the United States from 256.0 arrests per 100,000 citizens to 510.5 (U.S. Bureau of the Census, 1996, p. 210). Blacks, who comprise only 13% of the American population, make up 38% of these increasing arrests (U.S. Bureau of the Census, 1996, p. 208). The upshot is that young black men, 2% of the nation's population, constitute half of America's prison population (Duke & Gross, 1993, p. 170).

Susan Mackey-Kollis and Dan Hahn (1994) observe, "Whether by intent or effect, U.S. drug policy's focus on law enforcement in the war on drugs has resulted in the targeting of inner-city and black neighborhoods" (p. 14). To determine how this extensive injustice actually transpires, reporter Dan Baum (1996) visited Chicago's Night Drug Court in May 1994. What he noticed immediately was that every one of the defendants was black. Public defender Phil Mullane (as quoted in Baum, 1996) explained ingenuously, "What we do here is process young black men for prison" (p. 334). Typically, a young man is arrested in a drug sweep—a police action cued by an informer that is almost always carried out in black neighborhoods. As a first-time offender, the arrested youth is given the choice of immediate probation by the Night Drug Court or a wait in jail until a court date becomes available; the youth will select the former. When he is arrested a second time, the young man finds that he has violated probation and is destined for jail. He has never had a trial and could conceivably not be guilty, but now he is a criminal with a record. Mullane told Baum, "We do maybe 400 a night, five nights a week" (p. 336).

The full-scale assault on blacks, disguised as a War on Drugs, is also disguised in the anti-television violence crusades. People do not worry about their own viewing of violent shows, and in fact they are so at peace with it that they are less likely to acknowledge the very violence present (British Broadcasting Corporation, 1972, p. 136; Greenberg & Gordon, 1972, p. 253; Hartnagel, Teevan, & McIntyre, 1975, p. 345). They worry extensively, however, about the violence viewing of the Dark Other. David Buckingham (1997) notes, "Debates about the negative effects of the media are almost always debates about *other* people" (p. 32). It is onto the Dark Other that "people like us" project a violence sequence in which viewing entertainment violence leads to real-life criminal behavior. This scenario is false in every detail—there exists no uniform Dark Other anywhere else than in the minds of whites, and symbolic violence does not produce aggression—but it is upheld due to the emotional conviction behind it and the handy availability of rationalizing "scientific proof." Fears of the Dark Other—fears of difference, of being preyed on, of having one's culture overturned, of invalidating one's identity—are denied expression elsewhere but are allowed to sneak into the attack on television violence.

Whites create a representation of the Dark Other fully invested with what they do not like about themselves—their own evil thoughts, their malice, and their menace. By having the Dark Other, they can define themselves contrastingly. The Dark Other is criminal, a threat to sacred social order, whereas whites are law-abiding and enforcers of social order. The Dark Other has no control over his urges; whites are always in control. The Dark Other is sneaky; whites are forthright. The Dark Other looks like that; whites look like this. In this way, the Dark Other, his culture, his viewing habits, and his behaviors are distanced and disparaged.

Therefore, the campaigns against television violence derive added energy from the sublimated desire to suppress the racial Other because it is always other people's viewing, never one's own, that is suspect and perilous. There is a curious twist to all this, however—a complexity revealing much about the intricacies of social life: Whereas whites push off the Dark Other with vigor, at the same time they subtly beckon him back. Peter Stallybrass and Allon White (1986), extending Mikhail Bakhtin's (1968, Chapter 3) groundbreaking analysis of the carnivalesque, observe that whatever is excluded and displaced to the Other then becomes an object of fascination and is summoned back (p. 193). The desire for cultural homogeneity produces instead a heterogeneous mix. Thus, whites are fascinated by the music and dance of blacks and by their clothing styles and their behaviors. Whites study black athletes, seeking to learn about the prowess of the Other. Whites welcome black entertainers and watch them raptly on their television screens, even when (or especially when) black actors are involved in violent scenarios.

Kids

Those who enlist in the antitelevision crusade, invariably adults, always insist that it is "impressionable youths" whom they wish to protect from the noxious effects of televised violence. (I define youths as those younger than the age of 22; beyond this age, they have been definitely sorted into the dominant or the dominated strata and are taking up their adult roles.) Saving the young as a motive for anti-television violence campaigns is mentioned in the congressional testimony of reformers and in the press releases of advocacy groups; this theme is reflected in the subjects of choice (young people) for the experimental literature. In the guise of shielding youths, however, adults are suppressing, denying, containing them. Elders are waging an invisible but savage war.

The eternal generational conflict emerges in contemporary polls: A 1997 survey of 2,000 randomly selected American adults found them ill disposed toward both younger children and adolescents (Farkas & Johnson, 1997). The majority of adult respondents used harsh terms to characterize 5- to 12-year-olds such as "lacking discipline," "rude," and "spoiled" (p. 11). Two thirds of the respondents were very critical of teenagers, calling them "irresponsible" and "wild" (p. 8). According to the survey report, "Most Americans look at today's teenagers with misgiving and trepidation, viewing them as undisciplined, disrespectful, and unfriendly" (p. 8). The 600 teenagers who were also surveyed, however, viewed things differently: Most felt happy in their lives and in their relationships with adults (p. 32). These discrepant attitudes indicate much about the essential nature of generational strife—of who deprecates whom.

Adults are charged with the rearing of children, and some of this responsibility may entail the strong restraint or disabusal of wayward behavior. Children sometimes may require punishment. The punitive energy that is expended against children, however, can become excessive because in addition to cultivating the next generation adults may simultaneously resent them. Older people may envy children's youth, vitality, and their apparent carefreeness and spontaneity. The morals of the young seem looser and only intermittently employed, perhaps imperiling social order. Antagonism toward the young can be especially strong in an adult population configured like that of the United States—one that rapidly is aging due to the baby boom phenomenon. As Dick Hebdige (1988) observes, in the consciousness of adult society, "youth is present only when its presence is a problem, or is regarded as a problem" (p. 17). Overall, adults may feel threatened by the next generation, whose destiny is, after all, to replace their seniors. Anti-youth animus, which will seek relief through sanctioned censures, also serves reactively in the definition of adults: Youths are callow, but adults view themselves as mature, responsible, and honorable, even if they are not.

In past centuries, the control of children was much more brutally and straightforwardly executed: Lloyd deMause (1974), introducing his *The History of Childhood,* declared, "The further back in history one goes, the lower the level of child care, and the more likely children are to be killed, abandoned, beaten, terrorized, and sexually abused" (p. 1). What was blatant then is now accomplished in either subtler or more formalized and institutionalized ways. Curfews and total schooling are among the legitimated instruments of control. Adult society compels, with legal penalties in the wings, the young to sit in classrooms until they are well into their teens, no matter how much the child may resist schooling or despise the confinement. Near the start of the third millennium, the education of the young is becoming ever more regulated and repressive. Citing "the generalized fear of youth," Charles Acland (1995) asks, "Is it any wonder that arrest rates are increasing or that high schools are increasingly calling in police officers for incidents that had previously been dealt with internally?" (p. 146). The suppression of children reached some sort of critical apogee when, in 1996, a North Carolina first grader was expelled from school for innocently kissing the cheek of a classmate he liked.

In the context of the widespread restraint of the young, Acland (1995) notes, "Youth's complex relationship with popular culture as a lived and expressive domain is menacing because the uses of culture cannot be policed completely" (p. 136). With adults able only partially to supervise the "menace" of popular culture, children and adolescents turn to their television shows, their movies, their computer games, and their musical selections to alleviate the oppression from adults that describes their everyday lives. Passing through a difficult stage in life, indeed perhaps the most strenuous one of all, youths turn to television violence for the release it can vicariously offer (Fowles, 1992, Chapter 10). The choice of symbolic violent content correlates highly with age. According to a study commissioned by the Times Mirror Center for People and the Press, age is the single most significant factor in the viewing of television violence—younger viewers watch much more than do older viewers (Rosenstiel, 1993). James Twitchell (1989) suggests,

> If you study the eager consumers of vulgarities, you will soon see that this audience is characterized not so much by class (as we tend to assume, due in part to Marxist interpretations of the culture industry) as by maturity. (p. 15)

Youths do not think it probable that there could be any transfer from television's violence to aggression in the real world; of all age groups, they are the least likely to believe there is a connection (U.S. Department of Justice, 1996, pp. 222-223). Elizabeth Kolbert (1994b), a *New York Times* reporter, interviewed three teenage felons on the subject and noted, "The three teenagers . . . all scoffed at the notion that what young people see on the screen bore any relation to the crimes they committed" (p. A13).

If youths perceive their television violence viewing one way, however, then adults, conducting a general war of containment, embrace the opposite interpretation. Disguising and rationalizing their true motives, adults convince themselves that youths' selections of video violence will lead them into destructive acts. Adults then work, either in the large through the anti-television violence movement or in the small through callous household decrees, to deny the next generation the pleasures and the relaxation found in freely chosen programming.

The Gender War

No discussion of the festering contentions that produce the antagonistic energy behind the anti-television violence crusades would be complete without reference to gender conflicts. Simmering near the surface of national life, the struggle between masculinity and femininity permeates social action and interior reflection, and does so relentlessly, from waking moments into nighttime dreamscapes. As the male expresses dominion and the female resists it, negotiates it, and eludes it, everything in culture becomes gendered, has reference to gender, or plays off of gender and so participates in this total conflict. Such a pervasive rivalry would be expected to find its way into the antitelevision campaign as another camouflaged exertion of the superordinate against the subordinate, but in this instance the thrust is curiously and completely reversed. That is, when the energy of the struggle between genders enters into the condemnation of television violence, it does not do so as an expression of the dominant against the dominated but rather as an act of resistance of the female against the male—as a small counterstrike.

The power of males is most pointedly and excruciatingly realized in the voluminous violence they direct toward women. Elizabeth Stanko (1985) writes, "It is not uncommon that, by the time women are adults, they have experienced some form of coercive, threatening, intimidating, or violent behavior from men" (p. 2). Stanko cites a study (Hanmer & Saunders, 1983) in which 59% of the women interviewed reported "threatening, violent, or sexually harassing behavior" toward them within the past year (p. 11). Similarly, Schlesinger, Dobash, Dobash, and Weaver (1992) reported that for a cross section of 91 women, 57% had been subjected to violence, usually at the hands of a male partner (p. 23). When women are victims of men at such high rates, it is not surprising that feminist reactions form; in the explicit words of Sandra Lee Bartky (1991), "Feminist consciousness is consciousness of *victimizations*" (p. 15).

It is not just that women are extensively the victims of male violence; the situation is famously compounded by the fact that women are then blamed for having invited the malice. The attacks are frequently construed as their fault rather than the aggressors' fault: The women dressed provocatively, they were not acquiescent, or they were in the wrong place at the wrong time. Subjected to both the threat of aggression and the subsequent onus of recrimination for it, "women are continually on guard to the possibility of men's violence. Women, in fact, are specialists in devising ways to minimize their exposure to the possibility of male violence" (Stanko, 1985, p. 1).

Forever alert to the chance of male animosity, women are prone to feeling wary about violence even in its flattened, symbolic form on the television screen. The figment may draw too close to the real thing, whether experienced or imagined, to permit the degree of unimpeded pleasure that male viewers might enjoy. Females are more likely than males to report there is "too much violence in television entertainment" (U.S. Department of Justice, 1995, p. 221) and have been so since the general question was first asked (British Broadcasting Corporation, 1972, p. 171). When queried about the amount of violence on specific action programs, women viewers will perceive more of it than will men (Greenberg & Gordon, 1972, p. 253), presumably because of their awareness of and uneasiness about the vicious content. Indeed, the very act of television viewing, whether of violent content or not, can replicate some of the strained power relationships between the sexes in the real world (Zoonen, 1994, p. 114). If a male possesses the remote control device and a female has no access to it, then she can be subjected to the same pattern of gendered domination that may describe her daytime existence (Morley, 1986, p. 148). What is a leisure activity for the male, whereby pleasure is sought and found, can for a female be a continuing reminder of repression and negation.

A moral crusade against television violence, whenever it occurs, can afford women a choice opportunity for retribution. The well-rationalized antitelevision critique can mask a maneuver against masculine aggression and against masculinity. Seemingly untainted by any overt hostility on its own part, the movement to purify televised entertainment, one that all agree is to be rhetorical only, would seem to be shielded from any possibility of retaliatory strikes. How much contention against males is bound up in the assertion of Barbara Hattemer (1994), president of the National Family Foundation, that "as media violence is absorbed into a person's thoughts, it activates related aggressive ideas and emotions that eventually lead to aggressive behavior" (p. 366)? How much gender strife is exposed in the hyperbolic statement of Dr. Carole Lieberman (1996), chairperson of the National Coalition Against Television, that "more lives are damaged or destroyed by the effects of on-screen violence than by any other medical problem"? She has forgotten heart disease, cancer, and others, and she has done so for a particular reason.

The Subconscious Rumbles

Just as there is a sociology behind the clashing forces that enter into the attack on television violence, so too is there a psychology. Particularized in everyone's mind, there exist interior strains that can contribute an abundance of psychic energy to the crusade; these strains occur in the discord between the conscious mind and the subconscious (or unconscious) one. We need not be diverted by the sometimes rancorous debates regarding the exact nature of the subconscious mind: Philosophers may question its existence (Elder, 1994), whereas empiricists may believe they have quantified it (Sherrin, Bond, Brakel, Hertel, & Williams, 1996), but their efforts need not detain us. It is sufficient to assume that minds have some sort of holding tank that constrains inappropriate psychic material. In the conventional version of Charles Ashbach (1994),

> Within consciousness reside those aspects of mental life dealing with rationality, memory, decision making, acceptable desires and wishes, communication, and social relations. The unconscious is the vast storehouse for the repressed: those wishes, needs, desires, fears, anxieties, dreams, and fantasies that are unacceptable to the conscious mind. (p. 118)

Among the many things contained in this holding tank, the "vast storehouse," are churning antisocial impulses and easily bruised vulnerabilities. The jobs of the conscious mind are to overlay and protect the weaknesses in the subconscious and to discharge reprehensible urges by converting them into acceptable behaviors.

Sometimes exhausted from wrestling with the subconscious, the conscious mind can become apprehensive about its psychic partner. What forbidden content will the subconscious broach next? How is it to be managed? The conscious mind often grows to fear the subconscious and to wish it shackled and concealed. The containment of the subconscious and its resulting inaccessibility are indicated in the arduous work of psychoanalysis; the bringing forth of this material, even under the most sterile, protected conditions, is invariably a trial for both analyst and patient. The pioneering psychoanalyst Carl Jung (1957) observed that "resistances to psychological enlightenment are based on fear—on panic fear of the discoveries that might be made in the realm of the unconscious" (p. 48). People are afraid to acknowledge their subconscious and to give it free play because that would seem to be an invitation to self-subversion.

One index of the uneasiness that Americans have regarding the subconscious mind and its irrationality is the perennial issue of subliminal persuasion in advertising. The widely held belief is that advertisers routinely encode tabooed words or imagery into their entreaties, doing so subliminally in images so light, sounds so low, words so faint that they are below the threshold of conscious perception but can still register on the subconscious mind. These subliminal stimuli are thought to infiltrate the subconscious, engage it through the display of scandalous, banned items (of a sexual or funereal nature), and plant notices of consumables (Key, 1989). It is true that the subconscious mind vaguely perceives some things of which the conscious mind is not aware (Dixon, 1971), but there is not a shred of evidence that advertisers have been able to use this to their advantage or have even attempted to do so (Haberstroh,

1994, Chapter 3). Several laboratory experiments have failed to demonstrate that subliminal stimuli can direct consumers to a specific product (McDaniel, Hart, & McNeal, 1982; Saegert, 1987), which is, after all, what the advertiser would be paying for. In addition to the fact that subliminal appeals do not sell, advertisers must also contemplate what the discovery of subliminal stimuli, or "embeds," would do to their standing with consumers. Although there are many disgruntled former art directors, separated from advertising agencies for various reasons, and as many vengeful individuals among graphics technicians as there are in any other industry, not a single person has come forward claiming to have regularly inserted subliminal embeds into print ads or broadcast commercials. Even if one did profess this, there would remain the matter of proof beyond that for a onetime prank—an unlikely happenstance. For those scaremongers who claim to see lascivious items in an advertisement's ice cubes, clouds, or drapery, such discoveries are more readily accounted for by the well-known psychological mechanism of projection, by which the observer's own deep-seated preoccupations are projected onto amorphous shapes.

If it is unreasonable to believe that subliminal persuasion occurs, then why do the majority (approximately 62%; Haberstroh, 1994, Chapter 6) of Americans believe it does occur? The answer, of course, is that people are afraid that their own subconscious can betray them. Belief in the remarkable myth of subliminal persuasion is testimony to the problematic standing of the subconscious in the conceptions of Americans. The subconscious is conceived of as an intimate site of possible treachery—an enemy within. The subconscious can undermine. Like an unruly child, it cannot be silenced forever; it can only be rebuked, reproved, chastised, denied, and negated.

When the conscious mind disdains the subconscious, it also disdains all that pertains to or administers to the subconscious. Here is where popular culture in general, and television violence in particular, enter the discussion. This metaphorical content, freely chosen, clearly addresses the subconscious regions of the mind in that the content is fantastical in nature. It abounds with sculpted characters in the prime of life, with astounding derring-do, and with nicely cropped endings—all the antitheses of conscious life in the real world. In the domain of television entertainment, a few themes are teased upright and then laid flat—the opposite of the multithematic real world in which everything is a jumble and little ever truly terminates. The themes of televised entertainment are the themes of the repressed material of the subconscious mind, giving symbolic form to needs to dominate, to violate, to attract in a wholesale fashion, and to act admirably adept. Here dance the perfect, the fearless, and the gorgeous—all missing in the daily world of conscious exertion.

This service to the subconscious, which is the stock-in-trade of televised amusement, giving it value to viewers and thus in turn to broadcasters, is also television's albatross. Viewers who relish in the dark the secret sin of violence viewing are loath to confess it in the daylight. When television violence is made the subject of discussion and is transported from the level of the subconscious mind to the level of the conscious one, then what is appreciated privately must be denied publicly. The articulated topic of television violence serves as an unpleasant reminder of the turbulent subconscious and becomes just as reproachable. Person after person professes to reject such programming.

The announced rejection of violent fiction accumulates into a social condition; not only does the individual pretend to disdain it but also so do scores of others (although Nielsen ratings disclose otherwise). The disparagement of television violence becomes an accepted norm. It then becomes evermore incumbent on individuals to register a disgust regarding video violence; doing so brings them in line with their fellows and creates a comforting unanimity. A person wants to represent himself or herself to others as psychologically sound and not as volatile, borderline anything, in need of fictive scrapes, or a threat.

Regarding the television violence controversy, David Link (1994) states, "What is really at issue here is the war within human nature, the conflicts between what we know to be the law and what we feel" (p. 26)—that is, between rationality and irrationality, between the conscious and the subconscious minds. Those reproaching television violence may well be reproaching something they do not appreciate within themselves—the seething, unlicensed subconscious. Writing about media violence, Steven Starker (1989) ventures that those who most deny their own violent feelings, who are most defensive "against these aspects of their humanity, are also most shocked and offended, most likely to do battle against the offending source of stimulation" (p. 178). Attacking television violence can be a highly personal projection of inner discord.

Fear

The widely held belief that television fantasy violence stimulates aggression in the real world and should be censured is what propaganda experts might call "a big lie"—a grotesque fabrication to which all unreflectingly subscribe. A big lie usually exceeds any effort to question it and any attempt to ascertain its correctness; it is unapproachable and unimpeachable. What makes this particular big lie different from the propagandists' is that it is not bestowed on an acquiescent population for the ulterior, controlling motive of some cabal; rather, this is one that we all repeatedly tell one another, duping ourselves as we dupe others. We do this for reasons of convenience—that by repeating this uncontroverted big lie with ever-increasing volume, we can easily vent some of our own hostilities regarding other, truly confounding social and psychological conflicts.

The just-concluded tour of these conflictual rifts has disclosed an unexpected complexity: The censuring energy (only nominally against television violence) generally flows from the stronger party toward the weaker, but in some instances it flows in the opposite direction. Within the gender wars, and in the invectives of the religious Right, condemnatory energy flows from the weaker toward stronger targets. In this regard, Marxist thought comes up short. When John Fiske (1989) considers the anti-television violence critique solely in terms of the privileged against the disadvantaged (p. 135), his analysis omits the possibility of other struggles and other directional flows. Also, when Colin Sumner (1990), in his inquiry into social censures, finds that "it is inevitable that the class bloc which dominates the economy, owns the means of mass communication and controls the reins of political power, will have the greatest capacity to assert its censures in the legal and moral discourses of the day" (p. 27), he is likewise neglecting the possibility of other and reverse contentions.

The reproach that flows from femininity toward masculinity, or from religious fundamentalism toward more secular ideologies, can be understood as displays of moral power. Three other struggles discussed are instances of the social power familiar to Marxists: dominant over dominated classes, us versus the Dark Other, and adults against children. (Regarding the matter of the rivalry between the conscious and the subconscious mind, it may not be possible to determine which truly has the upper hand.) Whether the chastising energy flows from the stronger toward the weaker or from the weaker toward the stronger, however, has nothing to do with the actualities of television violence.

Whatever its immediate source, the energy that breathes life into the whipping boy, television violence, has its ultimate origins in fear—fear of the social disorder that, in the extreme, could overturn the human enterprise. Charles Acland (1995) comments, "A society is always concerned with normalization, with the organization of its order, to assure the continuation of its structures and distribution of power" (p. 11). Although social order is a perpetual preoccupation, at this point in history it would seem to be an obsessive one; witness the outsized emphasis on the containment of crime at a time when crime is on the decline and the reckless hysteria of the War on Drugs. Graham Murdock (1997) refers to the "fear about the precarious balance between anarchy and order in the modern age" (p. 70). Exactly why this fearful fixation on social order should be occurring now is open to question; perhaps it is a tardy response to the libertine excesses of the counterculture movement in the 1960s (Wagner, 1997, Chapter 5), or perhaps millennialism runs deeper than one might think. Its existence, however, should not be doubted. The need to strengthen social controls has a correlate in Americans' increasing imposition of self-controls: Per capita alcohol consumption and cigarette smoking are on the decline and health club memberships are on the rise (U.S. Bureau of the Census, 1996).

Driven by strong but unfocused apprehensions regarding social order, the American people scan the cultural landscape for fitting targets and settle quickly on television and its content. The medium is new enough that it is not embraced without reservations, and it has not yet accumulated the social equity that would allow it to be shielded by nostalgia. In addition to its relative novelty, it is enormous, filling up the day's nooks and crannies (television viewing is the third-ranked activity in terms of time spent doing it, trailing only work and sleep [Robinson, 1981]), and can be menacing on this count. Because everyone has access to television, its use cannot be regulated, and thus for those who want to control it, the medium is believed to be out of control and threatening (Starker, 1989, p. 176). Moreover, television brings to every place and every person imaged communication, whose power in comparison to linear text is believed to be sufficient to destroy traditions of close logic and reflective thought (Postman, 1985). The rise of television, observes Richard Sparks (1995), "has been taken to signify the drift of history beyond willed control or direction. The censure of television bears witness to the fear of the future" (p. 59).

The vague fears of disorder and evolving chaos that center first on television in general are then concentrated on television violence as the most plausible agent of destruction. General apprehension about the course of history is in several senses the inverse of video violence—the passivity of fear versus the frenzy of aggression, the amorphous versus the detailed, and the actual versus the symbolic—and the two find each other as if magnetized, whereupon the flaying of the whipping boy ensues.

In the final analysis, the television violence controversy is not about television violence: It is about fear and the expression of fear.

4

Viewing Violent Programs

From a certain perspective, there are no violent programs on television. There are only violent incidents within shows that proceed to the triumph of resolution and righteousness. Invariably, violence is contained, rectified, detonated, whereupon a moral commandment rises from the drama's shards. Violence is only a part of the schema that virtually always produces a contrasting last word, a proclamation of enduring American verities—of allegiance, justice, efficiency.

A case in point is a representative program from the 1996-1997 season of Fox's *New York Undercover*. Episodes in this series commonly begin with a wordless, rapidly paced scenario of brutal criminality, one with many ellipses to be filled in later. Here, ski-masked thieves in New York City's diamond district trap a departing diamond merchant's car between their vans and then viciously kill (shattered glass, automatic guns and loud retorts, corpses) the merchant, his son, and his driver, and steal the diamonds. When the cops arrive, one takes a statement from an aggrieved family friend of the merchant's, Rebecca Skolnik.

A stool pigeon tells two of the undercover squad members that a certain thief is buying any gambling debt markers owed by people working in the diamond district. The squad has one of its own, J. C. Williams, placed as a security guard at the diamond exchange and has the stoolie sell the undercover officer's faked marker to the thief, Luther. In an extended and gruesome scene, Luther and his two fellow thugs break J. C.'s little finger in a mail box cover, believing they are obtaining his compliance. J. C. arranges for another heist, but the gang notices the police presence and bolts.

Now the undercover J. C. is in trouble. The thieves are suspicious of him and hold him a virtual captive. Back at the station house, his wife bitterly complains to his lieutenant about J. C.'s neglect of herself and their son. J. C.'s devotion to duty comes at high personal cost.

The thieves embark on another robbery, and J. C. is forced to participate in order to maintain his cover. One of the thieves is oddly missing when the other men, dressed in police uniforms, burst into the tasteful residence of the Skolnik family. They dispatch Mr. Skolnik to remove gems from his safe in the diamond district while holding his wife and daughter Rebecca as hostages. It becomes clear to viewers that the police have staked out the house. Luther, the lead thief, says that this robbery is just a diversion, and that he plans to join his missing partner for an armored car heist at the Federal Reserve. As he prepares to escape alone through the basement, he tells his confederate to kill the wife and daughter once Skolnik returns with the jewels. "Oh, and whack him first," Luther says in a stage whisper, with reference to J. C. "He's a cop."

Skolnik returns home with the jewels and purposely spills them on the carpet. As the thief is groveling for the diamonds, in rush the undercover squad, guns drawn, nabbing the one thief and freeing J. C. Rebecca thanks J. C. tenderly.

The scene shifts to the street in front of the Federal Reserve, where the robbery of the armored car is being thwarted. Squad cars scream up, and a fusillade of gunfire erupts. Inside the armed car, a robber apparently is holding a guard hostage. The robber drags the hostage up the street. "It's a set-up," yells J. C., who has recognized that Luther is the "hostage." Luther breaks and runs, shooting at J. C. as J. C. shoots at him. Bang, bang, bang, over and over. Luther heads down a subway entrance. When J. C. catches up, Luther is slumped against the closed subway grate; the entrance had been closed off. "You're under arrest," J. C. says as he pulls the cowering criminal to his feet.

In the final scene, J. C. and his partner are relaxing in a nightclub, joshing as they listen to the performance of singer Phil Collins.

This program ably satisfies the well-established pattern for violence-laden dramas. Ritualistic as a church service, the plot moves—both predictably and excitingly—from one predetermined station to the next. As John Fraser (1974) notes in *Violence in the Arts,* "Works involving violence, like other kinds, tend to accumulate their conventions and to fall in certain patterns. And if one is out for relaxation, one can hardly have too many conventional elements" (p. 69). Protagonists and antagonists are identified early on through glimpses at their moral or immoral essences (Zillmann & Bryant, 1994, p. 448); here, the good guys are characterized by their interpersonal warmth, whereas the bad guys brutally kill and torture. The scriptwriters have established a suspenseful conflict between the undercover squad and the trio of criminals—a conflict dramatized and punctuated by spasms of viciousness. This violence is uncommon in the real world of the viewer and so has salience, but by the same token it is thoroughly conventional in the fantasy world of television and thus can be easily and familiarly accepted. Transgressions of the antagonists, transgressions that put the protagonists at risk, instigate the violence. For viewers to become deeply involved and to experience a sensation of suspense, there must be an apprehension that the heroes are subject to credible threats (Zillmann, 1980); J. C. is in greater peril and the rest of the squad in lesser. It then becomes dramatically justified for the protagonists to confront violence with sufficient retaliatory aggression on their own part to overcome the dangers posed; the cops burst into the Skolnik household with guns drawn, and then win the vicious shoot-out at the Federal Reserve. John Cawelti (1975) refers to this as "morally necessary violence" (p. 529). Resolution is depicted in the final scene at the nightclub, where it is clear that everything has been set back to rights. Light banter contains allusions to revalidated moral precepts—of duty, friendship, and justice. Unlike life, there is no troubling aftermath, no second thoughts, and no night sweats.

The violent incidents in television dramas draw far away from aggressive acts in real life; they are as stylized as the swordplay in Japanese Noh theater. Although most crimes in the United States are crimes against property (burglary, larceny, and auto theft), television specializes in crimes against people, most particularly in the rarest crime of all—murder. Prime-time television characters are 1,000 times more likely than real citizens to be murdered (Lichter, Lichter, & Rothman, 1994, p. 275). Whereas actual killers tend to be young, poor, black males, the television version is an older, well-off, white male (p. 291). Murderers and victims typically know each other in the real world but do not in the world of television fantasy: In the episode just reviewed, the jewel thieves did not know the diamond merchants they killed. Arguments lead to murder in everyday life, but on television the motive is avarice: "Murder on TV is usually a way to acquire someone else's money, possessions, or status" (p. 279). The television murder is a highly sanitary affair, with little blood or gore in evidence (*National Television Violence Study,* 1997, p. 109). If it is any consolation, violence on television is twice as likely to be committed by the bad guys as it is by the good guys (National Television Violence Survey, 1997, p. 97). Also, most of the bad guys will get their just desserts by the end of the show (National Television Violence Survey, 1997, p. 118).

All this action occurs in a territory that even the very young know is framed off from the real world. This framed-off terrain is that of entertainment, not reality; its content is merely symbolic, not palpable. That is, television offers two-dimensional images on a screen, bound by a script, and not the immediacy of live, interacting, unpredictable human beings. In the conjured sphere of television shows, emotions have a priority that they cannot have in the real world of obligations. In this diversionary sphere exist few of the demands of everyday life—meals, sicknesses, and dry cleaning. The television space is very different from worldly space.

Televised violent fictions are sometimes considered to be modern myths (Cawelti, 1975). James Taylor (1977) writes,

No society can live without myths. Myths provide the substructure of our collective social experience. Television crime shows are a vehicle for the communication of the dominant mythic patterns of contemporary American society, and within this genre, the portrayal of violence is a key element of mythic modes of expression. (p. 162)

Although this is an intriguing proposition and grants to television violence a significance it deserves as a key cultural phenomenon, this is not a fruitful line of thought. There are of course similarities in that both myths and shows are stories, are peopled with heroic figures, and feature heightened action. The myths of primitive peoples, however, typically centered on a single hero, whereas action-adventure shows are more likely to revolve around a duo or team of leading characters. Myths functioned as explanatory tales, narratively depicting the social relations among community members and the relationship of communities to the cosmos. If myths were not quite sense-making, at least they were question-answering. We can imagine a correspondence between the concerns of the myth-holders and the configuration of the myth. What they admired was often presented admirably in the myth. So valued were myths that they were held onto tightly, shared repeatedly among the many, and passed down as rotely as memory allowed.

Contemporary television violence in all its formats is quite different from the myths of preliterate peoples. Its primary function is not to articulate human and supernatural relations. It addresses not the large questions but the minute if excruciating ones of viewers' personal vexations. It speaks not to the community but to the individual. Its primary concerns are not cultural but psychological. It is not treasured and repeated; it is discarded. People do not remember a particular show or do not remember it for long. The activity in the performance may not be what the viewer generally endorses but just the opposite of it. Therefore, the notion of violent television programs as myths, especially as explanatory and value-illustrating myths, is a misleading one. J. C.'s escapades were not mythical.

In other words, the emphasis in myths is the reverse of the emphasis in television shows featuring violence. In general terms, the presentation of a myth will illustrate social norms first and secondarily deal in emotional material. In television crime shows, the emotional material, the action and so forth, occupies the foreground, whereas the endorsed social norms are present but receded. When James Twitchell (1989) says about violent programs that "the very stories we criticize most vociferously are indeed some of the most important socializing rituals that this culture has developed" (p. 13), we have to be very careful in delineating what "socializing rituals" might legitimately mean. Myths are clearly socializing rituals, but violent shows are so only in limited and specialized ways. At the level of emotions, these shows can provide a symbolic venue for the display and containment of the anger that rises from the ever-replenishing wellspring of human animosity. These programs must be formulaic and ritualistic in outline so that the viewer knows in advance which emotions will be addressed and how they will be manipulated. The viewer can then enter into the service with the sure knowledge that certain regular feelings are going to be channeled and converted. These shows socialize to the extent that they help exhaust antisocial emotions. Secondarily, at the normative level the socializing rituals of violent dramas teach repeatedly that illicit aggression is ultimately unavailing. Just as churchmen have described hell to steer parishioners away from it, so do violent entertainments inform the unwary. Occasionally, the ritual can be upended (i.e., evil triumphs), making the viewer aware of the ritual's existence and utility, but this cannot happen too often without viewers defecting. Voluntarily taking in this symbolic, ritualized, violence-flecked material, the television viewer then interprets it according to deeply personal needs.

Viewing Violence

It is important to understand that television is not watched by audiences. The word "audience" does not apply to the television experience: Viewers are disparate, perhaps solitary in their attendance, and certainly solitary in their minds; there is no unanimity in response as there may be for a live rock concert audience. It is individuals, one by one, who consume television. To clump all these viewers into an audience—to massify them—is to take the liveliness of reception away and to unbalance and demean the relationship between the purveyors of television programs and the purposive individuals who exploit the content. In the television context, the word audience perpetuates a derogatory misunderstanding of the conditions of reception and should be set aside. Viewers view individually, and as they do so they are working for themselves.

Viewers do not find the violence on their favorite programs to be excessive or objectionable, no matter how many violent incidents the show might contain by actual count. (Conversely, when television violence is found offensive, the judgment usually emanates from a crossover viewer—someone who prefers other content, who is not watching because of voluntary selection but because he or she has stumbled on the content accidentally, or who is being compelled to be in the presence of the content due to the wishes of a companion.) The violence on less liked shows is less tolerable, whereas the violence on chosen programs is found inoffensive and even enjoyable (British Broadcasting Corporation, 1972, p. 136). From a random sample of 303 adults, Greenberg and Gordon (1972) learned that the more frequent viewers of a violent program will judge it to be less violent than will nonviewers (p. 253). Among adolescents, Hartnagel, Teevan, and McIntyre (1975) discovered that only a small percentage perceive violence on their favorite shows (p. 345). For children, mayhem in frequently watched cartoons is not identified as scary or violent

(Van der Voort, 1986, p. 223). This prevailing misidentification is telling about the role of video violence in the lives of its viewers. For the individual fan, violent content of choice is not toxic but rather meshes with the viewer's mind in such a way that its toxicity vaporizes. There is no discrepancy, no tension, and no disagreeableness between the viewer and the viewed. The content has been selected because somehow it serves that viewer positively and well.

The viewer of television violence is more likely to be male than female (Greenberg & Gordon, 1972, p. 253; Murray, Cole, & Fedler, 1970, p. 255; Van der Voort, 1986, p. 334) and more likely to be younger than older (Rosenstiel, 1993); therefore, there are gender and generational aspects to the act of viewing violence—aspects that if found unsympathetic can interfere with one's comprehension of the activity. Viewing is typically done voluntarily, in anticipation of the pleasures it is designed to bring. The viewer usually watches the chosen content leisurely, in a relaxed frame of mind; there is no critical alertness that can hinder a blending of the material of the performance and the material of the viewer's mind. As they blend together, pleasure can occur either through the excitation of feelings that are scant but desired (e.g., being admired) or the lessening of feelings that are abundant but unwanted (e.g., hostility) (Fowles, 1996, pp. 105-106). Dolf Zillmann (1991) understands this bidirectional flow as facilitating "excitatory homeostasis" (p. 110). Thus, for the viewer, the entire activity operates first and foremost on the level of emotions in the effort to manage emotions by supplementing or diminishing feelings (Zillmann, 1988). The viewer also knows that toward the conclusion the show will attempt to move the corrected feelings in the direction of endorsed social norms (from violence to nonviolence, for instance). There are at least three distinct emotional services that violence viewing can accomplish; they correspond to the beginning, middle, and end of the dramatic structure.

Some viewers will choose aggressive content because they enter the viewing experience in a state of tedium and are searching for stimulating material. In an experimental demonstration of this, Bryant and Zillmann (1984) purposefully bored subjects by requiring them to do monotonous tasks for 1 hour such as threading washers on a shoelace. Each subject was then led to a viewing room in which he or she could choose from six programs—three action-packed and three not. Bored subjects were 10 times more likely to choose exciting programming than unexciting and on average experienced a sharp rise in their heart rates (p. 13). In an increasingly sedentary world, John Fraser (1974) remarks that the draw of symbolic violent action can be considerable: "In a culture as starved of physicality as ours, the enduring appeal of a good many violent works is not just that they are violent but that they reimmerse us vicariously in physical action" (p. 63). A listless viewer should find right from the start of the program enough arousing, conflictional material to lift him or her out of his or her doldrums. (Presumably, this is the sensation that viewers of reality-based programs such as *Cops* or demi-reality shows such as *America's Most Wanted* are pursuing.)

Another viewer of the same drama may be seeking an opposite treatment, and instead of an increase in excitement he or she could be searching for a diminishment in emotions. Some viewers (but certainly not all [Copeland & Slater, 1985; Gunter, 1980]) would want to experience cathartic relief instead of arousal. For this to occur, the content must be understood as fantasy; anything that draws too close to reality is not going to be experienced as soothing (Thomas & Tell, 1974). At lulling people, television has few peers. When researchers ask viewers why they watch the medium, the main response is invariably for rest and relaxation (Kubey & Csikszentmihalyi, 1990, p. 81; Winick, 1988, p. 224). Distressed viewers may select shows containing violent scenes because they have learned that, by empathizing with the protagonists as the characters exercise sanctioned aggression against evildoers, viewers can aggress vicariously, thereby discharging harbored and unwanted psychic energy. They also have the options of identifying with the victims or with the antagonists, and they may do so at moments to experience those states of mind; for most viewers most of the time, however, it is the good guys and their strenuous actions that offer the widest path to emotional redress (Zillmann, 1980, p. 143).

There are two affective states that might lead a viewer to seek out the possibly cathartic services of television violence. First, those with openly hostile feelings may turn to this symbolic arena to harmlessly vent their antagonisms. In one confirming experiment, Fenigstein (1979) induced aggressive sentiments in college-age male subjects (either through guided fantasies or through the encouraged administration of noxious noises) and then gave subjects the chance to select film clips succinctly labeled (i.e., "rioting at a rock concert" and "a student taking a test"). Students with elevated aggression, in contrast to the control group students, were much more likely to select violent clips. Aggressive feelings are also predictive of violence viewing for younger children, according to Atkin, Greenberg, Korzenny, and McDermott (1979). Measures from 227 fourth-, sixth-, and eighth-grade students were obtained for their violence viewing and their aggressive behavior and then obtained again 1 year later. The authors concluded that aggressive predispositions dictated subsequent choices of violent programs.

Although demonstrations of lowered hostility levels following exposure to televised violence are uncommon in the literature, they are not entirely lacking. Recall that Messner (1986) found lower rates of violent crime in the metropolitan areas in which violence viewing was the highest. Feshbach and Singer (1971) placed residents in four homes for wayward boys on either a television diet high in violent content or on a television diet low in such material. Their antisocial behavior was noted by trained observers before and after a 6-week test; the violence-exposed boys were less malicious and comparatively calmer than their peers. In another, smaller field experiment (Friedrich & Stein, 1973), highly aggressive preschoolers' levels of aggressiveness decreased after viewing violent cartoons such as *Batman* and *Superman* (p. 38). Linz,

Donnerstein, and Adams (1989) showed a 2-hour violent videotape to one group of subjects and an exciting but nonviolent videotape to a second group. When subsequently a brief clip of interpersonal violence was projected, the violence-exposed subjects were less readily aroused. Although the authors do not tender this interpretation, it is possible that for the experimental group a cathartic response had occurred, dampening reactions. Similarly, Rabinovitch, McLean, Markham, and Talbott (1972) demonstrated that sixth graders shown a violent program were the least prone to perceive subsequent violent scenes (p. 242). The lowering of aggressiveness in viewers is greater when the violent content proceeds to a happy resolution (Zillmann, Johnson, & Hanrahan, 1973). James Twitchell (1989) wisely indicates that the use of violent entertainment "is not finally escape, but a return, a return to our 'natural' selves, a safe return to levels of contained aggression" (p. 47).

It is unlikely, however, that the hostile viewer is ever completely purged of his or her animosities through the sedentary act of viewing dramatized violence. Violence viewing is only fully cathartic in intent, not in practice. What it does offer is a small, convenient, harmless, and symbolic venue for the discharge of some surplus hostility—a venue that does not entail real people or the repercussions of real life. Just as the reader of romance novels may not be fully satiated at the end, so to the viewer of violent fantasies cannot expel all his or her hostility.

It is not just angry viewers who can receive cathartic benefits from a selection of violent content, however. Evidence exists that a second group of individuals, the merely stressed, will also seek out this sort of programming. If an ingredient in everyday stress is repressed anger, then this makes sense in an obvious way because the stressed person, like the hostile person, would be seeking innocent ways to release pent-up feelings. In research by Anderson, Collins, Schmitt, and Jacobvitz (1996), 322 sets of parents completed viewing diaries and inventories of stressful events suffered within the preceding year. For fathers, it was determined that the more stress to which they had been exposed, the higher were the levels of violence viewing (whereas stressed mothers tended to watch more game and variety shows) (pp. 252-253).

Although the bored can use violent programs from the opening credits onwards to elevate feelings, and the hostile or distressed use scenes of protagonists' retaliation to alleviate feelings, the fearful must wait to the denouement for their gratification. Boyanowsky (1977) determined that people will turn to violent fantasy to placate their fears; following a campus murder, students flocked to a horror film at a neighborhood theater and ignored the competing offering (a light romance). Moreover, some people who are not initially fearful, particularly adolescents, attend to gory dramas to invoke the sensation of fear artificially in anticipation of adventurously carrying that feeling through to its resolution and rehearsing their own mastery of fear (Johnston, 1995, p. 543). Whatever the source of the fear, it is tugged along by a suspenseful plot line—one that usually arranges to place the protagonists in peril more than once (Zillmann, 1980, p. 140). For the truly apprehensive, this suspense may not be pleasurable, but if they continue to view they do so because they look forward to justice being done—and to a satisfying extent—at the end (Zillmann & Wakshlag, 1985, p. 154). An experiment by Wakshlag, Vial, and Tamborini (1983) suggests that people fearful about actual crime will favor dramas that feature the eventual restoration of justice; because justice is challenged by violent criminal behavior, the drama is likely to contain violent depictions, but these scenes are not the reasons why the fearful watch. In this study, apprehensions were raised by showing subjects a documentary about crime; the control group viewed a *National Geographic* documentary about Nepal. Both experimental and control subjects were then asked to select movies for additional viewing from a list with plot descriptions; the movie descriptions had been previously graded with reference to justice restoration and victimization themes. The authors noted, "Subjects in the experimental condition—who were exposed to the crime documentary—selected films with lower victimization ratings and higher justice ratings than subjects in the control condition" (pp. 236-237). To see justice prevail, however, the apprehensive viewer must hang on to the drama's close.

Lethargy, anger, stress, anxiety, and their variants are emotions that television violence works on for those who freely choose it. Some viewers need one feeling addressed, some need another, and some need all in sequence or all at once. Dolf Zillmann and Jennings Bryant (1994) observe,

> The fact remains that much entertainment is consumed to alter moods, affects, and emotions in the specified fashion; moreover, the fact remains that the desired effects come about with considerable regularity. De facto, then, the consumption of much entertainment has beneficial consequences. It is adaptive, recreational, restorative, and in this sense, therapeutic. (p. 457)

The main effects of viewing television violence are not outward manifestations, the supposed behaviors that give rise to much public hand-wringing, but rather are interior and emotional and therefore are nearly traceless. We can scarcely locate these effects because they are highly private, inside the minds of the individuals who have freely elected to watch this framed-off material for the emotional compensation it brings them.

Televised Sports

It may be the dissimilarities between action-adventure shows and televised sporting events (I concentrate on the most-watched American varieties—football, basketball, and baseball) that are more apparent at first. The game is broadcast live, after all, and is unlike other television shows that are the manufactured result of a lengthy production process at a Hollywood studio. Viewers certainly believe, and have to believe, that the contest has not been previously scripted.

The conclusion of the televised drama is known before it begins because the good guys are sure to be victorious, but the outcome of the athletic event is not guaranteed. It is the high level of uncertainty that attracts gamblers to games; no one is going to wager on how *NYPD Blue* will end. The guileless sports broadcast may be thought of as "real," like news. In fact, at some networks news and sports comprise one division and entertainment another.

On closer examination, however, both crime dramas and sports contests share much in common, and in description extensively overlap each other. The two orders of content center on struggles and ideally are wracked with tensions. The framed-off territories of both are highly conventionalized in differing but corresponding ways. Just as the action show is going to last an hour, the game is usually going to last four quarters or nine innings. Inside its boundaries of time and space, what happens is highly prescribed; the rulebooks are thick and thorough. No football team is going to line up perpendicular to the goal line or send in female players with field hockey equipment; no umpire is going to trip a base runner. Rules, supplemented by conventions of fair play, largely define the performance. The experienced viewer knows what to expect almost all the time because the space for something exceptional is a narrow one. Within that corridor of possibility, however, winning or losing will occur. Just as there are winners and losers in the crime drama so too there are in the athletic event. In both cases, participants strive toward their goals mightily, even violently. Violence lends a sought-after tonality to the two.

In analyses of sporting events, the word "violence" is often reserved for aggressive actions that are illegal and reproachable, but it is clear that much of what occurs within the rules is also violent by everyday standards. This is indisputable for football, in which players are maimed on a regular basis, sometimes to a paralyzing, life-threatening extent. In basketball, bodies are checked fiercely, topple and skid across the hardwood floor, and crash into the stands. Although baseball is not considered to be a contact sport, in addition to occasional bench-clearing rhubarbs, batters can be painfully struck by pitched balls, and base runners can spike and rip defensive players without penalty. The violence that lies near or on the surface of sporting events underscores the contesting, the drama marching on to a conclusion.

It has been experimentally demonstrated that, just as intuition suggests, "tense and hostile play not only proved to facilitate enjoyment, but made the entire contest more exciting, more involving, and more interesting to the audience" (Zillmann, Sapolsky, & Bryant, 1979, p. 321). To enhance the contest for the pleasure of television viewers, all three major sports have adjusted their rules to emphasize offensive action (Rader, 1984). The National Basketball Association instituted a 24-second clock, compelling quicker shots; baseball's American League had "designated hitters" bat for unproductive pitchers; and the National Football League opened up the passing game with rules that protected quarterbacks and allowed receivers, once downfield, to proceed unmolested.

The televised game depicts competition and struggle at its most naked, in purely physical, irrefutably explicit terms. No motives are concealed, no words are required, because all is spelled out clearly in the actions of the athletes (commentary does increase gratification, however; Comisky, Bryant, & Zillmann, 1977). In the end, there will be a winner and a loser—a definitive resolution of the competition. The struggle and the conclusion—in more pristine forms than the real world can deliver—transpire under the aegis of rules that ensure the integrity of the performance and the succession of comparable performances over time.

The viewer of a televised sporting event conceivably receives many of the same emotional rewards that are received by the viewer of a crime drama. The comparative advantage of a sports broadcast is that the content has immediacy and impact because it is telecast live. Like the understimulated viewer of an action-adventure show, the bored fan is likely to find excitement in the opening minutes of the event. In fact, most experimental evidence suggests that arousal is the most likely outcome of sports spectating (Russell, 1983). Nevertheless, angry or stressed viewers of the very same game, entering into it empathetically, may experience some degree of relief. Although such a cathartic result has not been demonstrated in any of the sports studies designed to detect it, Allen Guttmann (1986) pointed out that all these studies conducted their posttests immediately after the contest (p. 156): "The proper time to measure levels of hostility and aggression is not immediately before and after the game itself, but before and after the lengthier period of time which frames the entire sports experience" (p. 157). For the modern individual, whose hostile feelings must largely be restrained in the course of everyday life, the game offers an opportunity for "an enjoyable and controlled decontrolling of emotions" (Elias & Dunning, 1986, p. 44). Studies do indicate that the most aggressive spectators will experience the greatest pleasure from a violent sporting event, whereas the least aggressive can become uneasy (Bryant, 1989, p. 280). Within the framed-off space of the televised game, the spectator can do things he or she is not allowed to do normally—shout, rant, stomp, applaud, challenge, punch the air, and otherwise aggress by proxy—and do so without jeopardy.

Of course, the game will be most emotionally satisfying if the fan's favored team wins (Wenner & Gantz, 1989, p. 266). An outcome always at risk, this is the signal disadvantage of viewing sports: A loss may produce dismay and churlishness. In one study of fans' responses (Hirt, Zillmann, Erickson, & Kennedy, 1992), boosters were required to watch videotapes of their favorite team either winning or losing. Those who saw a losing effort had lower estimates of both their own and the team's future accomplishments and had diminished measures of mood and self-esteem. Even a loss, however, can have emotional utility in that it may steel a person to meet the adversities and deprivations that life can bring.

Television viewing cannot offer emotional depth comparable to that experienced when seeing the event in person, which would explain why people go to the trouble and expense to attend a game that is available to them free on their sets at home. The sensory excitement in the stadium can elicit reactions grander than are heard in most living rooms. Television, however, does strive to approximate the live experience, and in some few ways manages to surpass it. The ability to replay scenes means that thundering action will be seen repeatedly with no chance that the spectator will miss it. Moreover, close-ups of the athlete's faces capture the sensations of the victorious and the vanquished to an extent impossible to witness from most ballpark seats. Television also has play-by-play commentary that can clarify and enhance the observed action on the playing field.

Some viewers may not be emotionally committed to one team or the other and may draw subtler pleasures from the confrontation. For them, enduring values may have been illustrated by the players themselves, who have been taken to exhibit loyalty, teamwork, discipline, and obedience. In the aftermath, the endurance of the rules of the game may offer some satisfaction. All spectators incidentally learn and relearn principles of fairness and justice. According to Jennings Bryant's (1989) research, "Unsanctioned sports violence tends to result in impaired enjoyment, even if a disliked opponent is defeated via such unfair aggressive tactics" (p. 288). Postgame discussions, by which spectators may try to re-create in miniature the camaraderie witnessed among the athletes, often revolve around infractions, either against written rules or unwritten etiquette, and by doing so reinforce the norms of the sport. Crabb and Goldstein (1991) note, "In sports talk, we acquire, maintain, and perpetuate a belief system about aggression, justice, and fair play" (p. 368). In a never-ending morality tale, violence has been made to speak and then is silenced.

Music Videos

One person who has disapproved of the rowdy content of the music videos shown on MTV since 1981 and also on VH-1 and BET is Tipper Gore, the wife of Vice President Al Gore and mother of four children. In 1985, she cofounded the Parents Music Resource Center (PMRC), an advocacy group that strongly pressured the recording industry to tidy up its productions. The same year, at a Senate hearing she proposed that advisories be issued for music products (Gore, 1985). In another chapter in the endless generational contest, the parental was working—and working hard—to contain the juvenile and juvenile pleasures. Criticized by entertainment figures who viewed her proposal as tantamount to censorship, Mrs. Gore partially recanted her position in 1987 (Molotsky, 1987). Following her husband's election in 1992, she quietly resigned from the PMRC early in 1993, saying the organization had accomplished its goals (Gowen, 1993).

The broadcast minutes given to music videos on MTV have been reduced in recent years perhaps due to their controversial content and perhaps due to weakness in the ratings as the baby boomers' children age out of adolescence.

Also, there is evidence that the amount of violence within this reduced airtime is also on the decline. In a study of music videos broadcast in 1983, Caplan (1985) estimated there were 10.18 violent acts per hour, about twice the number shown in regular prime-time broadcasting. Similarly, Kalis and Neuendorf (1989) found that during the 1985 season 61% of videos contained at least one aggressive act; for concept videos (i.e., those that were not filmed at live performances), this figure was 75% (p. 151). Recent studies, however, found lower counts. According to the *National Television Violence Study* (1997), only 31% of music videos contain violence (p. 150). Victor Strasburger (1997) reports this number to be 22% (p. 441). A constant during this decline is the fact that rap music videos continue to contain the largest number of violent depictions (Strasburger, 1997, p. 442). Thus, the antipathy toward violent music videos is not only generational in nature but also can be magnified by racial attitudes.

Whatever the declines, and for whatever reasons, violent music videos remain the signature entertainment genre of adolescent viewers and must be discussed on this basis. The video content viewers see is not only rife with violence but also heavily gendered, and in arguably sexist ways. Males predominate; approximately 8 of 10 lead singers are males (Brown & Campbell, 1986, p. 98; Sherman & Dominick, 1986, p. 84). Overall, males outnumber females three to one (Seidman, 1992, p. 212). These male figures flagrantly act out caricatures of masculinity—they strut, flex, preen, and command. The female performers likewise epitomize a glossy version of femininity—slender perfected "boy toys," they flirt, flounce, discard clothes, and become prone. For both genders, chests are everywhere.

The disproportionate demographics of music videos and the patina of violence can easily lead to the thought that male dominance will take the form of the suppression of females, and that males will be the aggressors and females the victims. Although many commentators intuit this is the case and insist on reform, this conclusion cannot be confirmed in research data. Caplan (1985) reports, "No significant difference was found between sex and protagonist/victim status in individuals involved in violence" (p. 146). That is, once a female appears, she is as likely as a male to be an aggressor. Brown and Campbell (1986) also found no gender imbalances between those who were the aggressors and those who were the victims. In Sherman and Dominicks's (1986) study, males were the aggressors in 73.3% of the incidents and the victims in 76.8%: females were the aggressors in 26.7% of the incidents and the victims in 23.2% (p. 87). Females were victims to the same extent that they were aggressors, and males were aggressors to the same extent that they were victims. Caplan (1985) adds, "One repeated element in music videos is a man attacking a woman and in the next scene the woman attacking a man" (p. 146). Those who feel women are being excessively victimized in music videos must routinely view only the first scene of each pair.

What do adolescent viewers derive from this rambunctious musical entertainment? It must be underscored is that the content is music, an expressive mode that slips in under the discursive and rational layers of the mind to establish contact with elemental feelings and tempos. It is the emotions of teenagers that are being serviced by the music and also by the fantastical visual content. The fan of music videos will see and hear content that gives form to that person's inner tensions and dilemmas. At a stage in life in which people are reframing themselves as attractive members of their gender, learning how to negotiate with the other gender, and becoming sexually active, the sexuality of music videos directly addresses their primary emotional, if not to say hormonal, concerns. In the sphere of music videos, the young adult finds his or her own personal emotional turmoils articulated and worked on, if not worked out. Moreover, adolescence is the stage of life in which the transition from child to adult is in its most difficult phase—when apprehension about the upcoming condition is woven into resentments about the strictures and reproofs being applied by parents and schools in the attempt to move the adolescent successfully through this passage. It is a period of extreme personal turbulence, resentment, and rebelliousness. Because he or she has much hostility to deal with, the adolescent may find in music videos a symbolic venue in which some of that emotion may be identified and released. After viewing, the music video fan is likely to report exuberantly on such personal sensations as "open," "free," and "out-of-control" (Sherman & Dominick, 1986, p. 82). The content has provided delicious if momentary release from the noxious impositions of the maturation process.

Exploding Heads

Although the amount of violence in adult programming is substantial, the amount in children's cartoons (their favorite television genre) is truly remarkable. According to calculations by George Gerbner's team (Gerbner, Morgan, & Signorielli, 1995), throughout the years there have been an average of 5.3 acts of violence in each prime-time hour, whereas for children's Saturday morning programming the average number has been 23.0 acts, more than a fourfold difference. Nearly all this child-directed violence (97%) is in animated form (National Television Violence Study, 1997, p. 114). The younger viewer is awash in sequenced drawings of exploding heads, flattened bodies, and jettisoned limbs.

Other sorts of televised violence, such as the noncartooned action and virulent language on adult programs, are assiduously shunned by young children. An arresting study of preschoolers' facial expressions while viewing different varieties of televised violence was conducted by Lagerspetz, Wahlroos, and Wendelin (1978). Judges viewed and coded viewers' reactions recorded on silent videotapes, but the judges could not see the matching televised scenes that stimulated the children. When researchers paired the tapes, it was determined that verbal violence among filmed adults led children to withdraw from viewing and to find other activities within the screening room. Similarly, responses to filmed physical violence registered as fear, worry, tenseness, and anger on the young faces (p. 220). Cartooned violence, however, produced expressions of pure joy (p. 220).

Once within the joyful precincts of the cartoon world, children elect not to judge the antics they see as noticeably violent (Lyle & Hoffman, 1972; Snow, 1974; Tulloch, 1995; Van der Yoort, 1986, p. 223). Like adults, youngsters find the mayhem on their best-liked programs to be congenial. It is the unbelievability of violent cartoons that renders them delectable to children. Not only do the impossible mishaps and lightning resurrections make the shows unbelievable but also so does the very art form that delivers this material to the child (Winick & Winick, 1979, pp. 176-177). Unlike photographed fictive action, which for children can carry the stigma of being overly realistic portrayals, cartooning reduces everything to unreal and highly stylized outlines and by doing so takes the sting out of what would be frightening, converting it into the amusing. In addition, cartooning, by reducing the visual scene to a few essential elements, allows even very young viewers to focus on the characters and their contretemps and not be diverted by irrelevant cues.

The cartoon falls into the child's developing sense of fantasy as opposed to reality. The young viewer, entering into these fanciful fictions, can playfully violate the physics of the natural world and the logic and conventions of the social world (Winick & Winick, 1979, p. 176). The rift between the cartoon world and the real world helps reflexively to define the dimensions of reality: "Far from the fantastic nature of cartoons causing confusion between fantasy and reality, the largeness of the gap is helpful to young children in building up precisely that capacity to discriminate" (Hodge & Tripp, 1986, p. 9). With the help of cartoons, this distinction slowly forms in the mind of the child between the ages of 3 and 8 (Hawkins, 1977). Apparently, the sorting out of separate spheres begins with the division between commercials and noncommercial minutes; preschoolers are able to accomplish this (Levin, Petros, & Petralla, 1982). According to Jaglom and Gardner (1981), "between the ages of 3 and 4, children recognize the fact that the television world is in fact separate from their world" (p. 45). Separate in what way? It is not until the age of 7 (Nikken & Peeters, 1988, p. 450) or 8 (Gunter & McAteer, 1990, p. 43) that the categories of fantasy and reality are well established. The sets of rules that pertain to these two domains—designating which one is potentially perilous and which one is not—are by then mastered in no small part. By the time the child reaches 10 years, his or her discrimination between fiction and fact will duplicate that of adults' (Fitch, Huston, & Wright, 1993).

Children, voluntary participants in the television experience (as they are not in the experience of the real world), derive great pleasure from their hours with their chosen violent cartoons, as any parent knows. Similar to the joyous faces found by Lagerspetz et al.'s study (1978), in Patricia Palmer's (1986) study of children's responses to television, 8- and 9-year-olds were asked to draw pictures of themselves viewing; they consistently depicted themselves wearing broad smiles (p. 33). Just as for their elders, this sensation of pleasure can be understood as the correction of feelings that are either too slight or too overwhelming; pleasurable relief occurs as mental redress and balance are accomplished through the use of the cartooned fantasy. In this process, meanings offered on the screen are constantly being interpreted and negotiated by the child in the interest of bringing about corrected moods (Hodge & Tripp, 1986, p. 10). That young children are fully capable of using television to improve moods has been empirically illustrated: Four- and 5-year-old boys who had been treated callously by an experimenter watched *Mr. Rogers' Neighborhood* more than twice as long as boys in another group who had been treated warmly (Masters, Ford, & Arend, 1983).

Some child viewers may use cartons to release hostile feelings they have been keeping suppressed. Grant Noble (1975) reported the following from his research on actual viewing practices: "When the child viewer feels aggressive and he watches stylistically televised aggression he acts out his aggressive impulses by participating in the 'drama' " (p. 125). People may question that very young children would naturally feel aggressive because they are, for the most part, in protected if not nurturant settings; the view that violent cartoons are teaching rather than relieving hostility may reemerge. Jerome Lopiparo (1977) provides a sympathetic explanation of why children feel angry and why they need opportunities for symbolic redress:

> Probably the most important reason aggression must be part of a child's life is that it helps him cope with his feelings of powerlessness. Children do not feel powerful! They do not feel that they can effect change either in their own lives or in the lives of others. If they want to do something, they must ask an adult; if they want to have something changed, they have to hope adults feel the same way, for that is the only way it is going to happen. It is for this reason that children are drawn to TV violence. Many of the frustrations they feel can be effectively worked out via the TV screen. It is safe, the person you are attacking cannot retaliate, you can be a hero or a villain with just a flip of the dial, and most important, you can experience that elusive feeling of *power.* (p. 346)

To the attribute of powerlessness can be added other conditions that may precipitate a need for symbolic retribution. A child may feel invaded and displaced by younger, more needful siblings; older siblings will certainly try to rule the child; and parents, teachers, and caregivers will be reproving the child at every misstep. All this bears down on the young viewer and causes him or her to seek out the balm found in violent cartoon viewing. It can be difficult for some adults to acknowledge how arduous the socializing process is for the child and how much the vicarious aggression of cartoons is needed as relief. Charles Ashbach

(1994) believes that the chief plot structure that brings about this vicarious relief is that of the underdog (the disguised child) triumphing over the top dog (the adult antagonist) (p. 120). Thus, Bugs Bunny outsmarts Elmer Fudd, the Road-runner outlasts Wile E. Coyote, and Bart Simpson, the Teenage Mutant Ninja Turtles, and Beavis and Butt-head live to fight another day.

After viewing, the symbolic aggression may instigate rough-and-tumble play among viewers, although the extent of this can be exaggerated. Hap-kiewicz (1979) reported on two experiments in which aggressive cartoons pro-duced no more interpersonal squabbling than that which followed a neutral film shown to a control group (p. 32). Perhaps releasing this kinetic energy, when it does occur after a show, is "not only normal, but, in many respects, quite beneficial" (Lopiparo, 1977, p. 346). Any transfer from violent cartoons to real-life activities decreases rapidly with age (Noble, 1975, p. 126). In any case, if one were to test for a cathartic effect (or the lack of it) from viewing car-toon violence, it should not be done until any roughhousing had subsided; one control group shown nothing and another shown tame programming should be tested after an identical interval. Such a study is not found in the literature.

Alternatively, other viewers of violent cartoons are seeking to discharge tensions through laughter. For them, the humor will have primacy above the stylized violence. According to Palmer (1986), nearly every child interviewed said he or she liked cartoons because they were "funny" (p. 33). Girls found their fun in comic turns and contorted faces, whereas boys defined fun as ag-gressive deeds and distorted bodies (p. 44).

A correct analysis of children's selection of cartoon violence must represent these younger viewers as highly purposive, picking their way through car-tooned offerings in search of the emotional benefits (minus repercussions) that these fictions can offer. Children are constitutionally active, not passive, view-ers (Gunter & McAteer, 1990, p. 34). They choose some shows rather than oth-ers, they interact assertively with the programs, and they discuss what they have seen with other children (Palmer, 1986, p. 138). Even when they sit qui-etly in front of the TV, their minds are working and reworking the content. Why is the "passivity" of book readers never proclaimed but this attribute is con-stantly imputed to the television experience? Only a determination to demean the medium can explain this wrong-headed insistence on the passive viewer.

As surprising as it may sound, children's long and therapeutic hours before the screen have had no deleterious effect on their reading abilities, as Susan Neumann's (1991) thorough investigation of the matter has ably disclosed. Kubey and Csikszentmihalyi (1990) reluctantly conceded from their research of children's viewing that "the amount of time spent watching TV was also positively correlated with the amount of time spent in the classroom and with better school performance as measured by grade point average and controlling for aptitude" (p. 114). There are no adverse consequences, and many personal benefits, from the child's use of violent content. Hodge and Tripp (1986) con-cluded their invaluable study of children's use of television by noting, "We believe that that anxiety [regarding antisocial effects of violence in children's television] has had more than enough time and money and expertise devoted to substantiating it, and the attempt to do so should now be regarded as discredited" (p. 211).

Situation Comedies

It is incontestable that action programs, sports broadcasts, music videos, and cartoon shows offer violent segments to viewers. That situation comedies also traffic in violence would at first seem doubtful. These frivolous half-hour shows appear innocent, harmless, and devoid of corporeal threats. They evoke pleasant laughter, not crasser sensations. Any malice would seem to be denied by the breadth of the sitcom audience because these shows, the most popular on the medium, regale the older and the younger, females and males, and do so without reservation. Because these programs invite no controversy, they have attracted little reflection from scholars and others. At least one effort, however, has been made to tally and categorize the types of jokes in prime-time television (Stocking, Sapolsky, & Zillmann, 1977). These authors determined that the most common type of jokes by far (approximately 69%) are clearly hostile in intent (p. 451). These jokes disparage, demean, or ridicule someone, putting the laughingstock in an inferior position and the joke-teller in a superior one.

Part of the work of a situation comedy, therefore, is to set up characters who are butts to be belittled repeatedly (but, according to the rules of the genre, not painfully to a noticeable extent). The eccentric, the vacuous, the arrogant, the heavily accented, the elderly, the corpulent—in fact, anyone different at all—can be a suitable target for the gibes of situation comedy. They must take the verbal abuse and, like the Bobo doll that rolls to the upright position, return for more. An interesting development of the 1990s is that an increasing amount of the comedic attack is directed not at others but at oneself. Harking back to the style of Jack Benny, comedians such as Jerry Seinfeld, Drew Carey, and Ellen DeGeneres make jokes at their own expense. This turnabout could be interpreted as resulting from some uneasiness about traditional scapegoats, but more likely it suits a reflective age, a period in which many individuals have equivocal attitudes toward themselves.

How do viewers manage to convince themselves that the aggressiveness rampant in situation comedies is inoffensive? First, with each weekly broadcast the viewer is reinvited into a familiar and warming clutch of personalities. At a time in American history when one fourth of all households consist of a single person living alone, when connectedness is at an all-time low, here is effortless membership and congeniality. Even if the group members make fun of one another from time to time, the group is bound to endure—at least until the show is canceled, although then the possibility exists that a well-liked gang will return on a daily basis via syndication. The group members sustain one another through fondness and fellow-feeling; even the more despised outliers will from time to time receive the benefice of others. Into this welcoming circle the viewer enters vicariously to experience a nuturance that counterbalances any offensive hostility.

Next, the viewer is drawn through the half hour by the contrivances of the plot line—more often two plot lines and, in the case of *Seinfeld,* three or four knit together. Although the plots distinguish one episode from another, and bring the novelties that entice weekly viewing, they too have their regular and comforting features that help deflect recognition of the hostile jokes embedded in them. The episode will begin with something that upsets, or threatens to upset, the presumably normal arrangements or decorum. Complications arise that have to be worked out. In the end, however, as always, everything will be set back to rights. Order reigns once more.

The third feature that obscures the hostility at the core of situation comedy is that the whole episode is cloaked in mirth. We take humor categorically to be healthful, spirited, and, at its thinnest, "not serious." It cannot be damaging as long as people are laughing—and the world of situation comedy rollicks with audience laughter.

The jokes that precipitate laughter, for all their concealed murderous intent, are delicate, ingenious items. Efforts to explain how humor works are, even at this date, still rooted in Sigmund Freud's diagnosis delivered at the start of the century (1905/1960). There is a format (Freud's "joke-work") to a joke that gives comedic cues through pacing; we know the dialogue is leading to something unexpected—an incongruity at the end. Sometimes this format is occupied with truly innocent material, such as word play, and elicits little more than a smile; 31% of prime-time jokes are not disparaging (Stocking et al., 1977, p. 451). The majority of jokes, however, use the format to mask hostile or sexual imperatives, according to Freud. The forbidden subject is introduced as the tempo signals a joke is under way, and then the punch line, with its unexpected twist, tricks the censoring mechanism in the minds of spectators, and busts of repressed psychic energy come out in the form of laughter.

Broadcasters learned when the radio era was young that they could elicit more laughter from listeners if they "sweetened" the sound track with prerecorded guffaws and twitters. When television began, canned laughter was routinely and artfully added to programs, heightening the studio audience's responses and smoothing out uneven mirth. Social scientists subsequently confirmed that such added material did indeed enhance the pleasure of viewers: Comparing the same show with and without canned laughter, the sweetened show produced an increased number of laughs, each being longer and louder than those from the "unsweetened" version (Fuller, 1977).

The payoff for the viewer who laughs along with this camouflaged aggression is clearly a decrease in tension, just as popular wisdom suggests. In a series of experiments conducted by Thomas Scheff and Stephen Scheele (1980), subjects who had seen comedies, in comparison to others who had not, afterwards had lower heart rates and improved moods (tabulated with a mood adjective checklist). The authors noted, "In all three tests (the two audiences in the field study and the experiment) the findings support the hypothesis that humor lowers tensions" (p. 179). Similarly, Tan and Tan (1986) report that watching situation comedies is linked to positive mental health (p. 111). These great benefits occur at the butt's expense, however.

Balancing Emotions

Violent television content is a self-selected instrument for the management of emotions. In the viewer's search for emotional balance, this material can stimulate some feelings and reduce others. It can conquer boredom through excitation, and it can diminish excess hostility and stress. Moreover, it can control apprehension and restore a sense of well-being. As it does these things, and does them with great regularity, its operations have much to tell about the fundamental emotional construction of the humans who seek it out.

5

Human Violence in Perspective

In the title of her widely read *The Harmless People,* Elizabeth Marshall Thomas (1959) disclosed her essential understanding of the Kalahari Bushmen whom she lived with and studied. She believed that her foraging tribespeople, among the last remaining examples of the hunting-and-gathering lifestyle that had been humanity's first and universal cultural mode, would always go to great lengths to avoid violent conflict. Thomas reported that "it is not in their nature to fight" (p. 21), and she claimed, "Their hold on life is too tenuous to permit quarreling among themselves" (p. 22). Implications of her research would be that all hunters and gatherers in history were naturally peaceable, and that nonviolence was the basis of human existence. The ramifications of this depiction would extend to the television violence controversy in that television violence might be a violation of human nature—a violation needing correction.

Whether or not primitive human beings were free of violent impulses is an important question whose answer will help in understanding the true social functions—beyond that of a whipping boy—of violent television content. Therefore, to comprehend the significance of television violence several wider contexts must first be considered. We must shift our attention from symbolized violence to actual violence, from individual viewers to whole societies, and from a fixation on the present affording no perspective to the grand lessons of the past.

As the French thinker Roland Barthes (1985) realized, the more one concentrates on the subject of violence, the more things it can become (p. 307)— legitimate and illegitimate (as defined by whom and for which purposes?), offensive or defensive, physical and verbal, state-sponsored or not, gendered or not, sexual or not, wanted and not, pleasurable or not, explicit and implicit ("All power inescapably contains violence," noted Barthes [1985, p. 309]). For present purposes, however, we must think of violence finitely, and so I define it, with Siann (1985), as physical assault, unwanted by the recipient, aimed at eliminating the recipient, issuing from social units ranging from the individual to whole civilizations, and largely a male activity. On the last point, Daly and Wilson (1988) report, "There is no known human society in which the level of lethal violence among women even begins to approach that among men" (p. 146).

Elizabeth Thomas was probably wrong about her own respondents, and her work was certainly misleading with regard to inferences that could be drawn from it. Whether because of the small sample of foragers she was able to investigate, the limited time she could spend with them, or her own opinions about people she admittedly found attractive, she came to misrepresent the actual levels of hostility prevailing among hunters and gatherers. Richard Lee (1979) identified 22 homicides during 50 years for the Bushmen tribe he investigated (p. 382), which converts to an annual murder rate of 29.3 per 100,000 hunters and gatherers (p. 398) or about three times the present-day homicide rates in America's cities (U.S. Bureau of the Census, 1996, p. 201).

What is the case for the Kalahari Bushmen is also the case for the other hunters and gatherers whose ways of life overlapped the arrival of Western observers and ethnographers. From a review of 50 pertinent studies (Ember, 1978), it was determined that 64% of foraging peoples experienced warfare at least once every 2 years; for 26% warfare was somewhat less common; only five of the societies were exposed to little or no warfare, and most of those had been recently vanquished. Ember notes, "In sum, hunter-gatherers could hardly be described as peaceful" (p. 443). Among American Plains tribes who followed the buffalo herds, "counting coup"—bringing back the scalp of a man from a rival tribe—was the standard rite of passage (Daly & Wilson, 1988, p. 223). Inuit Eskimos were enmeshed in constant cycles of violence: "The acquisition of wives by murder. Vengeance by the murder victim's kin. The targeting of the original murderer's kinsmen. Occasional revenge massacres far in access of 'an eye for an eye' " (Daly & Wilson, 1988, p. 222).

An early account of the behaviors of the largest surviving hunting-and-gathering group, the Aborigines of Australia, occurs in the dictated memoirs of William Buckley, an escaped convict who lived among the natives for 32 years in the first half of the nineteenth century (Morgan, 1852/1979). Brutal combat between bands was a frequent occurrence, according to Buckley, who narrates many fights, some of them reprehensible:

> We saw another tribe on the opposite shore. In the middle of the night we heard a dreadful uproar in that direction, and in the morning learned that those we had seen before dark had been fallen upon by some others whilst they were sleeping, on so hearing this we went to their assistance. On our arrival a horrid scene presented itself, many women and children laying about in all directions, wounded and sadly

mutilated. Several of the poor creatures had rushed into the lake and were drowned. (pp. 71-72)

David McKnight (1986) reports about the twentieth-century Australian Aborigines he studied at a remote mission that "the people were polite, friendly, warm-hearted, and good-humored" (p. 138), but that

> everyday there was usually one fight; each week there was at least one brawl involving a couple of dozen people; about once a month there was a melee involving at least a hundred people; and every once in a while there was a tremendous upheaval which involved most of the community. (p. 138)

McKnight states that although most of the fights were not lethal, some did lead to severe wounds and even deaths (p. 161). He writes, "Fighting was an expected and accepted method of standing up for one's rights and exerting political influence" (p. 161).

What is found in the modern ethnographic record can be legitimately applied to the chronicle of prehistoric humans. Daly and Wilson (1988) point out that many archaic skeletons bear evidence of cranial fractures and broken ribs on their left sides (p. 144). Because handedness is a human feature, it is probable these blows were received from right-handed opponents. The occasional appearance of arrowheads lodged in skeletons adds credence to this theory. The authors observe, "There can be no doubt that men have killed one another at high rates for as long as there have been men" (p. 143). In light of this analysis, the many broken ribs on the mummified remains of a Neolithic male found frozen high in the Alps in 1991 (Spindler, 1994, p. 179) can be interpreted as something other than the results of hunting mishaps; it is more likely he had encountered the working end of an antagonist's staff.

The human capacity for violence seems to be everlasting and indeed inbred. The sociobiologist Edward O. Wilson (1978) asks, "Are human beings innately aggressive?" and answers, "Yes" (p. 99). Although the particular expressions of violence are culturally determined, Wilson explains, "We are strongly predisposed to slide into deep, irrational hostility under certain definable conditions" (p. 105). This predisposition is biological or genetic in character. What are the "certain definable conditions"? Wilson says that humans are programmed to divide the social world into "us" and "them" and to regard them with a hostility that can lead to aggression and war (p. 110). The impulse toward violence has its evolutionary source in the conflict between groups; a result is that the genes of the more antagonistic, and the less submissive, would be favored.

Primatologists Richard Wrangham and Dale Peterson (1996) examined the violence inherent in the evolutionary lineage that leads up to human beings. It had long been thought that chimpanzees, a species older than humans and also our closest evolutionary relation, were congenitally peaceful and harmonious;

an inference some drew was that violent human behavior was an aberration, perhaps one that could be corrected. Recently, however, chimpanzee troops have been observed raiding the territory of adjoining troops and maiming or killing one of their neighbors (p. 6). Chimps are not so gracious after all. Like humans, they will kill their own kind. The murderous instincts built into them are also built into us.

Of what evolutionary benefit to chimps and humans is violence? "Lethal raids" are ways to maintain not only a group, as Wilson suggested, but also a territory (Wrangham & Peterson, 1996, p. 170). Thus, there are geographical and social aspects to aggression. Those males who have this trait in abundance become dominant within their own troop, or tribe, and are able to commandeer and mate with more females (p. 191), ensuring that the trait will be reproduced. Therefore, the propensity for violence, aggrandized up to the point that it may turn ruinous, is guaranteed survival. Wrangham and Peterson (1996) state, "Chimpanzee-like violence preceded and paved the way for human war, making modern humans the dazed survivors of a continuous, 5-million-year habit of lethal aggression" (p. 63). The often-violent capacities to defend territory, control the group, and master females have been evolutionarily selected for in the human male.

The propensity for violence evident among hunters and gatherers becomes indisputably vivid at the next stage of human cultural evolution—that of simple gardening or horticultural life. A larger number of these societies have survived into the modern era, including the Yanomamo, dwelling along the border between Venezuela and Brazil. Yanomamo culture, as documented by anthropologist Napoleon Chagnon (1983), is rife with violent behavior. Disputes within a village compound may be settled by chest pounding, in which one man with a closed fist lands blows on the chest of another, sometimes as many as four in a row; the two then reverse roles until eventually one of them drops (p. 165). More serious altercations take the form of side slapping, when a man with an open hand strikes the area on his opponents' side between the hip and the ribs; sooner or later one of them will lose consciousness (p. 166). Escalation leads to fighting with clubs shaped like pool cues but up to 10 feet long; one man offers his head to be struck and then strikes his opponent, aiming to draw blood (p. 171). Warfare proper occurs in raids between villages, typically initiated when one group of males with a grudge locates and kills someone who is outside their compound (p. 175). The raiders are also trying to steal women, whom they are intent on raping and enslaving. The violated villagers will, needless to say, counterattack as soon as feasible. Recurrent strife is standard in intervillage relations and is reflected domestically; Yanomamo husbands regularly and savagely beat their wives for minor infractions (p. 112).

Again, the ethnographic story restates the historical one. Lawrence Keeley (1996) excavated many Neolithic (early horticultural) sites of ancient Europe, finding that they were often fortified; the residents clearly went to the effort to protect themselves from their violent neighbors. He notes that although some apparently pacifist communities did exist, the vast majority of Neolithic villages offered strong indications of frequent warfare and violence. In several camps, thousands of flint arrowheads were found where the perimeter palisade and ditch once stood, evidence of archery attacks (p. 18). Keeley notes, "The archeological evidence indicates that homicide has been practiced since the appearance of modern humankind and that warfare is documented in the archaeological record of the past 10,000 years in every well-studied region" (p. 39). Evolution, both physical and cultural, has produced the inherently violent creature we are considering.

The State Management of Violence

The formation of the state did not occur until agriculture and settled, indeed stratified, life were well advanced. Several millennia after horticulture first began in approximately 10,000 B.C. in the Middle East, states began to emerge with a strong central government, the ability to raise taxes and armies, and with a monopoly over aggression. We can understand state development as a response to the contesting of adjoining social entities, each successful in providing sustenance for a close, growing, and tiered population. Among the responsibilities of the new states, as for all states from that point forward, was the management of violence within their citizenry. The state would have to control interpersonal violence so that the fabric of new societies would not be rent while at the same time promoting the violence that fueled controlled battlefield aggression in the name of state defense or offense. Social tranquility would have to be coupled with military ferocity. From the outset, two sets of social regulations were called for—a legal apparatus complete with penalties that could constrain untoward behaviors of the people within the state and a military apparatus that could ensure the state's survival vis-à-vis other states and carry out expansionist agendas. If violent impulses were to be censured in the conduct of everyday life and allowed full expression only intermittently in warfare, however, then a third imperative opened up: The animosities of the population—probably heightened due to the pressures of life at close quarters—had to be managed and diverted during the normal course of events. This too became the responsibility of the state.

Chronologically, states with the triple obligations regarding violence existed before writing systems appeared. Sagan (1985) discusses several such states that endured into the nineteenth century when, before their demises, their practices were carefully noted by curious Westerners: the Buganda state in East Africa and, in the Pacific, Hawaiian and Tahitian societies. In addition to their large populations and their standing armies, these states were characterized by "a centralized monarchy, a political bureaucracy, the systematic collection of taxes, an organized priesthood, and a hierarchically ordered social system" (p. xxi). We can use these near-contemporary examples to shed light on the historical progression that first occurred in the Middle East in the fourth millennium B.C. In the New World, Aztec and Inca societies, with their barely nascent systems of notation, probably also qualify as prewriting states. Universally, such states practiced human sacrifice, perhaps as a means of releasing bloodthirsty impulses and placating their subjects (Sagan, 1974, Chapter 4).

It is with the arrival of writing systems—first appearing at approximately 3000 B.C. in Sumer (located where modern-day Iraq stands)—that state formation received its greatest impetus. By making words visible and numbers abstract, and both permanent, cuneiform writing was a miraculous means for the state to systematize its operations and regulate its population. A dozen Sumerian city-states prospered as a result, and Sumerian civilization came to dominate the region for the next 1,000 years. With a writing system in place, tax rolls could be fixed and payments accounted for firmly. The laws that regulated behavior could achieve a uniform application and thus a credibility that previously, owing to fickle memory, they could not. From 2700 B.C., there are extant Sumerian deeds of sale, clearly formatted according to legal formulas that have not survived (Kramer, 1963, p. 79). Sumerologist Samuel Noah Kramer (1963) stated that the promulgation of laws and legal regulations was commonplace by 2400 B.C. and in all likelihood much earlier (p. 83). From 2050 B.C., near the close of the Sumerian era, comes a surviving law code that ensures that "the orphan did not fall a prey to the wealthy," "the widow did not fall a prey to the powerful," and "the man of one shekel did not fall a prey to the man of sixty shekels" (p. 84). The violation of the weak was forever proscribed in writing.

Writing was no doubt a powerful asset in the operation of Sumerian armies. Goods could be requisitioned, material ordered, payrolls maintained, battles planned, and widows compensated. The wheel was invented in Sumer, and one of its primary uses, if not its first one, was on war chariots. Kramer (1963) notes:

> The kings established a regular army, with the chariot—the ancient "tank"—as the main offensive weapon and a heavily armored infantry which attacked in phalanx formation. Sumer's victories and conquests were due largely to this superiority in military weapons, tactics, organization, and leadership. (p. 74)

Thus, there is evidence that the first states with writing systems were able to regulate malice internally and to exert themselves aggressively against their enemies. What form did the diversions take that could siphon off the excess spleen generated in such a driven civilization? On this count we have no knowledge.

To determine how advanced states diverted the sometimes violent urges of their citizens, and thus sustained civil life, we must move forward in time to a better documented civilization. Sufficient information regarding life in the Roman Empire (27 B.C. to 467 A.D.) has survived that a nearly complete picture exists of the social mechanisms used to redirect the hostilities of the citizens.

The Romans were highly capable and successful militarists, conquering and ruling the largest state that area of the world has seen before or since. Their elaborate legal system, one without peer, thoroughly regulated the internal operations of the empire. Closed off in much of civil life, violent impulses found their sanctioned outlets in the highly developed institution of the Roman games or *ludi*.

By the fourth century A.D., the Roman calendar allowed fully 176 days for staged games each year, with the proportions suggesting the relative popularity of the types—102 days for theater, 64 days for chariot races, and 10 days in December set aside for gladiatorial contests (Wiedemann, 1992, p. 12). These games, free to citizens, became central to the operation of the empire, and according to Roland Auguet (1972), more important than bread (p. 187), at least metaphorically. On the theater days, the productions began with macabre, bone-chilling dramas featuring mythological personages and horrendous crimes. Dupont (1989) noted, "It was all so appalling that the tragedy had at once to be followed by a knock-about farce designed to put everyone back in a good mood" (p. 210)—an alteration between the malicious and the light-hearted akin to the present-day prime-time broadcast schedule. For single events, the largest attendance occurred at the chariot races; the Circus Maximus could hold 200,000 highly partisan Romans at one time—half cheering the vehicles from the Blue stables and half supporting the Green. Betting on the outcomes only inflamed the passions of the spectators. Of all the games, however, it is the least common variety that most explicitly captures the success of the empire at channeling the aggressions and the fears of the citizenry and of doing so successfully for centuries.

Gladiatorial contests, pitting a single fighter against another in a highly stylized struggle leading to death, had not originally been public spectacles; their history is more circuitous. In the early days of the republic, gladiators were hired, through their owners, to carry out their mortal combat at the funeral ceremonies of important figures. To understand this brutal ritual, one must understand not only the mourners' horror at losing a hallowed leader, who had no doubt protected and represented them, but also their horror of the underworld—altogether real to them—in which the departed would come to reside and from which he might return with hostile intent.

Confronting death doubly, they expiated their fear by observing it in reality, although at a safe and ceremonial distance. This costly pagentry told in heightened terms of their regard both for the dead and for death. Over time, such cruel ceremonies attracted increasingly larger crowds, and in addition to marking the deaths of individuals, by the third century B.C. they came to be linked with the terrors of military excursions (Plass, 1995, p. 30). Until the end of the republic, the staging of gladiatorial contests remained in private hands, increasingly done not only to honor and appease the dead but also to appease the mesmerized throng, sometimes so that the sponsor could earn honor with the public and perhaps political support. A transition was under way from rite to spectacle.

The secularization of gladiatorial combat was completed in the reign of the first emperor, Augustus (27 B.C. to 14 A.D.), when the state took over total responsibility for the performances. Wiedemann (1992) notes, "From the time when Augustus monopolized power, emperors consequently had an obligation to share that power with the people by providing them with games" (p. 169). To secure popular endorsement, the successive emperors maintained costly gladiatorial schools, constructed the special amphitheaters in which the contests took place, and financed the annual spectacles. The first stone amphitheater was built in Rome during Augustus's reign, and was replaced by the coliseum started by the Emperor Vespasian (69-79 A.D.). The coliseum's proportions would be the template for all the other amphitheaters built throughout the Roman Empire.

Entering an amphitheater on the day of a gladiatorial contest, members of the crowd would have their free tickets in hand that assigned them to particular seats in particular areas of the arena. Seating was determined by social rank, with senators and other luminaries closest to the ring and women and noncitizens furthest away. Roman society, therefore, was present in micròcosm. The emperor was expected to be in attendance and, moreover, to take as much obvious enjoyment in the proceedings as the audience did; Julius Caesar had been faulted for reading his correspondence while the combat was occurring (Hopkins, 1983, p. 19). The spectacle was an opportunity for the emperor and the plebeians to interact at close quarters and for the political dance to unfold; citizens were beholden to the emperor for his munificence in providing the games, but the crowd also wished to make its will known, primarily on the reprieve (or not) of vanquished gladiators but also on other issues between the ruler and the ruled (Futrell, 1997, p. 46). Roland Auguet (1972) comments, "The crowd, as may be imagined, was the leading actor in these bloody dramas" (p. 67).

A day-long affair, the contests (*munera*) were typically preceded in the mornings by the slaughter of wild beasts imported for such occasions. Lions were set against bulls, tigers against rhinoceroses, and elephants against armed hunters: The slaughter extended for hours. At approximately midday, the execution of criminals and prisoners of war occurred, sometimes unelaborately and sometimes staged as reenactments of famous military battles or (in a cleverly flooded tank) of naval engagements. Observes Thomas Wiedemann (1992) about the animal and human executions, "The arena was the place where these categories of threats to civilized life were destroyed—not just symbolically, but in actual fact" (p. 90). The *munera,* to begin in the afternoon, were paradoxically the least vicious of the day's events, although they were the most awaited, the most ritualistic, and the most gratifying—the culmination.

The objects of the crowd's rapt attention, the gladiators, had been carefully trained for the event. Drawn from the lowest reaches of society, they were condemned criminals, prisoners of war, or slaves who had entered into this profession as a way of improving their wretched lot in life. At the gladiator school (there were three in Rome), they learned the rituals of both fighting and dying, practicing with comrades who may well be their opponents in the arena. On completion of their training, they took oaths to behave as their profession dictated. They could aspire to prizes, to a regaining of lost status, to eventual freedom from their masters, or—of utmost importance in Roman culture—to a noble death (Auguet, 1972, p. 98).

A pair of these highly conditioned athletes would enter the arena together. Their records in previous combats were known to the crowd, and applause would greet the favorite or acknowledge the chances of a well-matched fight. Dupont (1989) stated, "Asymmetrical pairs were selected for combat, although an effort was made to ensure a fair match" (p. 88). For example, one gladiator might be armed with a net, a trident, and a dagger, whereas his opponent bore a shield, short sword, and helmet. These types and their equipment were exactly specified and conventional; other types displayed the regalia of peoples conquered and absorbed into the empire: Samnites, Thracians, and Gauls. At a signal from an official, the highly stylized, highly strategized combat would ensue. For minute after minute, the two fighters would strive to disarm or disable each other, thrusting and parrying, with the crowd's excitement building all the while. Raucous applause broke out when a weapon was dislodged or a tendon sliced. In the stands, furious betting was under way. Eventually, one gladiator would sink to his knee, unable to continue, and raise the forefinger of his left hand, supplicating the assemblage for his life. The victor would stand above, unmoving. The crowd, on it feet, shouted its feelings to the emperor, who was duty-bound to signal them to the officials and fighters. If the vanquished was to be reprieved, he would be carried from the arena. If he was to die, he would sit on his heel and grasp the left knee of the victor and offer his throat to the victor's weapon; the killing was done with dispatch, to the roar of the audience. An official with a hot iron would poke the body to ensure that death had occurred, and the body would be removed. Laborers cleaned the arena in anticipation of the next pair.

Although gladiatorial contests may appear to be simple affairs—a man against a man, all or nothing—on analysis they reveal themselves to be highly convoluted, many-layered events designed to tug at the harbored animosities and fears of Romans in a variety of ways. Comment must be made on the dichotomy between the spectator (forever safe) and the spectacle (forever dangerous). At a safe remove, the spectator could observe and experience peril without ever being imperiled; "The aim was to acknowledge danger without losing control" (Plass, 1995, p. 32). What were these dangers to be so judiciously entertained and overcome? They fall into two categories. First, in personal terms, the Romans had a heightened (from a current perspective) fear of death and the horrors of the afterlife. Living at a time when life spans were brief, when medical aid was minimal, and when the toll of warfare was glorified, they experienced death in repeated and terrifying ways. The need to rehearse and minimize the torment of death was always with them. This is the relief that the gladiatorial contests offered. Watching the trained combatants give up their lives, the Roman spectator could apply the culture's strong injunctions regarding virtuous death and condemn or praise the gladiators' manner of dying. Lessons in the society's construction of manliness, bravery, and self-control were retaught and relearned (Toner, 1995, p. 39). Recall that the contests were held during the last month of the year, just before the winter solstice; it was the season of death and the time to confront death. Having witnessed it, the spectator knew that he or she had also cheated it; "Instead of seeing a gladiatorial combat as a public display of killing, it might be useful to see it as a demonstration of the power to overcome death" (Wiedemann, 1992, p. 35).

Second, in terms of society, the gladiatorial contests spoke loudly to perceived threats regarding Roman civilization and the spectator's way of life (Futrell, 1997, p. 209). Roman citizens were highly aware of the grandeur of their empire, of what it had cost to assemble it, and of the possibility that what had been so arduously constructed could, under certain conditions, fall apart. Deep fears of the breakdown of Roman civilization were stayed off through the slaying of a gladiator. The gladiators were from the underbelly of society and represented the lawless and the sinister. No matter which one died, it would mean a victory over criminality—a victory for civilization. Moreover, the gladiators were costumed and trained to represent the barbarians at the frontiers of the Roman Empire; the death of either one would dramatize the empire's ability to suppress its distant enemies. Florence Dupont (1989) stated,

> For a fleeting instant the edges of the world would meet at its center, immediately to be hurled back, separated by blood, to the far ends of the universe. Romans, creatures of equilibrium, remained in the centre, at an equal distance from every excess and from every margin. (p. 89)

The gladiatorial contests identified the special and most profound fears of Roman citizens and dramatically allowed those fears to be confronted and cut down. Hopkins (1983) commented, "The enthusiastic participation by spectators, rich and poor, raised and then released collective tensions, in a society which traditionally idealized impassivity *(gravitas)*. The gladiatorial shows provided a psychic and a political safety valve for the population of the capital" (pp. 29-30). Roaring furiously at the duel and at the death, the crowd assaulted doubly—at the lowly gladiators and at the losing one—and became twice a victor—over the vanquished and over death. Identifying with the victorious gladiator had allowed for vicarious aggression, for a violent attack against symbolized threats. Having met and overcome death, the purged spectator was in a position to be reinvigorated. Emotions had been managed, and on a large scale.

The public nature of the spectacle did much to knit the society together communally in the aftermath (Dupont, 1989, p. 213). Citizen to citizen, class to class, patricians and plebeians, the emperor and the people were all linked by the enormity of what they had witnessed together. Conflicts were set to rest, and animosities were put on hold. There is some sense of the pacifying nature of the contests from the observation that there were no documented riots following gladiatorial combats, whereas there were many after chariot races (Guttmann, 1986, p. 34). A sense of well-being had been inculcated; Plass (1995) refers to an increase in "a feeling of security and solidarity through aggressive energy" (p. 31).

This Roman extravagance must be seen in broader perspective if it is to be understood. Although the Romans were brutal militarists, they were not cruel governors of the vast territories they conquered. Had they been, their reign would not have lasted so long. They ruled in an evenhanded fashion, mixing Roman legal codes with the power of local authorities. The period when the gladiatorial contests were the most popular was during the centuries of Pax Romana—of nearly universal peace and orderliness. J. P. Toner (1995) observes that "the Roman empire did not consist only of buildings and land, it was also an empire of the mind" (p. 39)—a very well-balanced mind.

No amount of explication, however, can remove current repulsion about this Roman spectacle. Gladiatorial contests were generally not seen as a moral problem to any of the Roman thinkers and philosophers of the time (Wistrand, 1992), but they certainly are to us. The difference between their views and ours is testimony to what the macrosociologist Norbert Elias (1897-1990) called "the civilizing process" (1939/1978, 1939/1982).

The Civilizing Process

The role of the state diminished in Europe for nearly 1,000 years following the expiration of the Roman Empire in the fifth century A.D. When in the 15th century states reemerged, coincidental with the appearance of the printing press and movable type (a machine of great usefulness to the resurgence of state power because it was capable of quickly replicating numerous exact copies of state documents), it did so with little regard for the third of the violence imperatives. That is, the reborn state once again directed violence outwards through well-controlled armies and navies and suppressed internal violence through newly developed legal codes, printed in the vernacular, but it did not take responsibility for the redirection of violent feelings through sponsored diversions or spectacles. In Christian Europe, there was no Renaissance equivalent of the state-run Roman *ludi*. How was the management of violence to be accomplished?

Examining more than 500 years of European history from the end of the feudal period to the twentieth century, the German-born scholar Norbert Elias thought he discerned a particular set of interacting forces—an evolving process. This process, he observed, "moves along in a long sequence of spurts and counterspurts" (1939/1982, p. 251). Considering that he was writing during one of history's bleakest "counterspurts," as the 1930s' global economic depression was turning into the bestiality of World War II (Elias's mother was to die at the Auschwitz concentration camp), his interpretation of that process was a remarkable one. What Elias saw as the longer term phenomenon was an increase in pacification—in civility. This new order was the product not of state control but of the centuries-long expansion of habits of self-control.

As laid out in Elias's two-volume *The Civilizing Process* (1939/1978, 1939/1982), Europe in the fifteenth, sixteenth, and seventeenth centuries experienced the close of loosely organized feudal societies and the rise of sturdy states, usually monarchical in form. The new states reserved to themselves the right to use force, removing that privilege from the hands of the lesser nobility in a transition that Elias describes as from "warriors to courtiers" (1939/1982, p. 259). As these new, larger political entities capped by absolutist rulers came into existence, societies grew in size and complexity. The functions of society were progressively differentiated, as revealed in the increased number of professions and specializations, and what Elias calls "the chain of interdependency" grew more extensive and intricate. People no longer produced what they consumed and consumed what they produced; they increasingly entered into marketplace transactions and were beholden to a sequence of preceding transactions, from producers to wholesalers to shippers and so on. He refers to "the progressive division of functions and growth of the interdependency chain into which, directly or indirectly, every impulse, every move of an individual becomes integrated" (1939/1982, p. 233).

The continuation of "the civilizing process" involved a subsequent decentralization of control, with power passing from the hands of one absolute monarch to the hands of many people—a "functional democratization"—in the interest of preserving and strengthening the proliferating chains of interdependence (Elias, 1939/1982, p. 115). The sharing of power among increasingly more people had consequences for the behaviors between people; manners grew refined, etiquette became inclusive, and more considerateness was imparted toward more types of people (1939/1978). To convey the flavor of the difference between the simpler and the more complex societies, Elias employs the metaphor of contrasting highway systems: Feudal roads and lanes carried little traffic; the main problem for the wayfarer was that of roadside brigands; the traveler always had to be wary and to be prepared for violent conflict. With modern roadways, however, traffic increased, as did speed; travelers had to regulate their vehicles, and their behaviors, with regard to the progress of others; violence and other emotions had to be held in check (1939/1982, pp. 233-234).

These social transitions, as Elias envisions them, are reflective of psychological transitions—of long-term changes in the organization and display of mental life. Here is where we witness the grandeur of Elias's scheme because, unlike other prominent thinkers, Elias is not concerned with social, political, or economic evolution alone; all these developments are to be woven into the changing nature of individual deportment, which is in the final analysis the very core of the process—the means by which it is transported from generation to generation. His civilizing process is rooted in personality, and in the evolution of personality. For the civilizing process to continue, throughout the centuries "the regulation of the whole instinctual and affective life by steady self-control becomes more and more stable, more even and more all-embracing" (1939/1982, p. 230). Increasing emotional self-control is the key to Elias's view of Western history. In particular, men have come to "restrain their own violence through foresight or reflection" (1939/1982, p. 239) or conscience or the superego. None of this restraint, of course, has happened without cost; Elias recognizes, "The drives, the passionate affects, that can no longer directly manifest themselves in the relationships *between* people, often struggle no less violently *within* the individual against this supervising part of himself" (1939/1982, p. 242).

Elias (1939/1982) summarizes the civilizing process as follows:

> The closer the web of interdependence becomes in which the individual is enmeshed with the advancing division of functions, the larger the social spaces over which this network extends and which becomes integrated into functional or institutional units—the more threatened is the social existence of the individual who gives way to spontaneous impulses and emotions, the greater is the social advantage of those able to moderate their affects, and the more strongly is each individual constrained from an early age to take account of the effects of his own or other people's actions on a whole series of links in the social chain. The moderation of spontaneous emotions, the tempering of affects, the extension of mental space beyond the moment into the past and future, the habit of connecting events in terms of chains of cause and effect—all these are different aspects of the same transformation of conduct which necessarily takes place with the monopolization of physical violence, and the lengthening of the chains of social action and interdependence. It is a "civilizing" change of behavior (p. 236)

In passing, it is of interest that Elias's chosen term, *civility,* was coined by Erasmus of Rotterdam in the early sixteenth century (Elias & Dunning, 1986, p. 21). Erasmus was perhaps the first celebrity author—a status made possible by the advent of the printing press. Although Elias does not refer to this, the conflux of developments that attract his attention—the rise in size and power of the state, the sharing of power with an increasingly literate public, the schooling and direction of behavior, and the evolving saliency of the individual—are all stimulated by the arrival of the typographic revolution (Eisenstein, 1983).

Elias's theories, presented without empirical support, have been vulnerable to critics who brandish the interminable examples of modern-day barbarities, greater and lesser. When these instances, from World War I gas warfare to "ethnic cleansing" in Bosnia, are fixed on with sufficient intensity and disgust, then inhumanity would seem to be nowhere in retreat. Pearson (1983) writes of a human proclivity to view the present as increasingly rife with destructive activity and the past as comparatively more placid. What has supported Elias since his works' original publication in 1939 are an increasing number of often ingenious studies examining European crime, especially homicide statistics, since the end of the Middle Ages. The methodological problems with such studies are immense because historical records are spotty and court documents from different times and places are open to a variety of interpretations. When this body of studies is considered in its entirety, however, the results are abundantly clear: Just as Elias would predict, in general terms interpersonal violence has been declining in Europe for 500 years (Johnson & Monkkonen, 1996, p. 2).

A prerequisite for the curtailment of interpersonal violence was the development of court systems—a slow and fitful process, but in the large a constant one—in the new European nation-states. Soman (1980) describes how between 1300 and 1800 criminal courts came to hold sway, removing the rights of retribution for illegal acts from the hands of individuals: "A long and uneven evolution—the work of more than five centuries—was necessary before the vast majority of the population would come to view the criminal courts as the primary locus of redress" (p. 21). It is clear to Soman that "increasing recourse to official justice is part of the great long-term trends of sensitization to violence and consolidation of nation-states" (p. 21).

As criminal courts became more common, concomitantly the rates of criminal behavior declined; both trends speak to the general pacification of Western civilization. The evidence comes from throughout Europe; Johnson and Monkkonen (1996) present 10 quantitative studies from various countries and summarize as follows:

> They provide remarkably consistent evidence from several different national contexts that the distant past was far more violent than the more recent past and indeed even the present; and that the great decline in the level of interpersonal violence took place sometime between the seventeenth and eighteenth centuries—a period marked by the rise of state control over the population. (p. 6)

In a representative European study, Spierenburg (1994) studied Amsterdam's official investigations of homicide corpses (from a scholastic perspective, this is a shrewd analysis because it moved him away from fluctuating legal definitions of murder and guilt) and learned that homicide rates had been declining since the middle of the fifteenth century (p. 712).

Of all European countries, England offers the firmest and most researched data on long-term homicide rates. Gurr (1989) begins his review of the available studies with the eyre court records from 1202 to 1276; homicide rates at that time annually averaged about 20 per 100,000 population or about 10 times the modern rates (p. 29). From assize court records of the late sixteenth century comes documentation that homicide rates then were lower than they were during medieval centuries but higher than modern rates. Gurr notes, "Beginning in 1805, English officials compiled national data on committals to trial for indictable (serious) offenses. . . . They reflect a real decline in interpersonal violence" (p. 31). In Lawrence Stone's (1983) summary of approximately 20 applicable studies, England's aggregate homicide rate was 20 per 100,000 in the thirteenth century, 15 at the end of the Middle Ages, 7 in approximately 1600, 4 or 5 in 1700, 2 in 1800, and approximately 1 at the start of the twentieth century (pp. 25-26).

In the case of the United States, a steady decrease in homicide rates as England experienced is not quite so clear. Violent crime has been much more prevalent in America—homicide rates average 10 times that of Europe's—and this has shifted analysts' attention away from historical trends toward atemporal concern and chastisement. When trends are sought, they are more difficult to discern because the time frame is much shorter, and therefore long-term tendencies are more likely to be obscured by periodic cycles. Gurr (1989) points to a decrease in executions (80% of them for murder) from 25 to 30 annually per 100,000 population in the seventeenth century to a much lower number in the twentieth, and he ventures, "Thus we can infer that the longer-run downward trend in executions probably tracks, in an imperfect way, a long historical decline in murder" (p. 35). Data from several municipalities would seem to support this conclusion. Ferdinand (1967) reported that "the aggregate crime rate in Boston has shown an almost uninterrupted decline from 1875-1878 to the present" (p. 87). Boston's murder rate, for example, decreased from more than 7 per 100,000 in 1855 to 2 in 1951 (p. 89). Examining arrest statistics in Buffalo, New York, Powell (1966) found that violent crime peaked in 1870, declined until 1900, rose until 1918, and then continued to decline through the 1940s. Monkkonen (1981) disclosed that arrest data in 23 United States cities descended steadily from 1860 to 1920, although between 1890 and 1920 there was a large increase in homicides. Weiner and Zahn (1989) summarize, "Together these three studies suggest an overall decline in violent crime from the mid-nineteenth to the mid-twentieth century" (p. 105), but then they report that their own study of Philadelphia arrest rates contradicts the earlier studies and indicates an increase in crime.

It is difficult to generate a general picture from municipal data, but national statistics were not available until the twentieth century, and a complete set of national data was not issued until 1933. Death registration records collected by the Bureau of the Census and issued as *Mortality Statistics* apparently recite a sharp increase in homicide rates between 1900 and 1933. Douglas Eckberg (1995), however, conducted a thorough reexamination of these data and concluded that the rise may well have been illusory. The Bureau of Census's "death registration area" expanded only as states standardized their counts according to the bureau's criteria; early counts were derived from more pacified and well-administered states and thus were in all likelihood below the nation's norm, deflating homicide rates. Because with the passage of time more westerly states met the bureau's standards for data collection, the overall rates appeared to increase. According to Eckberg's reanalysis, "Apparently no enormous explosion of homicide occurred early in the century. In fact, a moderating trend extended to the period after World War II" (p. 14).

When all evidence is taken into consideration, America's homicide trends appear to conform to the European "civilizing" model, although at a higher count. Homicide evidently decreased through the nineteenth century as law enforcement and criminal courts spread across the continent. The rates then neither increased nor decreased significantly until the 1930s, when a steep decline ensued. As discussed in Chapter 3, homicide rates in the 1960s regained previous heights due in large part to the maturing of the baby boom cohort, but then in the 1990s they again decreased in the direction of the longer term decline.

Johnson and Monkkonen (1996) conclude, "Elias's significance has come to be recognized in part because his descriptions of the 'civilizing process' match so well what crime historians have been finding" (p. 4). Europe's 500-year decrease in homicide rates and the 200-year trends in the United States would seem to confirm Elias's belief that the display of violence is gradually being suppressed in human affairs. With the passage of centuries, increasingly more individuals are learning to curtail murderous sentiments, to turn retribution over to a gradually expanding legal system, and to live evermore restrained lives. By using homicide rates as a crude but telling measure of this tendency, we can examine the spread of the civilizing ethos into all manner of human affairs—ones not so readily calculable but altogether as real. It is not just that people are not killing each other as readily as they did a few centuries ago but also that decency, and the constraint of animosity, has come to characterize most human relations.

As the locus of social control has shifted to individuals, antisocial sentiments of all sorts have been increasingly repressed. For example, anger is no longer allowed the free expression it was allowed in earlier periods. In their book, *Anger: The Struggle for Emotional Control in American History,* Carol Stearns and Peter Stearns (1986) trace Americans' lengthy wrestling with angry impulses (which they state are "biologically programmed within us to help us respond appropriately to noxious outside stimuli" [p. 238]). They write,

> While our founding fathers felt relatively free to storm and rage when the mood seized them and even took temper to be a sign of manliness, we have become embarrassed by such displays today. Though our ancestors were certainly concerned about suppressing some behaviors that might result from anger, such as insubordi-

nation by servants and children, they saw no need to attack the emotional basis of those behaviors directly. Contemporary Americans have gone much further: They seek to regulate not only behavior but the feeling itself.

Indeed, during the past 200 years, Americans have shifted in their methods of controlling social behavior toward greater reliance on direct manipulation of emotions and, particularly, of anger. (p. 2)

The increasing repression of anger occurred gradually over generations as zones determined to be free of rancor widened. According to Stearns and Stearns, the process began in the eighteenth century within the family as husbands and wives expressed more regard for each other (p. 11). It spread in time to child rearing, to schooling in the nineteenth century, and to the workplace in the twentieth century. The authors noted, "Thus has the prolonged battle to control anger borne fruit, not only in the goal of seeking internal restraint over anger and disapproving those who lack this restraint, but also in the intensity with which the goal is held" (p. 211).

The Dutch sociologist Cas Wouters (1986) points to similar trends among European populations. Concentrating on the twentieth century, Wouters's study of etiquette indicates greater accommodation among classes, genders, and individuals—the result of increased emotional awareness and self-control. He refers to "the pressure to treat each other more as equal human beings under conditions of mutual respect" (p. 4). Wouters (1991) notes,

Particularly *within* industrialized Western states the use of violence has become increasingly tabooed and constraints on violent impulses and emotions have expanded to all walks of life: Even in the realm where until recently men as "heads of the family" could let themselves go and behave relatively passionately and unrestrainedly towards their "own" wife and children, they have come to be morally and legally constrained to curb their violent and sexual impulses. (p. 702)

Therefore, in both the United States and Europe the vitriol that used to be routinely showered on one's lessers is now increasingly proscribed. Both legally and normatively, what was once standard abrasion between husbands and their wives, parents and children, teachers and students, and bosses and underlings is now considered exceptional and sometimes a deviation worthy of criminal prosecution. The stifling of interpersonal malice has come to pertain to all the groups that were once the object of common, thoughtless derision—blacks, immigrants, the handicapped. No longer are defenseless others constituted as fit objects for the venting of personal animosity. These are outbursts that the individual, ever more civil, has learned to stem.

What is currently expected, as never before in history, is moderated, considerate, cordial behavior in all the departments of a person's life. The person who does otherwise, who raises his or her voice and becomes excessively animated, is worthy of censure. The mother who slaps her child in a public place, the customer who flies off the handle, and the boss who shouts are all now condemned as inappropriate or deviant, whereas decades or centuries ago they would not have been. Elias's civilizing process has permeated every corner of existence. We dwell in an age of extraordinary self-control of violent feelings.

The devolvement of social control to the level of the individual has been accompanied by, and perhaps stimulated by, the partial erasure of the midrange institutions that once regulated behavior. That is, between the overarching organizations of the state and national culture at the top, and the individual at the bottom, the onetime mediating constructions of class, church, and community no longer have the hold they once had. Stearns and Stearns (1986) relate that "the concentration on anger control was a response to the decline of traditional church and community supervision of behavior and desire to replace this supervision with internalized restraints" (p. 212). What had hitherto in history been imposed through institutional repression now had to be generated by ever-strengthening psychological controls. The turn from exterior to interior controls may explain the fact that, as homicide rates have been declining in Western civilization, suicide rates have been increasing (Chesnais, 1992, p. 226).

If the management of violence within societies has become the responsibility of the newly endowed individual, and has resulted in increased civility, then what about the management of violence between societies? If murder is down, is war down too?

The enormous scale of war in the twentieth century—including two world wars plus nearly incessant skirmishing, all carried out with increasingly murderous weaponry—would seem to cast doubt on any assertion that the waging of war is on the decline. Noting that interpersonal violence has historically decreased, Johnson and Monkkonen (1996) hypothesize that state violence (war) is on the ascent, but they admit that this has not yet been demonstrated. In fact, and as inconceivable as it may sound at first, the available evidence would seem to suggest that war too is on a long-term decline. Keeley (1996) examines the prevalence of war in primitive societies and concludes, "The primitive world was certainly not more peaceful than the modern one. The only reasonable conclusion is that wars are actually more frequent in nonstate societies than they are in state societies—especially modern nations" (p. 33). Dawson (1996) points out that among classic state societies, the waging of war was considered a glorified activity and was entered into frequently: "Until recent times, warfare was generally assumed to have a certain place in the cosmic order, assigned to it by divine or natural law" (p. 2). Only in the past 200 years has the exercise of war been subject to skepticism and reconsideration (Dawson, 1996, p. 189). It is during this recent period that, although the scale of war has increased as has the lethality of weapons, the casualty rates from engagements have been on a steady decline; military historians Richard Gabriel and Karen Metz (1992) observe, "Every war since 1600 has resulted in fewer and fewer casualties as a percentage of the committed forces for both the victor and defeated" (p. 108). They explain,

It is clear that as weapons became more and more destructive, armies reacted by adjusting their tactics to increase their dispersion of forces so as to minimize the targets provided to the new weapons. Again, the overall result has been a decline in battle casualties even as the lethality of weapons increased. (p. 108)

What can be said with some certainty is that the deadliness of war has been decreasing. Considering the high rates of warfare among primitive peoples, and the end of the glorification of war in the modern period, the occurrence of warfare may also be less nowadays.

We arrive at a puzzle. In the modern era, interpersonal hostility is suppressed, as is intersocietal hostility at least officially if not in actuality; what avenues are there for the discharge of the violent impulses generic to *Homo sapiens?*

Venues for Violence

During the past few centuries, the rise of a new social institution, that of organized sports, has complemented the long-term advances of the civilizing process. As people have increasingly had to restrain antagonism and strife in daily life, the venue of sports has opened within broadening leisured hours as an arena for the display and appreciation of aggressive but largely harmless action. The exuberant, excessive, and physically combative behaviors that are sublimated in everyday existence are allowed full expression here. Whether directly through competitors' struggles or indirectly through spectators' vicarious participation, individuals can now experience "an enjoyable and controlled decontrolling of emotions" (Elias & Dunning, 1986, p. 44) that is denied elsewhere.

In Elias and Dunning's (1986) analysis, the rise of sports, an antidote to the pressures of self-regulation that comprise the civilizing process, began in England in the eighteenth century and within the upper reaches of society (p. 27). In the aftermath of the tribulations of the seventeenth century revolution and the subsequent monarchial Restoration, the ruling classes settled into a calmer pattern for the apportioning of power through the establishment of a strong Parliament and of electoral vote. In this manner, the two upper-class political parties, the Whigs and the Tories, could duel without recourse to physical violence and the outbreak of internecine warfare. At the same time, members of this social class began to organize their sports in a more rule-governed manner; Elias and Dunning (1986) noted, "The 'parliamentarization' of the landed classes of England had its counterpart in the 'sportization' of their pastimes" (p. 34). Therefore, the eighteenth century was one of Elias's "civilizing spurts" during which political behavior became more stable and reliable as diversions became more regulated and rewarding. The pressures from the first domain were released efficaciously in the second. From England, according to Elias, came the formalized sports of boxing, rugby, football (soccer), tennis, cricket, horse racing, and track and field (Elias & Dunning, 1986, p. 21).

Over time, the practice of formalized sports seeped downward in British society, until the entire nation became familiar with the regularized pastimes. As this was occurring, sports additionally evolved in the direction of less blood-letting and more rule government. Boxing in England, for example, used to involve striking with bare fists and legs (Elias & Dunning, 1986, p. 21); gloves were added in the nineteenth century and padded gloves in the twentieth century. Richard Holt (1989) remarks about early nineteenth-century British sport: "A favorite form of sport involved a player holding a heavy stick in one hand to brain his opponent, while defending himself with a wicker shield" (p. 19)—a reminder of Roman games. " 'No head be deemed broke until the blood run an inch' specified an advertisement for a contest" (p. 19). The predecessor of rugby, to select another example, entailed large and unequal sides; most participants carried sticks to hit opponents; some of the participants would be on horseback; there was no referee; rules were loose and local; and there was no external regulating organization (Dunning, 1993, p. 52). The nineteenth century saw the institution of written rules for rugby, stated penalties for infractions, enforcement through a referee, and a supervising national body. Although such refinements were generally in a civilizing direction, they never reached the point that rough, even violent, play was extinguished, or that the pleasure of player or spectator in the mock combat was eliminated. Boxing and rugby remain combative sports but in tamer versions. They still gratify humans' lust for aggressiveness, experienced firsthand or secondhand. Even sports that seem to be free of interpersonal violence, such as tennis and cricket, still depend on the resolute aggressiveness of opponents and on the use of a swung implement to lash out at a surrogate ball, and they still lend players and spectators the satisfaction of attack.

As the concept of organized sports spread from England to the United States in the last quarter of the nineteenth century, it offered the new nation the same venue that it did the British: sites for the inculcation and venting of emotions within the carefully constructed framework of the contest. Baseball after the 1870s, football after the 1880s, and basketball after the 1890s were occasions for rabid partisanship, torrid sentiments, and the roaring discharge of emotions that were increasingly forbidden display in routine circumstances. No matter their origins, these sports and others spread rapidly geographically and spread down through the grades of the educational system, affording more players and spectators the pleasures of the ball game. Just as sports became more regulated, so did the behavior of fans—not in volume, because this was the justification of the new institution, but in appropriateness. Stated codes for players and unstated ones for spectators guided the gratifications of the contests. Stearns and Stearns (1986) write,.

In using sports to divert anger, and in developing new opportunities for spectator-
ship that may have vented anger as well through intense partisanship, the later
nineteenth century developed a durable outlet for expressing anger and enthusiasm
that could not be safely displayed in ordinary life. (p. 228)

Toward the end of the nineteenth century, sports pages began to appear regularly
in American newspapers in an attempt to address the unfilled appetites for this
new diversion (Guttmann, 1986, p. 85).

The institution of sports has expanded ferociously in twentieth-century
American life, which is testament to its successful role in the management of
newly curtailed and civilized emotions. The century-long increase in game attendance, the proliferating leagues, and the ascending sales of sporting goods
tell of Americans fascination and devotion to this historically new activity.
Nowadays, many boys and girls are expected to play in organized sports from
the age of 6, giving Mom and Dad more opportunities to root for favorites. One
of the first television broadcasts (May 17, 1939) was of a baseball game
(Barnouw, 1975, p. 90)—Princeton beat Columbia—and from that day forward
sports and the medium have been inseparable companions, growing to gargan-
tuan proportions together because of nearly insatiable audience interest.

Guttmann (1986) notes, "One of [sports'] strongest attractions is its ability
to present precisely defined dramatic encounters between clearly separate antagonists whose uniforms immediately mark them as 'our side' or 'their side' "
(p. 184). The two antagonists, as sports have developed, represent two different geographical settings so that the contests are not simply "our side" against
"their side" but "our locale" against "their locale"; in this characteristic, sports
hark back to their distant origins in intervillage warfare. What fans are seeing
as they enjoy a sports contest is a well-modulated battle; it is the ancient thrill
of savage combat that draws spectators to the games and loosens their emotions. There, they experience a violent war by proxy and in diminished but
reminiscent terms. Norbert Elias (1986) refers to sports as "the provision of
mimetic battles, battles enacted playfully in an imaginary context which can
produce enjoyable battle-excitement with a minimum of injuries to human beings" (p. 59). The sign of the "enjoyable battle-excitement" that spectators feel
is the volume of noise, the din of the crowd elicited by the struggle on the playing field. Fans are vocally releasing feelings of aggression and excitement that
are disallowed in normal contexts. Permissibly excessive in the sports stadium,
the spectator can then return to everyday life in a refreshed state of mind.

Sports, whether played or viewed and whether actual or broadcast, are not
the only modern venue for the exercising and exorcising of violent impulses.
Elias and Dunning (1986) write, "The drama of a good game of football as it
unfolds itself has something in common with a good theatrical play" (p. 51).
From the moment theaters received royal licenses in England in the sixteenth
century, violence has been a constant theme for the delectation of audiences.
All Shakespeare's tragedies had their violent moments, such as in the on-stage

blinding of Gloucester in *King Lear,* the drawn-out, blood-drenched suicide of Antony in *Antony and Cleopatra,* and the repeated appearances of Banguo's gashed ghost in *Macbeth.* Often, violence as scripted by Shakespeare took the form of simple swordplay (Barish, 1991, p. 102), but sometimes it was far worse, such as in his very early and goriest production, *Titus Andronicus.* The Roman ruler's daughter, Lavinia, is raped by two brothers who cut off her hands and her tongue. Then Titus's two sons fall into a pit and are trapped. To reclaim them, Titus chops off his own hand, but what is returned to him are their heads only. Titus slashes the throats of Lavinia's two ravishers and has their bones served in a pie to their mother. He then kills Lavinia to remove her shame. At every turn, the violence compounds.

According to Thomas Gould (1991), the greatest change in the 500-year history of violence in the English-speaking theater has been the transition from tragedy such as that which Shakespeare wrote to what Gould refers to generically as melodrama. Authentic tragedy depicts violent "suffering or death told or staged in such a way that we feel the terrible unfairness of life" (p. 2). The spectator would feel pity for Lear, Antony, Titus, and other beleaguered heroic figures, and in doing so feel pity by extension for all humanity suffering from unjust forces and, ultimately, pity for oneself and one's own situation. The melodramas that ripened into their fullest form in the nineteenth century, however, featured violence of another kind as well—and for other ends. Gould writes,

> A melodrama often begins with violence of the sort that defines tragedy—grave miscarriages of justice. In this kind of drama, however, there is always the promise that the perpetrators of the preliminary violence will eventually be the victims of a new round of death and mayhem. Our appetite is whetted for a guilt-free phantasy-fulfillment of revenge for all previous setbacks, humiliations, or frustrations. (p. 3)

It is the pleasure of violent retaliation that melodrama offered its audience—a chance to aggress vicariously and righteously. Gould finds this second form to be the lesser and possibly more dangerous variant; it "lends itself all too easily to the exploitation of some very unlovely instincts in the audiences" (p. 4).

A different analysis of the transition from tragic violence to melodramatic violence, one less patronizing of the modern audience, might offer insights. A taste for classic tragic violence in the theater and for the heightened sensations of pity that it elicits is a signal of an essential resignation to the forces of existence. The admirer of tragedy might have seen the underlying human condition as one of profound helplessness and professions otherwise as hubris. The admirer of melodrama, however, as Gould (1991) defines it, would have to be a believer in human agency and in the powers of redemption. Instead of tragic endings, and a tragic stamp on human existence, the melodrama enthusiast wants to witness happy endings, affirmations of human prowess, and of the hold of positive values. The transition in audience preferences from the nullifying violence of tragedy to the redemptive violence of melodrama conforms to Elias's civilizing process because in the second instance individuals are empowered to act productively and are directed by ennobling and efficacious values.

It is largely the energy of melodramatic violence that, in the twentieth century, continued into the dramatic productions of a newer medium—the movies. Whatever the genre of violent film—whether detective, Western, horror, or action hero—the ending is likely not to be bleak but rather to be affirmative and optimistic. To reach that point, the spectator must first experience feelings of intimidation or victimization and then feelings of sanctioned violence and triumph. Within this framework, moviegoers from 1910 onward have been able, in the closure of the theater, to peaceably acknowledge and release aggressive feelings. The dedication of the cinema to the tending of violent emotions has increased since the introduction of television as it became the nation's amusement mainstay and captured the tamer varieties of entertainment. Following the release of *Psycho* (1960), the film industry has viewed itself as free to explore the extremes of violent content. Alongside the ogre of fictional movie violence stands the comparatively meeker television version.

Television Violence

History instructs, even if we may not wish to acknowledge what it teaches. Human beings, especially males, have a violent streak in them; of this there is little doubt. The expanse of human evolution discloses no fully peaceful stretch, no era when people all set their cudgels aside and lived placidly next to each other. We may dream of such a stage—and at this point in cultural evolution it is our lot to do so—but we should not impose our dream on a past that is racked with bone-breaking attacks of human on human. It is undeniable that hunters and gatherers, given the opportunity, would turn viciously on their neighbors, and that the first farmers did this also in an organized, premeditated, and ruthless fashion.

History teaches us that there must be outlets for this violent impulse. As we shift our attention through time, we witness a sequence of rituals addressed to humans' bloody proclivities—from living sacrifices to gladiatorial contests, rough sports, and staged violence. Culture has grown more complex, and as humans have learned to rein in their animosities, the management of violence has grown more refined, but never to the vanishing point. Television violence is simply the latest stop along this continuum. As James Twitchell (1989) comments, "Historically, mass-produced images of aggression appeared as other forms of recreational violence have subsided" (p. 8). In isolation, television violence may seem reproachable and occupy the foreground with a menacing intensity, but with a longer perspective it can seem comparatively like an improvement—a purer distillation of the age-old processes for containing and redirecting violence.

We must keep in mind that television violence is symbolic only: No real hearts are being torn out, no gladiators are succumbing before our eyes, and no drops of blood spot our clothing. Although the depictions can be gory, they are far removed from actual bloodletting, occurring as they do on a Hollywood sound stage with the help of packets of ketchup. Nobody actually suffers for our pleasure. The whole event is so free of anything dire that witnessing it occurs in a domestic setting—in the confines of a leisured household. It is not a concentrated practice; it is diffused over hours and over days. In all ways, it pales in comparison to its horrific progenitors.

Lionel Tiger and Robin Fox (1971) point out that any human population must have certain amounts of internal aggression to account for functions, however disguised, such as sexual selection, but aggression "must be contained—usually by the process of 'ritualization'—so that it does not develop into internal violence and destroy the population" (p. 209). The viewing of television violence, a distilled and diluted experience, conforms to the requirement of ritual. It is entered into ceremoniously: The nightly spectator is likely to take the same seat, adopt the same posture, and partake of the same refreshments. The content is highly ritualistic: The sports event is always played with the same rules, and it always leads to a winner and a loser. The situation comedy (violence in humorous disguise) will have the same format of disorder and order, has the same coterie of characters, and has the same intermittent bursts of canned laughter. Television violence in its most explicit form contains good and evil, crime fighters and criminals, and guns and gunshots, all in a predictable medley. Frequently, the cop-gang nails down a single heinous wrongdoer—a maneuver strongly reminiscent of the horticultural band's strike at a straying neighbor. Viewers return to this ritual of violence viewing on almost a daily basis to take advantage of a proven panacea.

The ritualistic rewards include at least three kinds of gratification. For many viewers, the content offers the opportunity to feel violent and act violently. One can aggress vicariously with the running back, the point guard, the giber, or the detective and in doing so call forth and vent a modicum of hostile feelings. This may help with the modern requirement that one remain civil during the workday, no matter what the happenstance. Second, in a mode of life in which emotions are suppressed and regulated, television violence offers the opportunity to experience excitement in a safe haven. Elias and Dunning (1986) observed that

> many leisure pursuits provide an imaginary setting which is meant to elicit excitement of some kind imitating that produced by real-life situations, yet without its dangers and risks. Films, dances, paintings, card games, horse races, operas,

detective stories, and football matches; these and many other leisure pursuits belong in this category. (p. 42)

Elias, the consummate scholar, could not bring himself to say "television"; we
must add this most frequent of leisure pursuits for him.

Third, television violence serves the fearful viewer as well as the fearsome
one. All its genres produce resolution: The winner wins, order is restored, and
crime does not pay. The troubled mind is set to rest one more time.

In summary, television violence is of obvious benefit for those who select it.
Television violence is good for people.

If television violence performs such beneficial services, why is it seen as
reprehensible? This too is a comment on the civilizing process. The desire to
stomp out all violence extends even to the symbolic and diluted variety.
Jean-Claude Chesnais (1992) explains that "the more something unpleasant
diminishes, the more what remains of it becomes unbearable" (p. 233). At
some level, the connection between the symbolic and its actual predecessors is
recognized and reproved. Those most involved in the civilizing process want to
eliminate violence within themselves, and the subject of television violence
reminds them of their own perhaps furtive viewing of it. The greater the
premium on self-control—and except for communities of the cloistered, it has
probably at no time been greater in Western civilization than now—the more
this temperate reminder of unleashed violence is despised. Seen in correct and
longer perspective, however, television violence is not reprehensible; it is
instead sensible. It is not a most flagrant display; it is the least.

6

Backwards and Forwards

To this point, the argument has been that the assault on television violence is absolutely unwarranted. Seen within the broad context of human history, television violence is simply the most recent and least damaging venue for the routinized working out of innate aggressiveness and fear. Societies need to tame the maliciousness of their populaces in the interest of their own well-being, and symbolic displays of video violence is a late-twentieth-century response to that perpetual requirement. Without harm to himself or herself or others, the voluntary violence viewer steeps himself or herself in phantasms of vile play, derring-do, and deterrence, and emerges in an improved state of mind. This occurs not occasionally but nightly and by the tens of millions; the enormity of the project demands notice if not respect.

If healthful services are truly the outcome of television violence, why is the subject recurrently treated with such general contempt? The argument has been that television violence, the remnant of a strong but increasingly controlled violent streak in humanity, receives the approbation and censure that has intermittently befallen all manifestations of viciousness during the past 500 years, during the "civilizing process." Uncomfortable with violence and especially with personal violent feelings, critics and all those who acknowledge the criticism (which, when they are in a particular frame of mind, includes the majority of Americans) are quick to chastise the representation of malice on the surface of the cathode ray tube. Television violence becomes the object of this proscriptive pressure in part because it has no defenders—it goes forth unarmed. Vulnerable despite its nominal content, television violence becomes a scapegoat, a whipping boy for much that is contentious in society. Blame that should go elsewhere is heaped on television violence because it is a convenient and well-rationalized target.

The periodic vitriol directed at television violence belongs to the category of social phenomenon known as *moral panics,* a term generally credited to

Stanley Cohen (1972), although perhaps not first invented by him (Goode & Ben-Yehuda, 1994, p. 12). Cohen (1972) introduces his concept as follows:

> Societies appear to be subject, every now and then, to periods of moral panic. A condition, episode, person or group of persons emerges to be defined as a threat to societal values and interests; its nature is presented in a stylized and stereotypical fashion by the mass media, the moral barricades are manned by editors, bishops, politicians, and other right-thinking people; socially accredited experts pronounce their diagnoses and solutions; ways of coping are evolved or (more likely) resorted to; the condition then disappears, submerges, or deteriorates and becomes more visible. (p. 9)

Missing from Cohen's description is a sense of the inordinate fervor that accompanies a moral panic, the extreme righteousness of the condemners as they lash out at conjured or magnified transgressions. The response is always out of proportion to whatever instigates it. Cohen's seminal study was of the British public's outsized revulsion and trepidation shown toward post-World War II youth factions—the Mods and the Rockers. Other British studies of moral panics include Sindall's (1990) examination of street robberies in the latter half of the nineteenth century (a declining crime rate went unappreciated) and Pearson's (1983) study of twentieth-century hooliganism (the present is always compared unfavorably to the past). Moral panics in the United States have been analyzed in Gilbert's (1986) study of 1950s coverage of juvenile delinquency, in Victor's (1993) work on Satan worshipping as a social construct, and in Goode and Ben-Yehuda's (1994) examination of, among other episodes, the late-twentieth-century drug panic.

A sterling example of a debunked moral panic is David Berliner and Bruce Biddle's (1995) treatment of Americans' distress regarding the nation's educational system. Seemingly everywhere it is claimed that schools are failing, that students are not learning the basic skills they will need to be successful adults, and that educationally the United States is falling behind the rest of the world. One by one, Berliner and Biddle prove false the many specific charges. In response to the criticism that student achievement has been decreasing, the authors point out that this is not evident in standardized national tests. The National Assessment of Educational Progress (NAEP) tests are administered every 2 years to a large sample of students aged 9, 13, and 17: They note, "In general, the NAEP tests have shown very little change over the past two decades" (p. 26). The aggregated scores of the Scholastic Aptitude Test (SAT) given to college aspirants, have decreased slightly since the 1950s, but this is testimony to the increasing proportion of students who want a bachelor's degree, "which should have been a cause for celebration, not alarm" (p. 23). When the SAT scores are disaggregated by subject or by race, they reveal themselves to be steady or increasing (p. 23). College students are not dumber than they were in previous generations; Graduate Record Examination scores have remained level since the 1960s even though the percentage of college graduates taking them has doubled (p. 38). The authors conclude, "Since the early 1980s, Americans have been subjected to a massive campaign of criticism directed at their public school and colleges. . . . These charges are errant nonsense" (p. 64).

Campaigns against television violence also qualify as episodes of moral panic. They qualify first because of their breadth, since significant segments of the population are involved or aware. As Goode and Ben-Yehuda (1994) wrote, in a moral panic "there is strong, widespread (although not necessarily universal) fear or concern that evildoings are afoot, that certain enemies of society are trying to harm some or all of the rest of us" (p. 11). Here, the "enemies of society" are the venal broadcasters said to be undermining child viewers. The second criterion, according to Goode and Ben-Yehuda, is that the fear or concern is out of proportion to the threat; if television violence is functional, as argued here, then its fervent chastisement is out of place. Finally, "the fear and concern had a social foundation, a dynamic that revealed the inner workings of the society in which it took place" (p. 11); as discussed in Chapter 3, the issue of television violence is a guise for many other, deeper-lying contentions. In summary, campaigns against television violence qualify as moral panics because of their broadness, their pretext of defending social stability, the underlying fears, the sanctimonious tones of the accusers, and the inappropriate extent of the censure.

Among those enlisted in the moral panic against television violence is Sissela Bok, whose *Mayhem: Violence as Public Entertainment* (1998) is the clearest possible statement of the reformist position. She questions rhetorically, "Is it alarmist or merely sensible to ask about what happens to the souls of children nurtured, as in no past society, on images of rape, torture, bombings, and massacre that are channeled into their homes from infancy?" (p. 3). "The souls of children" is fancy and suspicious language; one has to wonder how Bok knows what these are and why her claims are any better than anyone else's version. Moreover, to say that modern children observe carnage "as in no past society" is to do a disservice to the true horrors of history: What children enjoy on their television screens is different in every essential way from the real barbarities of the past. Implicit in Bok's version of the television-viewing experience is the notion of the imprisoned child viewer, compelled to watch unwanted atrocities. Again, the child viewer, like every viewer, is voluntary and purposeful, on the lookout for the kind and amount of content that serves personal needs and not a speck more.

Bok (1998) builds her case for the curtailment of television violence on her rendition of the quantitative violence effects literature. Although she insists that "the vast majority of the studies now concur that media violence can have both short-term and long-term debilitating effects" (p. 57), many well-executed studies find nothing of the sort, and many even suggest positive, or reductive, effects. As explained in Chapter 2, the scientific literature, considered in its entirety, lacks concurrence or consensus. On the basis of her version of this literature, Bok levels four indictments against television violence: I use her four points to review the counterarguments discussed in Chapter 2.

First, according to Bok (1998), viewing violence adds to real-world aggression: "There is near-unanimity by now among investigators that exposure to media violence contributes to lowering barriers to aggression among some viewers" (p. 84). This "near-unanimity," however, disappears when the entire community of violence scholars is taken into consideration. Detailed literature reviews by Freedman (1984, 1986, 1988), Cumberbatch and Howitt (1989), and Gauntlett (1995) conclude that the case against television violence has not been made, and that the evidence linking video mayhem and real-world aggression is insubstantial. In addition, specific large-scale naturalistic studies by Hennigan et al. (1982) and Messner (1986) found no positive relationship between the two variables of violence viewing and crime rates in American metropolitan populations. In fact, Messner found a negative correlation: The more popular violent shows were in a particular city, the lower the crime rate (p. 228).

It was shown that each of the three standard methodologies for studying any connection between television violence and aggressiveness—laboratory studies, field experiments, and longitudinal correlation studies—had severe drawbacks. Closely monitored laboratory studies, which constitute the bulk of the anti-television violence evidence, are highly susceptible to "experimenter expectancy bias," in which the biases of the researchers are likely to be realized in the findings, and to the "good subject effect," in which subjects try to behave in ways they intuit are expected of them (Rosnow & Rosenthal, 1997). To reduce the contamination of the laboratory setting has been the goal of field experiments, but according to one review of the few that have been done, "the findings from the field experiments offer little support for the media aggression hypothesis" (Gadow & Sprafkin, 1989, p. 404). Correlation studies are forever vexed by the fact that correlations, which indicate the tendency of two variables to exist simultaneously or sequentially, cannot prove causation. The best known correlational study is a longitudinal one by Leonard Eron and associates (Eron, Huesmann, Leftkowitz, & Walder, 1972) in which preferences for violent television shows at age 9 were compared to aggressiveness ratings at age 19 for more than 400 subjects. For six possible correlations (three for males and three for females), only one was statistically significant, and just moderately so. Cumberbatch and Howitt (1989) refer to Eron et al.'s efforts as "inferior in every respect" (p. 45).

Second on Bok's list of television violence's effects is fearfulness: "Studies show that the sense that threats abound in the outside world is common among heavy TV viewers of all ages" (p. 62). Most, and the best known, of these studies were conducted by George Gerbner, who correlated viewing hours with perceptions of crime. According to Gerbner, the greater a person's viewing time, the more likely that person is to overestimate the chances of being a crime victim and to express heightened fears of crime (Gerbner, Gross, Jackson-Beeck, Jeffries-Fox, & Signorielli, 1978, p. 206). Television is supposed to have instilled these misperceptions.

Gerbner's analysis has received much scholarly scrutiny and has been roundly criticized. Doob and Macdonald (1979), Jackson-Beeck and Sobal (1980), and Tyler and Cook (1984) determined that both variables are accounted for by a missing third factor, such as the crime rates in the viewer's locale: Those living in high-crime neighborhoods are likely to stay home and watch television and correctly to fear being victims. Other researchers presented evidence that the missing third variable is psychological (Wober & Gunter, 1982; Zillmann & Wakshlag, 1985): Those who are apprehensive to begin with may huddle by their sets, fearing crime. Still other scholars wondered if Gerbner's correlations existed at all. Michael Hughes (1980) demonstrated that if Gerbner had better controlled for variables known to indicate higher viewing times, such as gender, race, and age, then the correlations virtually disappear. Paul Hirsch (1980, 1981) also found, once he had introduced the requisite controls, that the relationship between viewing times and fearfulness was highly inconsistent. The linkage that Gerbner insists occurs in the United States has not been found in other countries (Bouwman, 1984; Hedinsson & Windahl, 1984; Piepe, Crough, & Emerson, 1977; Wober, 1978).

Third, Bok (1998) believes that

> to the extent that people seek out violent programming for the enjoyment and the excitement that the violence itself can provide, they may run a higher risk of suppressing empathy—the crucial ability to feel with and for others and to respond to their suffering. (p. 70)

This is the charge of "desensitization," whose purported existence is based almost entirely on four experiments by one research team (Drabman & Thomas, 1974a, 1974b, 1976; Thomas & Drabman, 1975). Attempts to replicate these experiments were not successful (Horton & Santogrossi, 1978; Woodfield, 1988). Even if the phenomenon exists in the laboratory, there is no evidence that it would generalize to the real world; Belson (1978) found no correlation between levels of violence viewing and callousness to real violence or inconsiderateness to others (pp. 471-475, 511-516). Reviewers of the small desensitization literature conclude that there is no empirical proof that television numbs people to real-world calamities (Comstock, 1989, p. 275; Gauntlett, 1995, p. 39; Van der Voort, 1986, p. 327; Zillmann, 1991, p. 124).

Fourth, Bok (1998) believes that the first three heinous effects can only increase as the condition of violence addiction sets in. She postulates that an appetite for television violence, "much like appetites for other activities found pleasurable, can turn into an addiction, characterized by higher and higher tolerance levels and by withdrawal symptoms for those who try to stop" (p. 80). Because Bok cites no empirical evidence (and indeed there does not appear to be any), her claim seems to represent unsubstantiated fear-mongering. At this point, she has departed the realm of reason and logic. The following is the pertinent fact: Violence viewing is heaviest among teenagers and declines as people age (Rosenstiel, 1993). Viewers do not need increasingly more but rather increasingly less.

In her determination to conquer any lingering resistance to her argument, Bok (1998) constructs an analogy between "reports of studies showing harm from TV viewing" and "research pointing to harm from smoking" (p. 145). Like the research on television, the research on smoking was, until recently, correlational, pointing to a statistical correspondence between smoking and cancer; the chemical path from one to the other was difficult to discern, so causality could not be proven impeccably. The implication is supposed to be that, just as it was widely accepted on correlational evidence that smoking caused cancer, and social censure resulted, so should it be accepted that violence viewing causes aggression and appropriate responses should be initiated. Bok is not alone in employing this analogy; many advocates of television reform use it, including Leonard Eron (1996). In congressional testimony, Eron claimed, "If you are still skeptical about the cause and effect relation between television violence and aggression, let me remind you that the size of the relation is about the same as that between smoking and lung cancer" (p. 230).

Analogies can be illuminating, but this particular one is false and cannot withstand scrutiny. The evidence that smoking correlates with cancer was based on studies with massive numbers of subjects. Both the hypothesized cause and the effect were carefully defined biological events, leaving little room for interpretations and little opportunity for the interjection of personal values. There is a simplicity to the basic concepts that invites causal deductions. None of this pertains to television violence research, in which the studies are characterized by small sample sizes. The stimuli are varying (all television content? just some shows? cartoons?), and the results are equivocal, sometimes to the point of invisibility. Instead of biological entities, the variables are cultural and subject to a variety of readings. Can the total show, including the ending, be said to be violent? How is the scenario interpreted by the individual viewer? Might the associated behaviors, however categorized, be stimulated by any number of other factors? The psychological and cultural complexities of the violence-viewing experience may elude the rigid protocols of science. In addition, Bok's (1998) analogy is further weakened by the fact that, as violence viewing remains high, aggression as gauged by crime statistics is on the decline in the 1990s. Instead of claiming that smoking and violence viewing are similar, it would be more to the point to stress their differences: As smoking is to cancer, so violence viewing is to psychological relief. The first is pathological, and the second is not.

However unwarranted the assault is against television violence, the fact remains that it continues. Although the antiviolence fervor crested in the first half of the 1990s, in the second half the campaign continued; Sissela Bok

(1998) comments, "During the 1990s, much larger efforts by citizen advocacy groups, churches, professional organizations, public officials, and media groups have been launched to address the problems posed by media violence" (p. 146). It continues as it has previously—round after round of the contest over television violence. On the one side, the reformist position finds articulation time and again; on the other side, the public's incessant desire for violent entertainment is reluctantly (because there is no prestige or cachet to be had in it) serviced by television companies as they compete against each other for profits. We can contrast these two forces in the following way: The first, the anti-television violence campaign, is highly focused in its presentation, calling for the curtailment of violent content, but this concerted effort has underpinnings that are vague and various, as discussed in Chapter 3; the second force is highly diffused on the surface (the public nowhere speaks pointedly in favor of violent content), but its underpinnings are highly concentrated and functional, pertinent to the management of disapproved emotions. To date, neither force has triumphed decisively. The antiviolence advocates can be gratified by the righteousness of their cause and sense of moral superiority, but violent content continues as a mainstay of the medium's offerings and in viewers' attention. Over the longer term, equilibrium has been the result.

If the equilibrium were upset, however, unplanned consequences would result. The attack on television violence is not simply unwarranted; it carries the threat of unfortunate dangers should it succeed. As previously discussed, on a nationwide scale television violence is a successful site for the siphoning off of unwanted emotions. The French critic Michel Mourlet (1991) explains:

> Violence is a major theme in aesthetics. Violence is decompression: Arising out of a tension between the individual and the world, it explodes as the tension reaches its pitch, like an abscess burning. It has to be gone through before there can be any repose. (p. 233)

The loss or even diminishment of the venue of television violence would suggest that surplus psychic energy would have to find other outlets. What these outlets would be is open to question, but the possibility exists that some of them might be retrogressive, involving violence in more outright and vicious forms. It is in the nation's best interest not to curtail the symbolic displays that come in the form of television violence.

Policy

The official curbing of television violence is not an idle or empty threat. It has happened elsewhere, most close by in Canada. In 1993, the Canadian Radio-Television and Telecommunications Commission, the equivalent of the Federal Communications Commission (FCC) in the United States, banned any "gratuitous" violence, which was defined vaguely as violence not playing "an integral role in developing the plot, character, or theme of the material as a whole" (Scully, 1993, p. 12). Violence of any sort cannot be broadcast before 9 p.m. Totally forbidden are any programs promoting violence against women, minorities, or animals. Detailed codes regulate violence in children's shows. In addition, the Canadian invention of the V (for violence) chip is to be implemented, which would permit parents to block out programming that exceeds preset levels for violence, sexuality, or strong language (DePalma, 1996).

The two houses of the United States Congress have held 28 hearings since 1954 on the topic of television violence (Cooper, 1996), but none of the hearings led to the passage of regulatory legislation until the Telecommunications Act of 1996. The Act alleges that

> studies have shown that children exposed to violent video programming at a young age have a higher tendency for violent and aggressive behavior later in life than children not so exposed, and that children exposed to violent video programming are prone to assume that acts of violence are acceptable behavior. (Section 551)

It then dictates that newly manufactured television sets must "be equipped with a feature designed to enable viewers to block display of all programs with a common rating" (Telecommunications Act of 1996, Section 551). The V-chip, the only available "feature" to meet the requirements, was to be imported from Canada to the United States. Owing to a rating system reluctantly and haltingly developed by the television industry, parents on behalf of their children would be able to black out offensive content. Censorship had passed down to the family level.

Although the V-chip represents the first legislated regulation of television violence, there was an earlier episode of violence censorship whose outcome may be telling about the fate of the chip. This occurred in the aftermath of the 1972 "Report to the Surgeon General on Television and Social Behavior," which, in highly equivocal language, appeared to give some credence to the notion that violent content can activate violent behavior in some younger viewers. Pressure from influential congressmen and from the FCC and its chairman, Richard Wiley, led the broadcasting industry in 1975 to institute what came to be known as the Family Viewing Hour. Formulated as an amendment to the Television Code of the National Association of Broadcasters, the stipulation decreed that before 9:00 p.m. "entertainment programming inappropriate for viewing by a general family audience should not be broadcast" (Cowan, 1979, p. 113). The definition of "inappropriate programming" was left to the individual networks to determine, but as the 1975-1976 television season drew near, it became clear to the production community in Los Angeles that the definitions would be strict. The producers of *M*A*S*H* (which aired at 8:30 p.m.) learned from the CBS censor assigned to them that three of their proposed programs—dealing with venereal disease, impotence, and adultery—would not be allowed to go into production (Cowan, 1979, p. 125). *Rhoda* could not discuss birth control (p. 131), and *Phyllis* would have to cancel a show on virginity (p. 136). Television writers and producers began to rebel, and in late 1975 their Writers Guild brought a lawsuit against the FCC and the networks with regard to the creative impositions of the Family Viewing Hour. Actor Carroll O'Connor (as quoted in Cowan, 1979, p. 179) complained, "Congress has no right whatsoever to interfere in the content of the medium," and writer Larry Gelbart voiced dismay (as quoted in Cowan, 1979, p. 177): "Situation comedies have become the theater of ideas, and those ideas have been very, very restricted." The judge who heard the case in April and May of 1976 took until November to issue his decision, but when it emerged it was polished and clear: Family Viewing Hour was the result of "backroom bludgeoning" by the FCC and was to be rescinded. According to the judge, "The existence of threats, and the attempted securing of commitments coupled with the promise to publicize noncompliance . . . constituted *per se* violations of the First Amendment" (Corn-Revere, 1995, p. 201). The fate of the Family Viewing Hour may prove to be premonitory: The American Civil Liberties Union is currently bringing a similar case against proponents of the V-chip—a case that may produce similar results.

Whether or not the V-chip will withstand judicial scrutiny, there are several problematic aspects to the device and to its successors, if any. Its usage would portend to impinge on the providers of violent content, on the viewers of it, and indeed on the fundamental legal structure of the nation.

To confront the first of these three impact areas, significant use of the V-chip by parents would measurably reduce the audience size for certain programs containing symbolic violence. Little else could have greater impact on the American television system as it is currently constituted. A decrease in audience numbers quickly translates to a decrease in advertising revenues. Advertisers may additionally shy away from a shunned program because of its loss of popularity or because its lowered ratings have clearly stamped it as violent. The decline in revenues would make the program less valuable in the eyes of network executives and perhaps a candidate for cancelation. The Hollywood production community would quickly take notice and begin tailoring its broadcast content to the new standards. Blander fare would be certain to result. Broadcast networks may begin losing viewers to bolder content on the less fastidious cable networks and in particular to the channels that are not supported by and influenced by advertising. Thus, we can anticipate a shift in the television system away from the more traditional and responsible channels toward the less so and away from advertising-supported channels in the direction of subscriber-supported channels. This shift would not transpire according to the traditional governing mechanism of television—audience preferences. Those to whom the censored content had been destined would have played no role in its neglect. Neglect would have transpired because of the artificial intercession of controls.

The second area to be impacted by the V-chip, should it prove successful, is the viewership, in particular younger viewers. Currently, young viewers have great license in most households to select the content they want to watch; this license would be greatly reduced with the introduction of the V-chip, which can block out entire genres. Screening for certain levels of violence, the parent could eliminate most cartoons and all action-adventure shows, whether the child desires some of these or not. A *New York Times* reporter, interviewing a Canadian mother who had been an early tester of a V-chip prototype, heard the mother's 12-year-old son protesting in the background, "We're not getting the V-chip back!" The mother explained to the reporter, "The kids didn't like the fact that they were not in control any longer" (as quoted in DePalma, 1995, p. C14)—with good reason. Children are losing the right to pick the content of which they are in psychological need. The V-chip represents another weapon in the generational war—a device that allows parents to eradicate the compensational content of which children have learned to make enjoyable use. The consequences of all this for the child and the family would be unpleasant. The chances that the V-chip will increase intergenerational friction are high. Not only will normal levels of tension and animosity be denied their outlet via television fiction but also so will the new superheated levels. It is not a congenial prospect.

Third, the V-chip constitutes a strong challenge to traditional First Amendment rights of free speech and a free press. Stoutly defended by post-World War II supreme courts, First Amendment rights can be voided "only in order to promote a compelling state interest, and then only if the government adopts the least restrictive means to further that interest" (Ballard, 1995, p. 211). The few restrictions allowed concern such matters as obscenity, libel, national security, and the sometimes conflicting right to a fair trial. According to legal scholar Ian Ballard (1995), there is no "compelling state interest" involved in the matter of television violence because "the social science evidence used to justify the regulation of televised violence is subject to such strong methodological criticism that the evidence is insufficient to support a massive regulatory assault on the television entertainment industry" (p. 185). Even if the goal of restricting television violence were acceptable, the V-chip is hardly "the least restrictive means" because it introduces a "chilling effect" on program producers and broadcasters that "clearly infringes on fundamental First Amendment rights" (p. 216). Moreover, states Ballard, "Fear of a slippery slope is not unfounded" (p. 216). If television violence can be censored, supposedly because it poses a threat to social order, then what topics might be next? It would not be long before challenging themes such as feminism or multiculturalism were deemed unfit for the same reason. An uninviting vista presents itself.

Taking all these matters into consideration, the best federal policy regarding television violence would be to have no policy—to leave the extent of violent depictions completely up to the dictates of viewer preferences, as expertly interpreted by the television industry. In this, I am in agreement with Ian Ballard

(1995), who finds that the best approach "is for the government to do nothing at all about television violence" (p. 218).

Politicians

In reviewing the half century of recurrent assaults on television violence, one matter becomes clear: It is in the halls of Congress where the attack invariably crystallizes. Nebulous concerns about video mayhem afloat among the public, plus a loose collection of published studies, become forged in the hands of astute politicians into an issue. Although most congressmen and congresswomen are stirred by a genuine if incorrect conviction that the violent content is damaging to the national fabric, we can nominate other, crasser motives for them to wield this particular topic. While many congressional items, though central to the maintenance of the world's most powerful country, are too dull to inspire reportage, this controversy, pertinent to the everyday lives of every sentient American, is covered by the press and does result in the senator's or representative's name and image being conveyed into households throughout the country. In addition, this fame is linked to an immaculate concern—the purification of American family life. Although there are many tawdry aspects to national politics, this is the cleanest one possible. The senator or representative is depicting himself or herself as a savior—purer than pure.

Situating himself as the enemy of violence in national life, it is easier for the congressman to go after television violence, which is undefended, than it is to go after the actual, and much more controversial, contributors to real-world mayhem. For example, if one truly wanted to reduce the harmful effects of violent crime, one would work to end the easy availability of handguns in the United States and lock horns with the powerful National Rifle Association. Violence is associated with inner-city life; a national program to increase job training and opportunities for inner-city youth would pay immediate dividends, although it would be costly. Our mythical congressman would have to confront national disinterest in helping black youngsters succeed. Finally, the congressman who really wants to decrease violence in America would also dare to think about decriminalizing drug usage.

It may well be inane to ask congressmen and congresswomen to abandon their periodically noble pose regarding television violence—to abandon this invalid issue. When the controversy returns once again, for some politicians it is too tempting to jump aboard and to be among those to articulate the issue and then to play a leadership role in its procedural evolution. The rewards are clear, and the risks are nonexistent. Rather than hope that congressmen and congresswomen will change their ways, it is more realistic to ask that members of the public give such displays less credence than they have in the past and try to effect a fuller understanding of the issue and of the reasons that some in power would use it to pander to the electorate.

Parents

Should young children be allowed to view the ilk of the *Mighty Morphin' Power Rangers?* In a typical episode, the five Power Rangers (Ashley, Cassie, Andros, Carlos, and T. J.—a racially and sexually balanced band) engage in three violent scrapes against evildoers. They may first battle in their street clothes, then morph into their Power Ranger persona and getups and karate kick their way out of trouble, and finally morph together into a gigantic warrior and do battle against an equally gigantic malefactor. Although the half-hour's worth of dramatic action is interrupted regularly with the mishaps of a comedic duo, the clear emotional center of the show is the violent struggle of the Power Rangers against their antagonists.

The answer to the question of whether children should be allowed to view this content is, of course it should be tolerated, if they have freely chosen it for themselves. They made the choice because of some inner need for such explosive content—a need that deserves to be respected. To be 6 years old is to be essentially powerless in the world of human affairs; even turning a door handle can be a challenge. Through the blend of the phantasms on the screen and the flight of imagination, however, the child viewer can become momentarily omnipotent, transcending all obstacles, and morphing at will. That the child would want to do this is not a reflection of relative failure but rather testimony to the child's resolve to resist weakness and to develop in time into a strongly mature human being. Time with the Power Rangers should be endorsed and not denigrated or denied. Thelma McCormack (1993), resisting the intrusion of Canadian authorities into children's selections, wrote,

> What is needed now rather than more regulation of television "in the interests of children," is a new understanding of how children create, process, and interpret television within the larger context of their historical culture, and the acceptance of a more robust children's aesthetic. (p. 22)

The same call applies to parents.

This is not to absolve parents of all responsibility regarding television viewing. They are the adults, after all, and need to lead youngsters into successful maturation. In the case of television, it is not the programs chosen but the time with the medium that should be controlled. Robert Hodge and David Tripp (1986) concur, "So it is generally more important for adults to limit the total time spent viewing than to select the programs viewed" (p. 214). Television should not be allowed to replace, or threaten to replace, the real world. Television has its role, but it must be a subsidiary one. The medium is compensation for the real world but not a substitute—never the be-all and end-all. Life is not all fun and diversion, and it is harmful to children to let them, by never leaving their television sets in their leisure hours, believe that it is. They need to develop their expertise with several different media, including reading.

Professors

The professoriate is the next group that has played a central role in the debate regarding television violence. Scholars have generated the studies that are used in the salvo against the rambunctious content. Although they would not like to think of themselves this way, they are the munitions makers in this war of words. Granted that a close reading of their total corpus reveals little consensus, there are more than enough studies with the "right" findings to provide ample ammunition for reformists. As nothing else, these studies are taken to legitimize the assault on television violence; they are cited in every attacking document and speech.

Not only do professors provide the accusatory studies but also they have much to do with amplifying the derogatory discourse. Recall from Chapter 2 that there are two concentric spheres of discourse regarding television violence: the inner ball of the violence effects literature and the immediate dialogues that it inspires, and the outer circle of more exhortatory discourse that draws selectively on the inner as it tries to make its case for the curtailment of television violence. Professors perform in both layers, with the few in the inner becoming a multitude in the outer. They are promulgators of the antiviolence position both directly by arguing for it in their lectures and other public utterances and indirectly by not contradicting the conventional wisdom on the topic found in textbooks and other classroom materials. From the perspective advanced in these pages, professors have compiled a disappointing record on this matter and have much to answer for.

Professors are privileged members of society whose classroom duties occupy them for only 30 weeks a year; no other employed people have a similar schedule. They are also well compensated, and if tenured they have a guaranteed sinecure. Being free of many worldly worries, there is every right to hope that they will meet the expectations for the profession—that they will be detached, thoughtful, and indeed wise. On the issue of television violence, however, this has not proven to be the case, for professors as a rule have been needlessly shortsighted. If they had stood back and examined television violence in its long-term historical context and seen where this matter ranks alongside the recurring atrocities in human history, then they would have realized that television violence is a relatively minor happenstance whose appearance suggests an improvement in the human condition and not a diminishment. This long-term perspective, however, is something professors cheated themselves out of as they took the easy path and considered the phenomenon ahistorically, as a present-day event only. Losing historical perspective is understandable for people in many walks of life, but it should not be excused for members of the Academy.

In addition, when work purporting to be scientific derives results that are consonant with prevailing values—as many studies within the violence effects literature have done—then that is not a moment for glee but rather a time for deep suspicion. Professors who try to teach their students to think critically cannot seem to think critically themselves when the subject is the television violence literature, so blinded are they by the fusion of the proper values and empirical findings. This happy occasion needs to be dealt with very cautiously, as the literature on "experimenter expectancy effects" suggests. This caution applies both to those professors doing the studies and to those who would cite them appreciatively.

People look to professors for intellectual leadership and, for the most part, with good reason. What can be asked for here is that professors also apply a high level of intellect to the issue of television violence. Both the historical and the scientific evidence needs to be sorted through very carefully. Only then can there be a full understanding of the role of television violence in the lives of modern humans.

People

Television violence deserves a much better reputation among people. As a product of Hollywood studios, it is the product of the largest creative community ever assembled. Although admittedly much of this product is hackneyed, the result of audience complacency and studio shortcuts, much is original. Trite or not, violent scenes are almost always captured with high production values. Although other television genres have risen and fallen, this finely wrought symbolic material has endured for decades and should be owed respect on this count alone.

Television violence survives because of viewers' preferences—not because of what people say they want but because of what they actually view. People who truly want to understand the role of television violence need to critically examine the role of this content, in its many guises, in their own lives. What truly are we viewing and why? Perhaps, to give television violence its due, we need first to respect ourselves more fully, to have greater regard for the complex, semiviolent creatures that we are.

References

A question for Michael Moriarty. (1996, June 30). *New York Times Magazine,* p. 13.

Acland, Charles R. (1995). *Youth, murder, spectacle: The cultural politics of "youth in crises."* Boulder, CO: Westview.

American Family Association. (1990). *Boycott Burger King.* Tupelo, MS: Author.

American Family Association. (1997). *AFA dirty dozen.* Tupelo, MS: Author.

American Medical Association. (1996). *Physicians' guide to media violence.* URL: *.ama-assn.org/ad-com/releases/1996/mvord909.*

American Psychological Association. (1993). *Violence and youth: Psychology's response.* Washington, DC: Author.

Anderson, Daniel R., Collins, Patricia, Schmitt, Kelly L., & Jacobvitz, Robin Smith. (1996). Stressful life events and television viewing. *Communication Research, 23*(3), 243-260.

Andişon, F. Scott. (1977). TV violence and viewer aggression: A cumulation of study results 1956-1976. *Public Opinion Quarterly, 41*(3), 314-331.

Argyle, Michael. (1994). *The psychology of social class.* London: Routledge.

Ashbach, Charles. (1994). Media images and personality development: The inner image and the outer world. In Dolf Zillmann, Jennings Bryant, & Aletha C. Huston (Eds.), *Media, children, and the family: Social scientific, psychodynamic, and clinical perspectives* (pp. 117-130). Hillsdale, NJ: Lawrence Erlbaum.

Atkin, Charles, Greenberg, Bradley, Korzenny, Felix, & McDermott, Steven. (1979). Selective exposure to televised violence. *Journal of Broadcasting, 23,* 5-13.

Auguet, Roland. (1972). *Cruelty and civilization: The Roman games.* London: Allen and Unwin.

Bakhtin, Mikhail. (1968). *Rabelais and his world.* Cambridge: MIT Press.

Ballard, Ian Matheson, Jr. (1995). See no evil, hear no evil: Television violence and the First Amendment. *Virginia Law Review, 81,* 175-222.

Balz, Dan. (1995, April 12). Dole projects dim view of Hollywood. *The Washington Post,* p. A4.

Bandura, Albert, Ross, Dorothea, & Ross, Shelia A. (1963). Imitation of film-mediated aggressive models. *Journal of Abnormal Social Psychology, 66*(3), 3-11.

133

Barish, Jonas. (1991). Shakespearean violence: A preliminary survey. In James Redmond (Ed.), *Violence in drama* (pp. 101-122). Cambridge, UK: Cambridge University Press.

Barnouw, Erik. (1975). *Tube of plenty: The evolution of American television.* New York: Oxford University Press.

Barrett, Myne M. (1994, September 14). Beavis and Butt-head: Social critics or the end of civilization as we know it? *USA Today,* pp. 86-88.

Barthes, Roland. (1985). On the subject of violence. In Roland Barthes (Ed.), *The grain of the voice* (pp. 306-311). New York: Hill & Wang.

Bartky, Sandra Lee. (1991). *Femininity and domination: Studies in the phenomenology of oppression.* New York: Routledge.

Baum, Dan. (1996). *Smoke and mirrors: The war on drugs and the politics of failure.* Boston: Little, Brown.

Belson, William A. (1978). *Television violence and the adolescent boy.* London: Saxon House.

Berliner, David C., & Biddle, Bruce J. (1995). *The manufactured crises: Myths, fraud and the attack on America's public schools.* Reading, MA: Addison-Wesley.

Blank, David M. (1977). The Gerbner Violence Profile. *Journal of Broadcasting, 21,* 273-279, 287-296.

Blau, Judith R. (1989). *The shape of culture: A study of contemporary cultural patterns in the U.S.* New York: Cambridge University Press.

Bok, Sissela. (1998). *Mayhem: Violence as public entertainment.* Reading, MA: Addison-Wesley.

Borden, Richard J. (1975). Witnessed aggression: Influence of an observer's sex and values on aggressive responding. *Journal of Personality and Social Psychology, 31*(3), 567-573.

Bourdieu, Pierre. (1984). *Distinction: A social critique of the judgment of taste.* Cambridge, MA: Harvard University Press.

Bouwman, Harry. (1984). Cultivation analysis: The Dutch case. In Gabriele Melischek, Karl Erik Rosengren, & James Stappers (Eds.), *Cultural indicators: An international symposium* (pp. 407-422). Vienna: Austrian Academy of Sciences.

Boyanowsky, Ehor O. (1977). Film preferences under condition of threat: Whetting the appetite for violence, information, or excitement? *Communication Research, 4,* 133-144.

British Broadcasting Corporation. (1972). *Violence on television: Programme content and viewer perceptions.* London: Author.

Brown, Jane D., & Campbell, Kenneth. (1986). Race and gender in music videos: The same beat but a different drummer. *Journal of Communication, 6,* 94-106.

Bruning, Fred. (1993, August 1). Public enemy No. 1? *Newsday,* pp. 7, 50-51.

Bryant, Jennings. (1989). Viewers' enjoyment of televised sports violence. In Lawrence A. Wenner (Ed.), *Media, sports, and society* (pp. 270-289). Newbury Park, CA: Sage.

Bryant, Jennings, & Zillmann, Dolf. (1984). Using television to alleviate boredom and stress: Selective exposure as a function of induced excitational rates. *Journal of Broadcasting, 22,* 1-20.

Buckingham, David. (1993). *Children talking television: The making of television literacy.* London: Falmer.

Buckingham, David. (1997). Electronic child abuse: Rethinking the media's effects on children. In Martin Barker & Julien Petley (Eds.), *Ill effects: The media/violence debate* (pp. 32-47). London: Routledge.

Butterfield, Fox. (1997, November 16). Report: Crime rate drops dramatically. *Houston Chronicle,* p. 10A.

Bybee, Carl, Robinson, Danny, & Turow, Joseph. (1982, Summer). Determinants of parental guidance of children's television viewing for a special subgroup: Mass media scholars. *Journal of Broadcasting, 3,* 697-710.

Caplan, Richard E. (1985). Violent program content in music video. *Journalism Quarterly, 62,* 144-147.

Carey, James W. (1989). *Communication as culture.* Boston: Unwin Hyman.

Carey, John. (1990, January 12). Revolted by the masses. *New York Times Literary Supplement,* pp. 34, 44.

Cater, Douglass, & Strickland, Stephen. (1975). *TV violence and the child: The evolution and fate of the surgeon general's report.* New York: Russell Sage.

Cawelti, John G. (1975). Myths of violence in American popular culture. *Critical Inquiry, 1*(3), 521-541.

Centerwall, Brandon S. (1989). Exposure to television as a cause of violence. In George Comstock (Ed.), *Public communication and behavior* (Vol. 2, pp. 1-58). Orlando, FL: Academic Press.

Centerwall, Brandon S. (1992, June 10). Television and violence: The scale of the problem and where to go from here. *Journal of the American Medical Association, 267*(22), 3059-3063.

Centerwall, Brandon S. (1993, Spring). Television and violent crime. *The Public Interest,* 56-71.

Chagnon, Napoleon A. (1983). *Yanomamo: The fierce people.* New York: Henry Holt.

Charters, W. W. (1933). *Motion pictures and youth.* New York: Macmillan.

Chesnais, Jean-Claude. (1992). The history of violence: Homicide and suicide through the ages. *International Social Science Journal, 44*(2), 217-234.

Clark, David G., & Blankenburg, William B. (1972). Trends in violent content in selected mass media. In George A. Comstock & Eli A. Rubinstein (Eds.), *Television and social behavior: Vol. 1. Media content and control* (pp. 188-243). Washington, DC: Government Printing Office.

Clifford, Brian R., Gunter, Barrie, & McAleer, Jill L. (1995). *Television and children: Program evaluation, comprehension and impact.* Mahwah, NJ: Lawrence Erlbaum.

Coates, Brian, Pusser, H. Ellison, & Goodman, Irene. (1976). The influence of *Sesame Street* and *Mister Rogers' Neighborhood* on children's social behavior in the preschool. *Child Development, 47,* 138-144.

Coffin, Thomas E., & Tuchman, Sam. (1972, Winter). Rating television programs for violence: A comparison of five surveys. *Journal of Broadcasting, 17,* 3-20.

Cohen, Stanley. (1972). *Folk devils and moral panics: The creation of the Mods and Rockers.* London: MacGibbon & Kee.

Cole, Jeffery. (1996). *The UCLA television violence monitoring report.* Los Angeles: University of California, Los Angeles, Center for Communication Policy.

Comisky, Paul, Bryant, Jennings, & Zillmann, Dolf. (1977). Commentary as a substitute for action. *Journal of Communication, 27*(3), 150-153.

Comstock, George. (1989). *The evolution of American television.* Newbury Park, CA: Sage.

Comstock, George, & Paik, Haejung. (1991). *Television and the American child.* San Diego: Academic Press.

Comstock, George, & Strasburger, Victor C. (1990). Deceptive appearances: Television violence and aggressive behavior. *Journal of Adolescent Health Care, 11,* 31-44.

Cook, Thomas C., Kendzierski, Deborah A., & Thomas, Stephen U. (1983). The implicit assumptions of television research: An analysis of the 1982 NIMA Report on Television and Behavior. *Public Opinion Quarterly, 47,* 161-201.

Cooper, Cynthia A. (1996). *Violence on television: Congressional inquiry, public criticism and industry response—A policy analysis.* Lanham, MD: University Press of America.

Copeland, Gary A., & Slater, Dan. (1985). Television, fantasy and vicarious catharsis. *Critical Studies in Mass Communication, 2,* 352-362.

Corn-Revere, Robert. (1995, Winter). Television violence and the limits of voluntarism. *Yale Journal on Regulation, 12,* 187-205.

Cowan, Geoffrey. (1979). *See no evil: The backstage battle over sex and violence on television.* New York: Simon & Schuster.

Crabb, Peter B., & Goldstein, Jeffrey H. (1991). The social psychology of watching sports: From Illium to living room. In Jennings Bryant & Dolf Zillmann (Eds.), *Responding to the screen: Reception and reaction processes* (pp. 355-372). Hillsdale, NJ: Lawrence Erlbaum.

Csikszentmihalyl, Mihaly, & Kubey, Robert. (1981). Television and the rest of life: A systematic comparison of subjective experience. *Public Opinion Quarterly, 45,* 317-328.

Cumberbatch, Guy, & Howitt, Dennis. (1989). *A measure of uncertainty: The effects of the mass media.* London: J. Libbey.

Cutler, Blayne. (1990, November). Where does the free time go? *American Demographics,* pp. 36-38.

Daly, Martin, & Wilson, Margo. (1988). *Homicide.* New York: Aldine.

Davis, David Brion. (1986). *From homicide to slavery: Studies in American culture.* New York: Oxford University Press.

Dawson, Doyne. (1996). *The origins of Western warfare: Militarism and morality in the ancient world.* Boulder, CO: Westview.

de Forest, Lee. (1950). *The father of radio: The autobiography of Lee de Forest.* Chicago: Wilcox & Follett.

deMause, Lloyd. (1974). *The history of childhood.* New York: Harper.

DePalma, Anthony. (1996, December 30). Canadian parents test limits on TV access. *New York Times,* pp. C9, C14.

Dixon, Norman F. (1971). *Subliminal perception.* London: McGraw-Hill.

Doctors push for less violence on TV. (1995, June 9). *Houston Chronicle,* p. A16.

Dominick, Joseph R. (1973). Crime and law enforcement on prime time television. *Public Opinion Quarterly, 37,* 241-250.

Doob, Anthony N., & Macdonald, Glenn E. (1979). Television viewing and fear of victimization. *Journal of Personality and Social Psychology, 37*(2), 170-179.

Drabman, Ronald S., & Thomas, Margaret Hanratty. (1974a). Does media violence increase children's toleration of real-life aggression? *Developmental Psychology, 10,* 418-421.

Drabman, Ronald S., & Thomas, Margaret Hanratty. (1974b). Exposure to filmed violence and children's toleration of real-life aggression. *Personality and Social Psychology Bulletin, 1,* 198-199.

Drabman, Ronald S., & Thomas, Margaret Hanratty. (1976). Does watching violence on television cause apathy? *Pediatrics, 57,* 329-331.

Duke, Steven B., & Gross, Albert. (1993). *America's longest war: Rethinking our tragic crusade against drugs.* New York: Tarcher/Putnam.

Dunning, Eric. (1993). Sport in the civilizing process: Aspects of the development of modern sport. In Eric G. Dunning, Joseph A. Maguire, & Robert E. Pearlon (Eds.), *The sports process: A comparative and developmental approach* (pp. 39-70). Champaign, IL: Human Kinetics.

Dupont, Florence. (1989). *Daily life in ancient Rome.* Oxford, UK: Blackwell.

Durkin, Kevin. (1985). *Television, sex roles and children: A developmental social psychological account.* Milton Keynes, UK: Open University Press.

Eckberg, Douglas Lee. (1995, February). Estimates of early twentieth-century U.S. homicide rates: An econometric forecasting approach. *Demography, 32,* 1-16.

Eggerton, John. (1994, January 31). Hundt hits television violence. *Broadcasting and Cable,* pp. 10, 12.

Eisenstein, Elizabeth L. (1983). *The printing revolution in early modern Europe.* Cambridge, UK: Cambridge University Press.

Elder, Charles R. (1994). *The grammar of the unconscious.* University Park: Pennsylvania State University Press.

Elias, Norbert. (1978). *The civilizing process: Vol. 1. The history of manners.* New York: Pantheon. (Original work published 1939)

Elias, Norbert. (1982). *The civilizing process: Vol. 2, Power and civility.* New York: Pantheon. (Original work published 1939)

Elias, Norbert, & Dunning, Eric. (1986). *Quest for excitement: Sport and leisure in the civilizing process.* Oxford, UK: Basil Blackwell.

Ember, Carol R. (1978). Myths about hunter-gatherers. *Ethnology, 27,* 439-448.

Eron, Leonard D. (1963). Relationship of television viewing habits and aggressive behavior in children. *Journal of Abnormal and Social Psychology, 67,* 193-196.

Eron, Leonard D. (1987). The development of aggressive behavior from the perspective of a developing behaviorism. *American Psychologist, 43*(5), 435-442.

Eron, Leonard D. (1993, Summer). No doubt about it, media violence affects behavior. *Media and Values, 64,* 14.

Eron, Leonard D. (1994). Testimony. In U.S. Senate Subcommittee on the Constitution and Subcommittee on Juvenile Justice, *Hearing on the implementation of the Television Program Improvement Act of 1990, June 8, 1993* (pp. 95-98). Washington, DC: Government Printing Office.

Eron, Leonard D. (1995). Media violence. *Pediatric Annals, 24*(2), 1-3.

Eron, Leonard D. (1996). Testimony. In U.S. Senate Committee on Commerce, Science, and Transportation, *Hearing on television violence, July 12, 1995* (pp. 227-232). Washington, DC: Government Printing Office.

Eron, Leonard D., Huesmann, L. Rowell, Lefkowitz, Monroe M., & Walder, Leopold O. (1972). Does television violence cause aggression? *American Psychologist, 27,* 253-263.

Farkas, Steve, & Johnson, Jean. (1997). *Kids these days: What Americans really think about the next generation.* New York: Public Agenda.

FBI reports crime decrease. (1997, November 24). *Houston Chronicle,* p. 7A.

Fenigstein, Allan. (1979). Does aggression cause a preference for viewing media violence? *Journal of Personality and Social Psychology, 37*(12), 2307-2317.

Ferdinand, Theodore N. (1967, July). The criminal patterns of Boston since 1849. *American Journal of Sociology, 73,* 84-99.

Feshbach, Seymour, & Singer, Robert D. (1971). *Television and aggression: An experimental field study.* San Francisco: Jossey-Bass.

Fiske, John. (1989). *Understanding popular culture.* Boston: Unwin Hyman.

Fiske, John, & Hartley, John. (1978). *Reading television.* London: Methuen.

Fitch, Marguerite, Huston, Althea C., & Wright, John C. (1993). From television forms to genre schemata: Children's perception of television reality. In Gordon L. Berry & Joy Keiko Asamen (Eds.), *Children and television: Images in a changing sociocultural world* (pp. 38-52). Newbury Park, CA: Sage.

Fowler, Bridget. (1997). *Pierre Bourdieu and cultural theory.* Thousand Oaks, CA: Sage.

Fowles, Jib. (1982). *Television viewers vs. media snobs: What TV does for people.* New York: Stein & Day.

Fowles, Jib. (1985). Could television violence be good for children? In U.S. Senate Subcommittee on Juvenile Justice, *Hearing on media violence, October 25, 1984* (pp. 58-66). Washington, DC: Government Printing Office.

Fowles, Jib. (1992). *Why viewers watch: A reappraisal of television's effects.* Newbury Park, CA: Sage.

Fowles, Jib. (1996). *Advertising and popular culture.* Thousand Oaks, CA: Sage.

Fowles, Jib. (1997, April). *On the periodicity of the television violence controversy.* Paper presented at the annual meeting of the Popular Culture Association, San Antonio, TX.

Fraser, John. (1974). *Violence in the arts.* Cambridge, UK: Cambridge University Press.

Freedman, Jonathan L. (1984). Effects of television violence on aggression. *Psychological Bulletin, 96,* 227-246.

Freedman, Jonathan L. (1986). Television violence and aggression: A rejoinder. *Psychological Bulletin, 100,* 372-373.

Freedman, Jonathan L. (1988). Television violence and aggression: What the research shows. In Stuart Oskamp (Ed.), *Television as a social issue* (pp. 144-162). Newbury Park, CA: Sage.

Freud, Sigmund. (1960). *Jokes and their relation to the unconscious* (James Strachey, Trans.). New York: Norton. (Original work published 1905)

Friedrich, Lynette Kohn, & Stein, Aletha Huston. (1973). Aggression and prosocial television programs and the natural behavior of preschool children. *Monographs of the Society for Research in Child Development, 38*(4, Serial No. 151).

Fuller, Ray. (1977). Uses and abuses of canned laughter. In Antony Chapman & Hugh C. Foot (Eds.), *It's a funny thing, humor* (pp. 395-398). Oxford, UK: Pergamon.

Futrell, Alison. (1997). *Blood in the arena: The spectacle of Roman power.* Austin: University of Texas Press.

Gabriel, Richard A., & Metz, Karen S. (1992). *A short history of war: The evolution of warfare and weapons.* Carlisle Barracks, PA: U.S. Army War College.

Gadow, Kenneth D., & Sprafkin, Joyce. (1989). Field experiments of television violence with children: Evidence for an environmental hazard? *Pediatrics, 83*(3), 399-405.

Gans, Herbert J. (1974). *Popular culture and high culture: An analysis and evaluation of taste.* New York: Basic Books.

Gauntlett, David. (1995). *Moving experiences: Understanding television's influences and effects.* London: J. Libbey.

Gerbner, George. (1972). Violence in television drama: Trends in symbolic functions. In George A. Comstock & Eli A. Rubinstein (Eds.), *Television social behavior: Vol. 1. Media content and control* (pp. 28-187). Washington, DC: Government Printing Office.

Gerbner, George. (1993). Testimony. In U.S. House of Representatives, Subcommittee on Crime and Criminal Justice, *Hearing on violence on television, December 15, 1992* (pp. 64-67). Washington, DC: Government Printing Office.

Gerbner, George. (1994, November). *Desensitization toward violence in our society as a result of violence in the media.* Paper presented at the International Conference on Violence in the Media, New York.

Gerbner, George, & Gross, Larry. (1976a). Living with television: The violence profile. *Journal of Communication, 26*(2), 173-199.

Gerbner, George, & Gross, Larry. (1976b, April). The scary world of TV's heavy viewer. *Psychology Today,* pp. 41-45, 89.

Gerbner, George, Gross, Larry, Eleey, Michael F., Jackson-Beeck, Marilyn, & Signorielli, Nancy. (1977). TV violence profile No. 8: The highlights. *Journal of Communication, 27*(2), 171-180.

Gerbner, George, Gross, Larry, Jackson-Beeck, Marilyn, Jeffries-Fox, Suzanne, & Signorielli, Nancy. (1978). Cultural indicators: Violence profile No. 9. *Journal of Communication, 28*(2), 176-207.

Gerbner, George, Gross, Larry, Morgan, Michael, & Signorielli, Nancy. (1980). The "mainstreaming" of America: Violence profile No. 11. *Journal of Communication, 30*(3), 10-29.

Gerbner, George, Gross, Larry, Morgan, Michael, & Signorielli, Nancy. (1982). Charting the mainstreaming: Television's contributions to political orientations. *Journal of Communication, 22*(2), 100-127.

Gerbner, George, Gross, Larry, Morgan, Michael, & Signorielli, Nancy. (1986). Living with television: The dynamics of the cultivation process. In Jennings Bryant & Dolf Zillman (Eds.), *Perspectives on media effects* (pp. 17-40). Hillsdale, NJ: Lawrence Erlbaum.

Gerbner, George, Morgan, Michael, & Signorielli, Nancy. (1995). Violence on television: The Cultural Indicators Project. *Journal of Broadcasting and Electronic Media, 39*(2), 278-283.

Gerbner, George, Signorielli, Nancy, Morgan, Michael, & Jackson-Beeck, Marilyn. (1979). The demonstration of power: Violence profile No. 10. *Journal of Communication, 29,* 177-196.

Gilbert, James. (1986). *A cycle of outrage: America's reaction to the juvenile delinquent in the 1950s.* New York: Oxford University Press.

Giroux, Henry. (1988). *Teachers as intellects.* New York: Bergin & Garvey.

Gitlin, Todd. (1994, February 23). The symbolic crusade against media violence is a confession of despair. *Chronicle of Higher Education,* p. B5.

Goode, Erick, & Ben-Yehuda, Nachman. (1994). *Moral panics: The social construction of deviance.* Oxford, UK: Blackwell.

Gore, Tipper. (1985). Testimony. In U.S. Senate Committee on Commerce, Science, and Transportation, *Hearing on the content of music and the lyrics of records, September 19, 1985* (pp. 12-13). Washington, DC: Government Printing Office.

Gould, Stephen Jay. (1981). *The mismeasure of man.* New York: Norton.

Gould, Thomas. (1991). The uses of violence in drama. In James Redmond (Ed.), *Violence in drama* (pp. 1-12). Cambridge, UK: Cambridge University Press.

Gowen, Anne. (1993, April 15). Tipper Gore quits PMRC. *Rolling Stone,* 20.

Greenberg, Bradley S. (1980). *Life on television: Content analysis of U.S. TV drama.* Norwood, NJ: Ablex.

Greenberg, Bradley S., & Gordon, Thomas F. (1972). Perceptions of violence in television programs: Critics and the public. In George A. Comstock & Eli A. Rubinstein (Eds.), *Television and social behavior: Vol. 1. Media content and control* (pp. 244-258). Washington, DC: Government Printing Office.

Greenberg, Bradley S., & Wotring, C. Edward. (1974). Television violence and its potential for aggressive driving behaviors. *Journal of Broadcasting, 18*(4), 473-480.

Greenhouse, Linda. (1978, August 9). Lawsuit dismissed against NBC-TV. *New York Times,* p. 8.

Grixti, Joe. (1985). Mass media violence and the study of behavior. *Educational Studies, 11,* 61-76.

Gunter, Barrie. (1980). The cathartic potential of television drama. *Bulletins of the British Psychological Society, 33,* 448-450.

Gunter, Barrie. (1985). *Dimensions of television violence.* New York: St. Martin's.

Gunter, Barrie. (1988, Spring). The importance of studying viewers' perceptions of television violence. *Current Psychology: Research and Reviews, 7,* 26-42.

Gunter, Barrie, & McAteer, Jill. (1990). *Children and television: The one-eyed monster?* New York: Routledge.

Gurr, Ted Robert. (1989). Historical trends in violent crime: Europe and the United States. In Ted Robert Gurr (Ed.), *Violence in America: Vol. 1. The history of crime* (pp. 21-54). Newbury Park, CA: Sage.

Guttmann, Allen. (1986). *Sports spectators.* New York: Columbia University Press.

Guttman, Monika. (1994, May 9). A kinder, gentler Hollywood. *U.S. News & World Report,* pp. 39-46.

Haberstroh, Jack. (1994). *Ice cube sex: The truth about subliminal advertising.* Notre Dame, IN: Cross Cultural.

Hagell, Ann, & Newburn, Tim. (1994). *Young offenders and the media: Viewing habits and preferences.* London: Policy Studies Institute.

Hanmer, Jalna, & Saunders, Shelia. (1983). Blowing the cover of the protective male: A community study of violence to women. In Eva Gamarnikow, David Morgan, June Purvis, & Daphne Taylorson (Eds.), *The public and the private* (pp. 28-46). London: Heinemann.

Hapkiewicz, Walter. (1979). Children's reactions to cartoon violence. *Journal of Clinical Child Psychology, 8,* 30-34.

Harding, Sandra. (1991). *Whose science? Whose knowledge?* Ithaca, NY: Cornell University Press.

Harris, Mary B. (1992). Television viewing, aggression, and ethnicity. *Psychological Reports, 70*(3), 137-138.

Hartnagel, Timothy F., Teevan, James J., Jr., & McIntyre, Jennie J. (1975). Television violence and violent behavior. *Social Form, 54*(2), 341-351.

Harvey, Susan E., Sprafkin, Joyce N., & Rubinstein, Eli. (1979). Prime-time television: A profile of aggressive and prosocial behaviors. *Journal of Broadcasting, 23*(2), 179-189.

Hattemer, Barbara. (1994, July). Cause and violent effect: Media and our youth. *The World and I*, pp. 358-369.

Hawkins, Robert P. (1977). The dimensional structure of children's perceptions of television reality. *Communication Research, 4*(3), 299-320.

Hawkins, Robert P., & Pingree, Suzanne. (1986). Activity in the effects of television on children. In Jennings Bryant & Dolf Zillmann (Eds.), *Perspectives on media effects* (pp. 233-250). Hillsdale, NJ: Lawrence Erlbaum.

Head, Stanley W. (1954). Content analysis of television drama programs. *Quarterly of Film, Radio and Television, 9*, 175-194.

Hearold, Susan. (1986). A synthesis of 1043 effects of television upon social behavior. In George Comstock (Ed.), *Public communication and behavior: Vol. 1* (pp. 65-133). New York: Academic Press.

Heath, Linda, Kruttschnitt, Candace, & Ward, David. (1986). Television and violent criminal behavior. *Violence and Victims, 1*, 177-190.

Hebdige, Dick. (1988). *Hiding in the light: On images and things.* New York: Routledge.

Hedinsson, Elias, & Windahl, Sven. (1984). Cultivation analysis: A Swedish illustration. In Gabrielle Melischek, Karl Erik Rosengren, & James Stappers (Eds.), *Cultural indicators: An international symposium* (pp. 389-406). Vienna: Austrian Academy of Science.

Hennigan, Karen M., DelRosario, Marilyn L., Heath, Linda, Cook, Thomas D., Wharton, J. D., & Calder, Bobby J. (1982). Impact of the introduction of television on crime in the United States: Empirical findings and theoretical implications. *Journal of Personality and Social Psychology, 42*, 461-477.

Hirsch, Paul. (1980). The scary world of the nonviewer and other anomalies: A reanalysis of Gerbner et al.'s findings on cultivation analysis: Part 1. *Communication Research, 7*(4), 403-456.

Hirsch, Paul. (1981). On not learning from one's mistakes: A reanalysis of Gerbner et al.'s findings on cultivation analysis: Part 2. *Communication Research, 8*, 3-37.

Hirt, Edward R., Zillmann, Dolf, Erickson, Grant A., & Kennedy, Chris. (1992). Costs and benefits of allegiance: Changes in fans' self-ascribed competencies after team victory or defeat. *Journal of Personality and Social Psychology, 63*(5), 724-738.

Hodge, Robert, & Tripp, David. (1986). *Children and television: A semiotic approach.* Stanford, CA: Stanford University Press.

Holt, Richard. (1989). *Sport and the British: A modern history.* Oxford, UK: Clarendon.

Holz, Robert. (1971, September). *Television violence: A paper tiger?* (CRC Report No. 57).

Hopkins, Keith. (1983). *Death and renewal.* Cambridge, UK: Cambridge University Press.

Horton, Robert W., & Santogrossi, David. (1978). The effect of adult commentary on reducing the influence of televised violence. *Personality and Social Psychology Bulletin, 4*(2), 337-340.

Howitt, Dennis, & Cumberbatch, Guy. (1974). Audience perceptions of violent television content. *Communication Research, 1,* 204-227.

Huesmann, L. Rowell, & Eron, Leonard O. (1986). *Television and the aggressive child: A cross-national comparison.* Hillsdale, NJ: Lawrence Erlbaum.

Huesmann, L. Rowell, Eron, Leonard D., Lefkowitz, Monroe, & Walder, Leopold. (1984). Stability of aggression over time and generations. *Developmental Psychology, 20*(6), 1120-1134.

Hughes, Michael. (1980). The fruits of cultivation analysis: A reexamination of some effects of television watching. *Public Opinion Quarterly, 44,* 287-302.

Huston, Aletha. (1992). *Big world, small screen: The role of television in American society.* Lincoln: University of Nebraska Press.

Irwin, Barbara J., & Cassata, Mary. (1994, October). *The Ronnie Zamora story: Why TV was not to blame.* Paper presented at the International Conference on Violence in the Media, New York.

Jackson-Beeck, Marilyn, & Sobal, Jeff. (1980). The social world of heavy television viewers. *Journal of Broadcasting, 24,* 5-11.

Jaglom, Leona M., & Gardner, Howard. (1981). Decoding the worlds of television. *Studies in Visual Communication, 7,* 33-47.

Johnnysee. (1995, August 28). Interview with Michael Moriarty. In *eWorld/Tinsel Talk: All about filmmaking.* URL: *.concentric.net/~~-stealth/mm* (accessed February 27, 1997).

Johnson, Eric A., & Monkkonen, Eric H. (Eds.). (1996). *The civilization of crime: Violence in town and country since the Middle Ages.* Urbana: University of Illinois Press.

Johnston, Deirdre D. (1995, June). Adolescents' motivations for viewing graphic horror. *Human Communication Research, 21*(4), 522-552.

Jones, Landon Y. (1980). *Great expectations: America and the baby boom generation.* New York: Coward, McCann, & Geoghegan.

Jones, Laurie. (1995, February 20). AMA among groups supporting TV anti-violence bill. *American Medical News, 38*(7), 6.

Jowett, Garth. (1976). *Film: The democratic art.* Boston: Little, Brown.

Jowett, Garth S., Jarvie, Ian C., & Fuller, Kathryn H. (1996). *Children and the movies: Media influences and the Payne Fund controversy.* New York: Cambridge University Press.

Joy, Lesley A., Kimball, Meredith M., & Zabrack, Merle L. (1986). Television and children's aggressive behavior. In Tannis MacBeth Williams (Ed.), *The impact of television: A natural experiment in three communities* (pp. 303-360). Orlando, FL: Academic Press.

Jung, C. G. (1957). *The undiscovered self.* Boston: Little, Brown.

Kalbacker, Warren. (1994, July). 20 questions: Michael Moriarty. *Playboy, 41*(7), 138-142.

Kalis, Pamela, & Neuendorf, Kimberly. (1989). Aggressive cue prominence and gender participation in MTV. *Journalism Quarterly, 66,* 148-154.

Kaplan, Robert M., & Singer, Robert D. (1976). Television violence and viewer aggression: A reexamination of the evidence. *Journal of Social Issues, 32*(4), 35-70.

Katz, Jon. (1994, March 24). Animated arguments. *Rolling Stone,* p. 45.

Keeley, Lawrence H. (1996). *War before civilization: The myth of the peaceful savage.* New York: Oxford University Press.

Key, Wilson B. (1989). *Age of manipulation.* New York: Henry Holt.

Kids' doctors call on TV biz. (1995, June 9). *Hollywood Reporter,* p. 6.

Kolbert, Elizabeth. (1994a, August 5). Study reports TV is considerably more violent despite outcry. *New York Times,* p. A13.

Kolbert, Elizabeth. (1994b, December 14). Television gets closer look as a factor in real violence. *New York Times,* pp. A1, A13.

Kolbert, Elizabeth. (1995, August 20). Americans despair of popular culture. *New York Times,* pp. H1, H23.

Kramer, Samuel Noah. (1963). *The Sumerians: Their history, culture, and character.* Chicago: University of Chicago Press.

Kubey, Robert, & Csikszentmihalyi, Mihaly. (1990). *Television and the quality of life.* Hillsdale, NJ: Lawrence Erlbaum.

Kurtz, Howard. (1997, August 12). The crime spree on network news. *The Washington Post,* pp. D1, D6.

Lagerspetz, Kirsti M. J., Wahlroos, Carita, & Wendelin, Carola. (1978). Facial expressions of pre-school children while watching television violence. *Scandinavian Journal of Psychology, 19,* 213-222.

Lamont, Michele. (1992). *Money, morals and manners: The culture of the French and American upper-middle class.* Chicago: University of Chicago Press.

Lee, Richard B. (1979). *The !Kung San: Men, women, and work in a foraging society.* Cambridge, UK: Cambridge University Press.

Levin, Stephen R., Petros, Thoman U., & Petralla, Florence W. (1982). Preschoolers awareness of television advertising. *Child Development, 51,* 933-937.

Lichter, S. Robert, Lichter, Linda S., & Rothman, Stanley. (1994). *Prime time: How TV portrays American culture.* Washington, DC: Regency.

Lieberman, Carole. (1996). Sweep violence off of television and off our streets. URL: *.newstalk.com/gpp/lieber* (accessed September 11, 1996).

Liebert, Robert M., & Sprafkin, Joyce. (1988). *The early window: Effects of television on children and youths.* New York: Pergamon.

Link, David. (1994, March). Facts about fiction: In defense of TV violence. *Reason, 25*(10), 22-26.

Linz, Daniel, Donnerstein, Edward, & Adams, Steven M. (1989). Physiological desensitization and judgments about female victims of violence. *Human Communication, 15,* 509-522.

Longino, Helen E. (1990). *Science as social knowledge: Values and objectivity in scientific inquiry.* Princeton, NJ: Princeton University Press.

Lopiparo, Jerome J. (1977, April). Aggression on TV could be helping out children. *Intellect, 105*(2583), 345-346.

Luke, Carmen. (1990). *Constructing the child viewer: A history of the American discourse on television and children.* New York: Praeger.

Lyle, Jack, & Hoffman, Heidi R. (1972). Children's use of television and other media. In Eli A. Rubinstein, George A. Comstock, & John P. Murray (Eds.), *Television and social behavior: Vol. 4. Television in day-to-day life: Patterns of use* (pp. 129-256). Washington, DC: Government Printing Office.

Lynn, Richard, Hampson, Susan, & Agahi, Edwina. (1989). Television violence and aggression: A genotype-environment, correlation and interaction theory. *Social Behavior and Personality, 17*(2), 143-164.

Mackey-Kollis, Susan, & Hahn, Dan. (1994, Winter). Who's to blame for America's drug problem? The search for scapegoats in the "war on drugs." *Communication Quarterly, 42,* 1-20.

MacLeod, Jay. (1987). *Ain't no making it.* Boulder, CO: Westview.

Malcolmson, Robert. (1982). Popular recreations under attack. In Bernard Waites, Tony Bennett, & Graham Martin (Eds.), *Popular culture past and present* (pp. 20-46). London: Croom Helm.

Mangan, Katherine S. (1997, September 26). Professor's comments on affirmative action inflame a campus. *Chronicle of Higher Education,* pp. A33-A34.

Masters, John C., Ford, Martin E., & Arend, Richard A. (1983). Children's strategies for controlling affective responses to aversive social experience. *Motivation and Emotion, 7,* 103-116.

McAvoy, Kim, & Coe, Steve. (1993, October 25). TV rocked by Reno ultimatum. *Broadcasting & Cable,* pp. 6, 14.

McCormack, Thelma. (1993, November). TV and the child savers. *Canadian Forum,* pp. 20-22.

McDaniel, Stephen W., Hart, Sandra H., & McNeal, James U. (1982). Subliminal stimulation as a marketing tool. *Mid-Atlantic Journal of Business, 20,* 41-48.

McGuire, William J. (1986). The myth of massive media impact: Savagings and salvagings. In George Comstock (Ed.), *Public communication and behavior* (pp. 175-259). Orlando, FL: Academic Press.

McKnight, David. (1986). Fighting in an Australian aboriginal supercamp. In David Riches (Ed.), *The anthropology of violence* (pp. 136-163). Oxford, UK: Basil Blackwell.

Messner, Steven F. (1986). Television violence and violent crime. *Social Problems, 32*(3), 218-235.

Mifflin, Lawrie. (1998, January 14). Study finds a decline in TV network violence. *New York Times,* p. B7.

Milavsky, J. Ronald, Kessler, Ronald, Stipp, Horst, & Rubens, William S. (1982). *Television and aggression: A panel study.* New York: Academic Press.

Milgram, Stanley, & Shotland, R. Lance. (1973). *Television and antisocial behavior: Field experiments.* New York: Academic Press.

Minow, Newton N., & LaMay, Craig L. (1995). *Abandoned in the wasteland: Children, television and the First Amendment.* New York: Hill & Wang.

Mitchell, Alison. (1996, January 24). Clinton offers challenges to nation. *New York Times,* pp. A1, A12.

Molitor, Fred, & Hirsch, Kenneth William. (1994). Children's toleration of real life aggression after exposure to media violence: A replication of the Drabman and Thomas studies. *Child Study Journal, 24*(3), 191-207.

Molotsky, Irvin. (1987, November 6). Gores see Hollywood leaders on issue of lewd rock lyrics. *New York Times,* p. A12.

Monkkonen, Eric. H. (1981). *Police in urban America 1860-1920.* Cambridge, UK: Cambridge University Press.

Morality in Media. (n.d.). *TV: The world's greatest mind-bender.* New York: Author.

Morgan, John. (1979). *The life and adventures of William Buckley: Thirty-two years a wanderer amongst the aborigines.* Sussex, UK: Caliban. (Original work published 1852)

Morgan, Michael. (1987). Television, sex-role attitudes, and sex-role behavior. *Journal of Early Adolescence, 7*(3), 269-282.

Morley, David. (1986). *Family television: Cultural power and domestic leisure.* London: Comedia.

Mortimer, Jeffrey. (1994, October). How TV violence hits kids. *Education Digest, 60,* 16-19.

Most believe TV violence begets crime. (1993, December 19). *Houston Post,* p. 26.

Mother blames MTV cartoon cretins for fatal fire. (1993, October 9). *Galveston Daily News,* p. 3A.

Mourlet, Michael. (1991). In defense of violence. In Christine Gledhill (Ed.), *Stardom: Industry of desire* (pp. 233-236). New York: Routledge.

MTV moves *Beavis and Butt-head.* (1993, October 25). *Broadcasting and Cable,* p. 29.

Mueller, Charles W., Donnerstein, Edward, & Hallam, John. (1983). Violent films and prosocial behavior. *Journal of Personality and Social Psychology, 9,* 83-89.

Murdock, Graham. (1997). Reservoirs of dogma: An archaeology of popular anxieties. In Martin Barker and Julien Petley (Eds.), *Ill effects: The media/violence debate* (pp. 67-86). London: Routledge.

Murphee, Randall. (1993, July). Murder, mayhem and morality. *AFA Journal,* p. 5.

Murray, Randall L., Cole, Richard R., & Fedler, Fred. (1970). Teenagers and TV violence: How they rate and view it. *Journalism Quarterly, 47*(2), 247-255.

National Foundation to Improve Television. (1996). *Mission statement.* Boston: Author.

National Television Violence Study: Vol. 1. (1997). Thousand Oaks, CA: Sage.

National Television Violence Study: Vol. 2. (1998). Thousand Oaks, CA: Sage.

Neuman, W. Russell. (1982). Television and American culture: The mass medium and the pluralist audience. *Public Opinion Quarterly, 46,* 471-487.

Neumann, Susan B. (1991). *Literacy in the television age: The myth of TV effect.* Norwood, NJ: Ablex.

Newcomb, Horace. (1978). Assessing the violence profiles of Gerbner and Gross: A humanistic critique and suggestion. *Communication Research, 5*(3), 264-282.

New York Times/CBS News. (1996). *Economic Insecurity Poll II.* New York: Author.

Nikken, Peter, & Peeters, Allerd L. (1988). Children's perceptions of television reality. *Journal of Broadcasting and Electronic Media, 32,* 441-452.

Noble, Grant. (1975). *Children in front of the small screen.* London: Constable/Sage.

Paik, Haejung, & Comstock, George. (1994). The effects of television violence on anti-social behavior: A meta-analysis. *Communication Research, 28*(4), 516-546.

Palmer, Patricia. (1986). *The lively audience: A study of children around the TV set.* Sydney: Allen and Unwin.

Pearson, Geoffrey. (1983). *Hooligan: A history of respectable fears.* London: Macmillan.

Pearson, Geoffrey. (1984). Failing standards: A short, sharp history of moral decline. In Martin Barker (Ed.), *Video nasties: Freedom and censorship in the media* (pp. 88-103). London: Pluto.

Petley, Julien. (1997). Us and them. In Martin Barker & Julien Petley (Eds.), *Ill effects: The media/violence debate* (pp. 87-101). London: Routledge.

Phillips, Phil, & Robie, Joan Hake. (1988). *Horror and violence: The deadly duo in the media*. Lancaster, PA: Starburst.

Piepe, Anthony, Crouch, Joyce, & Emerson, Miles. (1977). Violence and television. *New Society, 41,* 536-538.

Plass, Paul. (1995). *The game of death in ancient Rome: Arena sport and political suicide*. Madison: University of Wisconsin Press.

Postman, Neil. (1985). *Amusing ourselves to death: Public discourse in the age of show business*. New York: Viking.

Potter, W. James. (1991). The linearity assumption in cultivation research. *Human Communication Review, 17,* 562-584.

Potter, W. James. (1994). *Cultivation theory and research* (Journalism Monographs No. 147). Columbia, SC: Association for Education in Journalism and Mass Communication.

Potter, W. James, Vaughan, Misha, & Warren, Ron. (1995). How real is the portrayal of aggression in television entertainment programming? *Journal of Broadcasting and Electronic Media, 22,* 496-516.

Potter, W. James, & Ware, William. (1987). An analysis of the context of antisocial acts on prime-time television. *Communication Research, 14,* 27-46.

Powell, Elwin H. (1966). Crime as a function of anomie. *Journal of Criminal Law, Criminology, and Police Science, 57,* 161-171.

Preiss, Bob. (1997). Michael Moriarty. URL: *.speakers.com/spkr1076* (accessed February 27, 1997).

Prison population surge ebbs. (1997, June 23). *Houston Chronicle,* p. 3A.

Proffitt, Steve. (1994, March 6). Michael Moriarty: When fighting against censorship means defending television violence. *Los Angeles Times,* p. M3.

Rabinovitch, Martin S., McLean, Malcolm S., Jr., Markham, James W., & Talbott, Albert D. (1972). Children's violence perception as a function of television violence. In George A. Comstock, Eli A. Rubinstein, & John P. Murray (Eds.), *Television and social behavior: Vol. 5. Television's effects: Further explorations* (pp. 231-252). Washington, DC: Government Printing Office.

Rader, Benjamin G. (1984). *In its own image: How television has transformed sports*. New York: Free Press.

Roberts, Churchill. (1981). Children's and parents' television viewing and perceptions of violence. *Journalism Quarterly, 58,* 556-564, 581.

Robinson, John P. (1981). Television and leisure time: A new scenario. *Journal of Communication, 31,* 120-130.

Romanowski, William D. (1996). *Pop culture wars: Religion and the role of entertainment in American life*. Downers Grove, IL: InterVarsity Press.

Rosenberg, Mark L., O'Carroll, Patrick W., & Powell, Kenneth E. (1992, June 10). Let's be clear: Violence is a public health problem. *Journal of the American Medical Association, 267*(22), 3071-3072.

Rosenstiel, Thomas B. (1993, March 25). Views on TV violence reflect generation gap. *Los Angeles Times,* p. F2.

Rosenthal, Robert, & Fode, Kermit L. (1961). The problem of experimenter-outcome bias. In Donald P. Ray (Ed.), *Series research in social psychology* (No. 8, pp. 9-14). Washington, DC: National Institute of Social and Behavioral Science.

Rosnow, Ralph L., & Rosenthal, Robert. (1997). *People studying people: Artifacts and ethics in behavioral research.* New York: Freeman.

Rowland, Willard D., Jr. (1983). *The politics of TV violence: Policy uses of communication research.* Beverly Hills, CA: Sage.

Rowland, Willard D., Jr. (1997). Television violence redux: The continuing mythology of effects. In Martin Barker & Julien Petley (Eds.), *Ill effects: The media/violence debate* (pp. 102-124). London: Routledge.

Rubin, Alan M., Perse, Elizabeth M., & Taylor, Donald S. (1988). A methodological examination of cultivation. *Communication Research, 15*(2), 107-134.

Rubin, Ellis, & Matera, Dary. (1989). *"Get me Ellis Rubin!" The life, times and cases of a maverick lawyer.* New York: St. Martin's.

Russell, Gordon W. (1983). Psychological issues in sports aggression. In Jeffrey H. Goldstein (Ed.), *Sports violence* (pp. 157-182). New York: Springer-Verlag.

Saegert, Joel. (1987, Summer). Why marketing should quit giving subliminal advertising the benefit of the doubt. *Psychology & Marketing, 4,* 107-120.

Saferstein, Barry. (1994). Interaction and ideology at work: A case of constructing and constraining television violence. *Social Problems, 41*(2), 316-345.

Sagan, Eli. (1974). *Cannibalism: Human aggression and cultural form.* New York: Harper & Row.

Sagan, Eli. (1985). *At the dawn of tyranny: The origins of individualism, political oppression, and the state.* New York: Knopf.

Said, Edward. (1978). *Orientalism.* New York: Pantheon.

Scheff, Thomas J., & Scheele, Stephen C. (1980). Humor and catharsis: The effect of comedy on audiences. In Percy Tannenbaum (Ed.), *The entertainment functions of television* (pp. 165-182). Hillsdale, NJ: Lawrence Erlbaum.

Schlesinger, Philip, Dobash, R. Emerson, Dobash, Russell P., & Weaver, C. Kay. (1992). *Women viewing violence.* London: BFI.

Schwartz, Tony. (1978, August 14). TV on trial again. *Newsweek,* 41-42.

Scully, Sean. (1993, November 8). Canadians come down hard on television violence. *Broadcasting and Cable,* p. 12.

Seidman, Steven A. (1992, Spring). An investigation of sex-role stereotyping in music videos. *Journal of Broadcasting and Electronic Music, 31*(2), 209-216.

Seiter, Ellen. (1996). Notes on children as a television audience. In James Hay, Lawrence Grossberg, & Ellen Wartella (Eds.), *The audience and its landscape* (pp. 131-144). Boulder, CO: Westview.

Sherman, Barry L., & Dominick, Joseph R. (1986, Winter). Violence and sex in music videos: TV and rock 'n' roll. *Journal of Communication, 36,* 79-93.

Sherrin, Howard, Bond, James A., Brakel, Linda A. W., Hertel, Richard K., & Williams, William J. (1996). *Conscious and unconscious processes.* New York: Guilford.

Siann, Gerda. (1985). *Accounting for aggression: Perspectives on aggression and violence.* Boston: Allen and Unwin.

Signorielli, Nancy. (1990). Television's mean and dangerous world: A continuation of the Cultural Indicators perspective. In Nancy Signorielli and Michael Morgan (Eds.), *Cultivation analysis: New directions in media effects research* (pp. 85-106). Newbury Park, CA: Sage.

Signorielli, Nancy, Gerbner, George, & Morgan, Michael. (1995). Violence on television: The Cultural Indicators Project. *Journal of Broadcasting and Electronic Media, 39*(2), 278-283.

Sindall, Robin. (1990). *Street violence in the nineteenth century: Media panic or real danger?* Leicester, UK: Leicester University Press.

Singer, Jerome L., & Singer, Dorothy G. (1988). Some hazards of growing up in a television environment: Children's aggression and restlessness. In Stuart Oskamp (Ed.), *Television as a social issue* (pp. 171-188). Newbury Park, CA: Sage.

Skogan, Wesley G. (1989). Social change and the future of violent crime. In Ted Robert Gurr (Ed.), *Violence in America: Vol. 1. The history of crime* (pp. 235-250). Newbury Park, CA: Sage.

Skogan, Wesley G., & Maxfield, Michael G. (1981). *Coping with crime.* Beverly Hills, CA: Sage.

Slaby, Ronald G. (1994, January 5). Combating television violence. *Chronicle of Higher Education, 40*(18), B1-B2.

Slaby, Ronald G., Quarforth, Gary R., & McConnachie, Gene A. (1976). Television violence and its sponsors. *Journal of Communication, 26,* 88-96.

Smith, Buddy. (1997). AFA alert: CBS to show most violent program in their history—*Brooklyn South.* URL: *www.afa.net/alert/aa97O808.*

Smythe, Dallas. (1954). Reality as presented by television. *Public Opinion Quarterly, 18,* 143-156.

Snow, Robert P. (1974). How children interpret TV violence in play context. *Journalism Quarterly, 51,* 13-21.

Sohn, David. (1981). Television violence and aggression revisited. *American Psychologist, 36,* 229-231.

Sohn, David. (1982). On Eron on television violence and aggression. *American Psychologist, 37,* 1292-1293.

Soley, Lawrence C., & Reid, Leonard N. (1985, Spring). Baiting viewers: Violence and sex in television program advertisements. *Journalism Quarterly, 62,* 105-110.

Soman, Alfred. (1980). Deviance and criminal justice in Western Europe 1300-1800: An essay in structure. *Criminal Justice History: An International Annual, 1,* 3-28.

Sparks, Richard. (1992). *Television and the drama of crime: Moral tales and the place of crime in public life.* Buckingham, UK: Open University Press.

Sparks, Richard. (1995). Entertaining the crises: Television and moral enterprise. In David Hewitt-Kidd & Richard Osborne (Eds.), *Crime and the media: The postmodern spectacle* (pp. 49-66). London, Pluto.

Spierenburg, Pieter. (1994). Faces of violence: Homicide trends and cultural meanings: Amsterdam 1431-1816. *Journal of Social History, 27*(4), 701-716.

Spindler, Konrad. (1994). *The man in the ice.* New York: Harmony.

Stallybrass, Peter, & White, Allon. (1986). *The politics and poetics of transgression.* Ithaca, NY: Cornell University Press.

Stanko, Elizabeth. (1985). *Intimate instrusions: Women's experience of male violence.* London: Routledge.

Starker, Steven. (1989). *Evil influences: Crusades against the mass media.* New Brunswick, NJ: Transaction Publishers.

Stearns, Carol Zisowitz, & Stearns, Peter N. (1986). *Anger: The struggle for emotional control in America's history.* Chicago: University of Chicago Press.

Stocking, S. Holly, Sapolsky, Barry S., & Zillmann, Dolf. (1977). Sex discrimination in prime time humor. *Journal of Broadcasting, 21,* 447-457.

Stone, Lawrence. (1983). Interpersonal violence in English society 1300-1980. *Past and Present, 101,* 22-33.

Storm, Jonathan. (1994, December 28). Foes of TV violence turn up volume. *Philadelphia Inquirer,* pp. A1, A10.

Strasburger, Victor. (1997, May). Make love, not war: Violence and weapon carrying in music videos. *Archive of Pediatrics and Adolescent Medicine, 151,* 441-442.

Sumner, Colin S. (1990). Rethinking deviance: Towards a sociology of censures. In Colin S. Sumner (Ed.), *Censure, politics and criminal justice* (pp. 15-40). Buckingham, UK: Open University Press.

Surgeon General's Scientific Advisory Committee on Television and Social Behavior. (1972). *Television and growing up: The impact of televised violence* (Report to the surgeon general, United States Public Health Service). Washington, DC: Government Printing Office.

Takeuchi, Michio, Clausen, Tanya, & Scott, Ralph. (1995). Televised violence: A Japanese, Spanish, and American comparison. *Psychological Reports, 77,* 995-1000.

Tan, Alexis S., & Tan, Gordean K. (1986). Television use and mental health. *Journalism Quarterly, 63,* 106-113.

Tannenbaum, Percy H. (1972). Studies in film- and television-mediated arousal and aggression: A progress report. In George A. Comstock, Eli A. Rubinstein, & John P. Murray (Eds.), *Television and social behavior: Vol. 5. Television's effects: Further explorations* (pp. 309-350). Washington, DC: Government Printing Office.

Taylor, James. (1977). Television crime drama: A mythological interpretation. In the Royal Commission on Violence in the Communications Industry, *Report: Vol. 3, Violence in television, films and news* (pp. 157-219). Toronto: The Royal Commission.

Telecommunications Act of 1996. (1996). Washington, DC: Government Printing Office.

Thomas, Elizabeth Marshall. (1959). *The harmless people.* New York: Knopf.

Thomas, Margaret Hanratty, & Drabman, Ronald S. (1975). Toleration of real-life aggression as a function of exposure to televised violence and age of subject. *Merrill-Palmer Quarterly, 21*(3), 227-232.

Thomas, Margaret Hanratty, & Tell, Phillip M. (1974). Effects of viewing real versus fantasy violence upon interpersonal aggression. *Journal of Research in Personality, 8,* 153-160.

Tiger, Lionel, & Fox, Robin. (1971). *The imperial animal.* New York: Henry Holt.

Toner, J. P. (1995). *Leisure and ancient Rome.* Cambridge, UK: Polity.

Tulloch, Marion I. (1995). Evaluating aggression: School students' responses to television portrayals of institutionalized violence. *Journal of Youth and Adolescence, 24,* 95-115.

Turner, R. E. "Ted." (1994). Testimony. In *Violence on television: Hearings before the Subcommittee on Telecommunications and Finance, House of Representatives: May 12, June 25, July 1 and 29, and September 15, 1993* (pp. 105-121). Washington, DC: Government Printing Office.

TV wins a crucial case: Dismissal of suit blaming NBC for a rape. (1978, August 21). *Newsweek,* p. 85.

Twitchell, James B. (1989). *Preposterous violence: Fables of aggression in modern culture.* New York: Oxford University Press.

Tyler, Tom R., & Cook, Fay Lomax. (1984). The mass media and judgment of risk. *Journal of Personality and Social Psychology, 47*(4), 693-709.

U.S. Bureau of the Census. (1996). *Statistical abstract of the United States.* Washington, DC: Government Printing Office.

U.S. Department of Justice. (1994). *Sourcebook of criminal justice statistics 1993.* Washington, DC: Government Printing Office.

U.S. Department of Justice. (1995). *Sourcebook of criminal justice statistics 1994.* Washington, DC: Government Printing Office.

U.S. Department of Justice. (1996). *Sourcebook of criminal justice statistics 1995.* Washington, DC: Government Printing Office.

U.S. Department of Justice. (1997). *Sourcebook of criminal justice statistics 1996.* Washington, DC: Government Printing Office.

Van der Voort, T. H. A. (1986). *Television violence: A child eye's view.* Amsterdam: Elsevier.

Victor, Jeffrey S. (1993). *Satanic panic: The creation of a contemporary legend.* Chicago: Open Court.

Vine, Ian. (1997). The dangerous psycho-logic of media "effects." In Martin Barker & Julien Petley (Eds.), *Ill effects: The media/violence debate* (pp. 125-146). London: Routledge.

Wagner, David. (1997). *The new temperance: The American obsession with sin and vice.* Boulder, CO: Westview.

Wakshlag, Jacob, Vial, Virginia, & Tamborini, Ronald. (1983). Selecting crime drama and apprehension about crime. *Human Communication Research, 10*(2), 227-242.

Wartella, Ellen, & Reeves, Byron. (1985). Historical trends in research on children and the media. *Journal of Communication, 35*(2), 118-133.

Weiner, Neil Alan, & Zahn, Margaret A. (1989). Violent arrests in the city: The Philadelphia story 1857-1980. In Ted Robert Gurr (Ed.), *Violence in America: Vol. 1. The history of crime* (pp. 102-121). Newbury Park, CA: Sage.

Wenner, Lawrence A., & Gantz, Walter. (1989). The audience experience with sports on television. In Lawrence A. Wenner (Ed.), *Media, sports, and society* (pp. 241-269). Newbury Park, CA: Sage.

Wertham, Frederic. (1954). *The seduction of the innocent.* New York: Rinehart.

Wiedemann, Thomas. (1992). *Emperors and gladiators.* London: Routledge.

Wiegman, O., Kuttschreuter, M., & Baarda, B. (1992). A longitudinal study of the effects of television viewing on aggressive and prosocial behaviors. *British Journal of Social Psychology, 31,* 147-164.

Williams, Raymond. (1958). *Culture and society, 1780-1950.* New York: Columbia University Press.

Williams, Tannis MacBeth (Ed.). (1986). *The impact of television: A natural experiment in three communities.* Orlando, FL: Academic Press.

Wilson, Edward O. (1978). *On human nature.* Cambridge, MA: Harvard University Press.

Winick, Charles. (1988). The functions of television: Life without the big box. In Stuart Oskamp (Ed.), *Television as a social issue* (pp. 217-237). Newbury Park, CA: Sage.

Winick, Mariann Pezzella, & Winick, Charles. (1979). *The television experience: What children see.* Beverly Hills, CA: Sage.

Wistrand, Magnus. (1992). *Entertainment and violence in ancient Rome: The attitudes of Roman writers of the first century A.D.* Goteborg, Sweden: Acta Universitatis Gothoburgensis.

Wober, Mallory. (1978). Televised violence and paranoid perception: The view from Great Britain. *Public Opinion Quarterly, 42,* 315-321.

Wober, Mallory, & Gunter, Barrie. (1982). Television and personal threat: Fact or artifact? A British survey. *British Journal of Social Psychology, 21,* 239-247.

Wood, Wendy, Wong, Frank T., & Chachere, J. Gregory. (1991). Effects of media violence on viewers' aggression in unconstrained social interaction. *Psychological Bulletin, 109,* 371-383.

Woodfield, D. L. (1988, March). *Mass media viewing habits and toleration of real life violence.* Paper presented at the meeting of the Southeastern Psychological Association, New Orleans.

Woolgar, Steve. (1988). *Science: The very idea.* London: Tavistock.

Wouters, Cas. (1986). Formalization and informalization. *Theory, Culture and Society, 3*(2), 1-18.

Wouters, Cas. (1991). On status competition and emotional management. *Journal of Social History, 24*(4), 699-717.

Wrangham, Richard, & Peterson, Dale. (1996). *Demonic males: Apes and the origins of human violence.* New York: Houghton Mifflin.

Zillmann, Dolf. (1971). Excitation transfer of communication-mediated aggressive behavior. *Journal of Experimental Social Psychology, 7*(4), 419-434.

Zillmann, Dolf. (1980). Anatomy of suspense, In Percy H. Tannenbaum (Ed.), *The entertainment functions of television* (pp. 133-163). Hillsdale, NJ: Lawrence Erlbaum.

Zillmann, Dolf. (1988). Mood management: Using entertainment to full advantage. In Lewis Donohew, Howard E. Sypher, & E. Tory Higgins (Eds.), *Communication, social cognition, and affect* (pp. 147-171). Hillsdale, NJ: Lawrence Erlbaum.

Zillmann, Dolf. (1991). Television viewing and physiological arousal. In Jennings Bryant & Dolf Zillmann (Eds.), *Responding to the screen: Reception and reaction processes* (pp. 103-133). Hillsdale, NJ: Lawrence Erlbaum.

Zillmann, Dolf, & Bryant, Jennings. (1991). Responding to comedy: The sense and nonsense of humor. In Jennings Bryant & Dolf Zillmann (Eds.), *Responding to the screen: Reception and reaction processes* (pp. 261-280). Hillsdale, NJ: Lawrence Erlbaum.

Zillmann, Dolf, & Bryant, Jennings. (1994). Entertainment as media effects. In Jennings Bryant & Dolf Zillmann (Eds.), *Media effects: Advances in theory and research* (pp. 437-461). Hillsdale, NJ: Lawrence Erlbaum.

Zillmann, Doff, Johnson, Rolland C., & Hanrahan, John. (1973). Pacifying effect of happy endings of communications involving aggression. *Psychological Reports, 32,* 967-970.

Zillmann, Dolf, Sapolsky, Barry S., & Bryant, Jennings. (1979). The enjoyment of watching sports contests. In Jeffrey H. Goldstein (Ed.), *Sports, games, and play: Social and psychological viewpoints* (pp. 297-336). Hillsdale, NJ: Lawrence Erlbaum.

Zillmann, Dolf, & Wakshlag, Jacob. (1985). Fear of victimization and appeal of crime drama. In Dolf Zillmann & Jennings Bryant (Eds.), *Selective exposure to communication* (pp. 141-156). Hillsdale, NJ: Lawrence Erlbaum.

Ziman, John. (1984). *An introduction to science studies: The philosophical and social aspects of science and technology.* Cambridge, UK: Cambridge University Press.

Zoonen, Liesbet Van. (1994). *Feminist media studies.* Thousand Oaks, CA: Sage.

Zusne, Leonard. (1968). Measuring violence in children's cartoons. *Perceptual and Motor Skills, 27,* 901-902.

Index

About the Author

Jib Fowles is Professor of Communication at the University of Houston-Clear Lake. His previous books include *Why Viewers Watch* (1992) and *Advertising and Popular Culture* (1996). His articles have appeared in the *New York Times, Atlantic Monthly, TV Guide, Advertising Age, Chronicle of Higher Education,* and many scholarly journals.